SpeedPro Series

SECRETS OF SPEED

TODAY'S TECHNIQUES FOR 4-STROKE ENGINE BLUEPRINTING & TUNING

"You can think about only what you know ...
"You can know only what you have thought about"

Arthur Schopenhauer
Essays and Aphorisms

Also from Veloce Publishing –

Speedpro Series

4-cylinder Engine – How to Blueprint & Build a Short Block For High Performance (Hammill)
Alfa Romeo DOHC High-performance Manual (Kartalamakis)
Alfa Romeo V6 Engine High-performance Manual (Kartalamakis)
BMC 998cc A-series Engine – How to Power Tune (Hammill)
1275cc A-series High-performance Manual (Hammill)
Camshafts – How to Choose & Time Them For Maximum Power (Hammill)
Competition Car Datalogging Manual, The (Templeman)
Cylinder Heads – How to Build, Modify & Power Tune Updated & Revised Edition (Burgess & Gollan)
Distributor-type Ignition Systems – How to Build & Power Tune New 3rd Edition (Hammill)
Fast Road Car – How to Plan and Build Revised & Updated Colour New Edition (Stapleton)
Ford SOHC 'Pinto' & Sierra Cosworth DOHC Engines – How to Power Tune Updated & Enlarged Edition (Hammill)
Ford V8 – How to Power Tune Small Block Engines (Hammill)
Harley-Davidson Evolution Engines – How to Build & Power Tune (Hammill)
Holley Carburetors – How to Build & Power Tune Revised & Updated Edition (Hammill)
Honda Civic Type R, The – High-Performance Manual (Cowland & Clifford)
Jaguar XK Engines – How to Power Tune Revised & Updated Colour Edition (Hammill)
MG Midget & Austin-Healey Sprite – How to Power Tune New 3rd Edition (Stapleton)
MGB 4-cylinder Engine – How to Power Tune (Burgess)
MGB V8 Power – How to Give Your, Third Colour Edition (Williams)
MGB, MGC & MGB V8 – How to Improve New 2nd Edition (Williams)
Mini Engines – How to Power Tune On a Small Budget Colour Edition (Hammill)
Motorcycle-engined Racing Car – How to Build (Pashley)
Motorsport – Getting Started in (Collins)
Nissan GT-R High-performance Manual, The (Gorodji)
Nitrous Oxide High-performance Manual, The (Langfield)
Rover V8 Engines – How to Power Tune (Hammill)
Secrets of Speed – Today's techniques for 4-stroke engine blueprinting & tuning (Swager)
Sportscar & Kitcar Suspension & Brakes – How to Build & Modify Revised 3rd Edition (Hammill)
SU Carburettor High-performance Manual (Hammill)
Successful Low-Cost Rally Car, How to Build a (Young)
Suzuki 4x4 – How to Modify For Serious Off-road Action (Richardson)
Tiger Avon Sportscar – How to Build Your Own Updated & Revised 2nd Edition (Dudley)
TR2, 3 & TR4 – How to Improve (Williams)
TR5, 250 & TR6 – How to Improve (Williams)
TR7 & TR8 – How to Improve (Williams)
V8 Engine – How to Build a Short Block For High Performance (Hammill)
Volkswagen Beetle Suspension, Brakes & Chassis – How to Modify For High Performance (Hale)
Volkswagen Bus Suspension, Brakes & Chassis – How to Modify For High Performance (Hale)
Weber DCOE, & Dellorto DHLA Carburetors – How to Build & Power Tune 3rd Edition (Hammill)

General

Anatomy of the Works Minis (Moylan)
André Lefebvre, and the cars he created at Voisin and Citroën (Beck)
Art Deco and British Car Design (Down)
Automotive A-Z, Lane's Dictionary of Automotive Terms (Lane)
Bluebird CN7 (Stevens)
BMC Competitions Department Secrets (Turner, Chambers & Browning)
BRM – A Mechanic's Tale (Salmon)
Classic British Car Electrical Systems (Astley)
Concept Cars, How to illustrate and design (Dewey)
Coventry Climax Racing Engines (Hammill)
Drive on the Wild Side, A – 20 Extreme Driving Adventures From Around the World (Weaver)
Fast Ladies – Female Racing Drivers 1888 to 1970 (Bouzanquet)
Mazda MX-5/Miata 1.6 Enthusiast's Workshop Manual (Grainger & Shoemark)
Mazda MX-5/Miata 1.8 Enthusiast's Workshop Manual (Grainger & Shoemark)
MGB & MGB GT– Expert Guide (Auto-doc Series) (Williams)
MGB Electrical Systems Updated & Revised Edition (Astley)
Porsche 964, 993 & 996 Data Plate Code Breaker (Streather)
RX-7 – Mazda's Rotary Engine Sportscar (Updated & Revised New Edition) (Long)
SM – Citroën's Maserati-engined Supercar (Long & Claverol)
Subaru Impreza: The Road Car And WRC Story (Long)
Supercar, How to Build your own (Thompson)
Tales from the Toolbox (Oliver)
Virgil Exner – Visioneer: The Official Biography of Virgil M Exner Designer Extraordinaire (Grist)

From Veloce Publishing's new imprints:

Soviet General & field rank officer uniforms: 1955 to 1991 (Streather)
Red & Soviet military & paramilitary services: female uniforms 1941-1991 (Streather)

Complete Dog Massage Manual, The – Gentle Dog Care (Robertson)
Dinner with Rover (Paton-Ayre)
Dog Games – Stimulating play to entertain your dog and you (Blenski)
Dog Relax – Relaxed dogs, relaxed owners (Pilguj)
Know Your Dog – The guide to a beautiful relationship (Birmelin)
My dog is blind – but lives life to the full! (Horsky)
Smellorama – nose games for dogs (Theby)
Waggy Tails & Wheelchairs (Epp)
Winston ... the dog who changed my life (Klute)
You and Your Border Terrier – The Essential Guide (Alderton)
You and Your Cockapoo – The Essential Guide (Alderton)

www.veloce.co.uk

First published in June 2010 by Veloce Publishing Ltd., Veloce House, Parkway Farm Business Park, Middle Farm Way, Poundbury, Dorchester, Dorset, DT1 3AR, England. Fax 01305 268864/e-mail veloce@veloce.co.uk/web www.veloce.co.uk

ISBN 978-1-845842-97-0/UPC 6-36847-04297-4

SECRETS OF SPEED

TODAY'S TECHNIQUES FOR 4-STROKE ENGINE BLUEPRINTING & TUNING

NICHOLAS SWAGER

VELOCE PUBLISHING
THE PUBLISHER OF FINE AUTOMOTIVE BOOKS

Contents

SPEEDPRO SERIES

978-1-845840-05-1

978-1-845840-06-8

978-1-845840-19-8

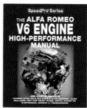
978-1-845840-21-1

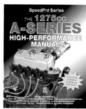
978-1-845840-23-5

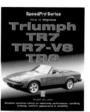
978-1-845840-45-7

978-1-845840-73-0

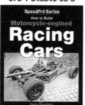
978-1-845841-23-2

978-1-845841-42-3

978-1-845841-62-1

978-1-845841-86-7

978-1-845841-87-4

978-1-845842-07-9

978-1-845842-08-6

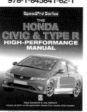
978-1-845842-24-6

978-1-845842-66-6

978-1-845842-97-0

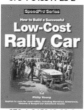
978-1-874105-70-1

978-1-901295-26-9

978-1-903706-14-5

978-1-903706-17-6

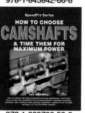
978-1-903706-59-6

978-1-903706-68-8

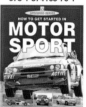
978-1-903706-70-1

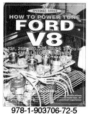
978-1-903706-72-5

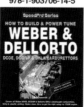
978-1-903706-75-6

978-1-903706-76-3

978-1-903706-77-0

978-1-903706-78-7

978-1-903706-80-0

978-1-903706-92-3

978-1-903706-94-7

978-1-903706-99-2

978-1-904788-22-5

978-1-904788-78-2

978-1-904788-84-3

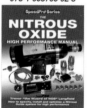
978-1-904788-89-8

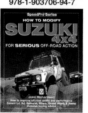
978-1-904788-91-1

978-1-904788-93-5

– more on the way!

About the author, introduction & acknowledgements

ABOUT THE AUTHOR

Nick Swager has been building motorsport engines for more than thirty years – more than half of this time in the USA. Amongst others, he has worked on drag racing and endurance engines, and built motors for Oval Racing, WRC and the Mille Millia. He is now based in Britain with his family, and is a World-Wide representative for a high-speed diesel manufacturer. He has served a City and Guilds apprenticeship and has a BA in English.

INTRODUCTION

The purpose of writing this book has been to bring together information that may be useful to people who want to improve the performance of their engines. For some makes of engine a reasonable body of facts-and-figures is in the public domain and yet for others, it is patchy or non-existent. It is hoped that this book's data adds to that which is already available, and also is of use to vehicle owners who have little printed guidance. The book is not engine specific. It deals with some of the engineering problems that may be encountered when building any high performance 4-stroke engine. It tries to explain from a hands-on perspective what to look for and why, and then suggests the best course of action. To help illustrate specific problems, a few anecdotes have been included. The material has been organised to explain how to strip and inspect, repair and modify, and build and test a performance engine.

ACKNOWLEDGEMENTS

Even when working alone, few people are totally unaided. A person may be the sole creator of a piece of work yet they are supported in their efforts by others: even if the support is indirect. Such people need to be recognised. I take this opportunity to thank Gavin King and Justin Dean for their help with photography. There is also intellectual support: thanks to Melanie Selfe and Gill Lowe, Senior Lecturers at University Campus Suffolk for their advice and encouragement. Then there is my immediate support group: I would like to thank my wife and children for their understanding.

Nick Swager
Woodbridge, Suffolk

7

Using this book & essential information

USING THIS BOOK

Throughout this book the text assumes that you, or your contractor, will have a workshop manual specific to your engine to follow for complete detail on dismantling, reassembly, adjustment procedure, clearances, torque figures, etc. This book's default is the standard manufacturer's specification for your engine model so, if a procedure is not described, a measurement not given, a torque figure ignored, you can assume that the standard manufacturer's procedure or specification for your engine needs to be used.

You'll find it helpful to read the whole book before you start work or give instructions to your contractor. This is because a modification or change in specification in one area may cause the need for changes in other areas. Get the whole picture so that you can finalize specification and component requirements as far as is possible before any work begins.

For those wishing to have even more information on high-performance short block building principles, ignition systems, Weber/Dellorto sidedraught carburettors and cylinder head work, the following Veloce titles are recommended further reading: *How To Blueprint & Build A 4-Cylinder Short Block For High Performance, How To Build & Power Tune Distributor-type Ignition Systems, How To Build & Power Tune Weber & Dellorto DCOE & DHLA Carburetors and How To Build, Modify & Power Tune Cylinder Heads.*

ESSENTIAL INFORMATION

This book contains information on practical procedures; however, this information is intended only for those with the qualifications, experience, tools and facilities to carry out the work in safety and with appropriately high levels of skill. Whenever working on a car or component, remember that your personal safety must ALWAYS be your FIRST consideration. The publisher, author, editors and retailer of this book cannot accept any responsibility for personal injury or mechanical damage which results from using this book, even if caused by errors or omissions in the information given. If this disclaimer is unacceptable to you, please return the pristine book to your retailer who will refund the purchase price.

In the text of this book **Warning!** means that a procedure could cause personal injury and **Caution!** that there is danger of mechanical damage if appropriate care is not taken. However, be aware that we cannot foresee every possibility of danger in every circumstance.

Note that changing component specification by modification is likely to void warranties and also to absolve manufacturers from any responsibility in the event of component failure and the consequences of such failure.

Increasing the engine's power will place additional stress on engine components and on the car's complete driveline: this may reduce service life and increase the frequency of breakdown. An increase in engine power, and therefore the vehicle's performance, will mean that your vehicle's braking and suspension systems will need to be kept in perfect condition and uprated as appropriate. It is also usually necessary to inform the vehicle's insurers of any changes to the vehicle's specification.

The importance of cleaning a component thoroughly before working on it cannot be overstressed. Always keep your working area and tools as clean as possible. Whatever specialist cleaning fluid or other chemicals you use, be sure to follow – completely – manufacturer's instructions and if you are using petrol (gasoline) or paraffin (kerosene) to clean parts, take every precaution necessary to protect your body and to avoid all risk of fire.

Foreword

Nick Swager has spent over 30 years working on drag racing and endurance engines. He has accumulated a wealth of experience during this time, and this book sets out this experience, whilst always concentrating on the practical aspects. Whether disassembling an engine, inspecting, part refurbishing, assembling, or testing, many practical hints and tricks of the trade may be found in these pages. Nick also gives in-depth descriptions of components and engine systems which will be of interest to any engine enthusiast. The text is fully supported by a comprehensive set of illustrations, and, where helpful, by rudimentary calculations.

Nick Swager and I are professional working colleagues working within the diesel service industry. Nick's book is presented both lucidly and logically and in a manner which I have come to expect from him.

Ian W Drake
Chief Design Engineer
MAN Diesel Limited Colchester
Business Unit

Because a lot ot the diagrams have had to be reproduced quite small in the book, we've made them available as high resolution JPEG files on our website: http://www.veloce.co.uk/secrets_of_speed/figures.zip

Chapter 1
Planning your project

OBJECTIVES

An internal combustion engine is a machine that converts the chemical energy contained in its fuel into mechanical power. Any unmodified engine can be altered to raise its power output and reliability. However, as greater rewards usually result from planning, it's best to define your objectives rather than make random modifications – identify what is wanted, and how it will be achieved. For example, an engine may be from a classic vehicle that is being restored to 'original' specification. Alternatively, an 'original appearance' motor may be required.

In most cases, the original specification or 'provenance' of a production engine is easy to establish. However, building an original spec engine and keeping pattern internal parts can be at the expense of practicality. An original appearance engine can incorporate upgraded components – silicon-chromium steel valves can be replaced by harder-wearing nimonic alloy items, for example, or a cast or forged crankshaft may be replaced with one made from an alloy billet. Many older engines had general purpose cork gaskets; these can be replaced with modern gasket material, or dispensed with entirely by using face-to-face joints and a modern sealer – thus improving stiffness. Today, components can be assembled to much more rigorous standards and tolerances than was possible when a period engine was first manufactured. This, in turn, may result in improved performance and reliability.

Performance is an important consideration, as some classic vehicles are hard to drive in modern traffic, so modest increases in power or better cooling, for example, can improve drivability. Therefore, non-visible upgrading can broaden a vehicle's practical use, arguably, without destroying provenance.

The original specification of racing machinery presents more of a problem. An engine may have been built to a certain pattern at the beginning of a racing season, but improved components may have been fitted, or modifications undertaken, as and when they were advantageous. What's more, any advantage is unlikely to have been made public, so records or build sheets for period race engines may be unavailable. As a result, at times, the original specification of racing engines can be somewhat subjective: in other words, open to interpretation. In contrast, with regard to a modern production engine, originality may not be a concern, as the object might be merely to extract more power.

Generally speaking, an engine becomes less user-friendly the higher its level of performance. For instance, a 4-cylinder, 2000 cubic centimetre (cc) eight-valve motor from a road vehicle might develop 150 horsepower (hp). To raise its level of performance, the engine's ports and valves could be enlarged, a high-lift cam fitted, and the compression increased. Such modifications would raise horsepower, but the point of maximum torque (low to medium speed pulling power) shifts further up the rev range. In addition, gas velocity through the ports would be low at slow engine speeds, as would vacuum. This could lead to reversion: a percentage of exhaust gas obstructs the inlet charge (see Chapter 3, 'Overlap'). As a result, such modifications may make the idle erratic, and upset the power delivery below 3000 revolutions-per-minute (rpm) due to poor combustion and the shifted torque point. Fuel consumption would probably be higher, and driving such a vehicle could be trying in an urban environment. Consider engine modifications carefully. What will be the common engine speed range? Will the vehicle be used for urban or track driving, or rallying?

Reliability is another concern as dependability is sometimes a trade off against performance. Nonetheless, powerful, reliable race engines exist. Although it's easy to see the huge differences between an engine for a Top Fuel dragster, and one for a 200-mile race – there must be a balance between usable power and reliability. Aside from fitting tuning components like high-compression pistons or high-lift cams, several modifications or assembly techniques can be applied to existing components and castings to increase horsepower and reliability for a relatively modest cost. Nevertheless, if the primary purpose is to raise horsepower, it is well to consider the principal theory of the 4-stroke cycle that makes increases possible, namely:

• To reduce or remove needless friction
• To fill a cylinder with the utmost charge as often as possible in any given minute

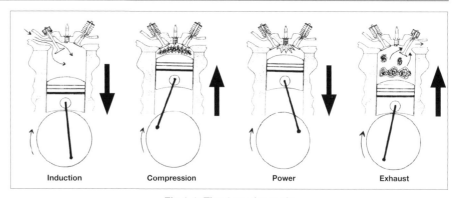

Fig 1-1: The 4-stroke cycle.

• To convert as much of the heat released by combustion into energy

Engines can always be modified; just because something has been made or fits together in a certain way does not mean it's best for the liberation of horsepower. The implication is not that most engines are badly designed. University-educated engine designers are hardly uninformed, but blank sheets of paper and unlimited budgets for designers to satisfy their creative talents rarely occur. Financial considerations, time constraints and metallurgical or machine shop limitations press on the professional just as they affect the amateur. As a result, the need for stronger parts, better materials or more thorough designs are sometimes secondary to other concerns.

TUNING

The word 'tuning' concerning internal combustion engines commonly refers to their level of performance; or how much power a given size of engine produces. This can be expressed as, horsepower-per-litre (hp/lt). When comparing power ratings, it's important to note that some European manufacturers may measure in metric horsepower, rather than the more common, Society of Automotive Engineers (SAE). Rating power output in kilowatts (kW) is unambiguous, which

is largely the reason for its adoption by commercial engine manufacturers.

One (1) metric horsepower = 0.736kW
One (1) SAE horsepower = 0.746kW
One (1) kW = 1000 watts

The origin of the word tuning, used in the context of engines, is unclear. Some people, versed in period history, credit it to George Dance, a highly successful British motorcycle racer in the inter-war years who was a development engineer for Sunbeam Motorcycles. The story goes that he was working on an engine in his shed-cum-garage when someone walked in and asked him what he was doing. In those days of magneto ignition, contact breaker points were tensioned by a series of two-inch long flat springs, formed in a gentle curve. Perhaps not wishing to disclose what he was really doing, he is supposed to have flicked a magneto spring so that it made a twang like a tuning fork and said, "Just tuning it up." Competitive motorsport is very secretive!

The common understanding of tuning is described best by example. Imagine a particular engine that had a modest compression ratio, valve timing and port sizes; it would have reasonable torque for its displacement but meagre horsepower (low hp/lt). Overall, the engine would not be highly stressed and it would possess docile and dependable characteristics. The engine's enhancement or level of tune could be increased by replacing components or making modifications to the engine castings. This would raise horsepower but lessen useable torque and at the same time, the engine castings and internal components would be subject to higher levels of stress. The engine could be further developed, producing more horsepower but less torque, until it became impractical or good for only one use. An example of such a motor is the V8 8.2-litre engine of a Top Fuel dragster. Fitted in a light projectile these engines put out a minimum 5000hp, yet the longevity of such an engine, when under load, is measurable in seconds before it will need to be overhauled. Such a 5000hp engine produces 609hp/lt but little torque. Compare this to the 36-cylinder, 127-litre, Lycoming XR-7755 engine. Its stated output is 5000hp, which works out to 40hp/lt. This engine was designed to have sufficient torque to power a large aircraft. When raising an engine's state of tune, strike a balance between horsepower (horsepower-per-litre) and torque, for high horsepower low torque engines are impractical except for specialist uses. Tuning, then, is a generic term to indicate a particular engine's level of performance enhancement.

BLUEPRINTING

Blueprinting came about when factory teams competed in race series that restricted engines to standard parts. To make engines run better, they used only the best standard parts. So, blueprinting is a colloquial term that, in its original sense, meant 'to assemble an engine with the best fitting original parts.' It entails matching parts to the most favourable dimension stated on a designer's blueprint. Yet without manufacturing tolerances, there would be no such thing as blueprinting. For example, if a designer wanted pistons made for an engine with a skirt diameter of 86.00 millimetres (mm) it is unlikely every piston would end up that size. There are a number of reasons: the limitations of machine tools (the inherent inaccuracy of shafts, bearings, chucks and feed screws); and worn grinding wheels and cutting tools. Wear-and-tear throughout machine life, and operator error compound the issue. As a result, there would be impossible wastage if every piston *had* to be *exactly* 86.00mm. This would increase manufacturing cost and make parts – in this case pistons – very expensive. Weighing these factors in mind, designers give components tolerances: optimum piston size is 86.00mm but the designer may also accept 0.0065mm (high) or 0.0127mm (low).

In that case the sizes become:

0.0065mm (+)
86.00mm optimum size
0.0127mm (-)

Adding the + and - values together, the total tolerance is 0.0192mm/ 0.00075in.

There would also be a tolerance on the engine's cylinder bore size, and another assembly tolerance (the running clearance) when the piston is fitted in its bore. A difficulty might arise when attempting to blueprint an engine with a piston finished on a low (-) tolerance and a cylinder bore on a high (+) tolerance (a small piston and a big bore). In which case, a large running clearance would exist that may lead to piston-to-bore gas leakage. To obviate this problem, try to match piston size to bore size.

Any precision part has a tolerance, and matching a cylinder head that gives a higher compression, a camshaft with a higher lift, and pistons that limit gas leakage, can result in a smoother more powerful engine. However, blueprinting involves more than clearances. Blueprinting is also concerned with reducing frictional losses, whether they result from surface finish, or the misalignment of shafts or bearings. Aim for the finest surface finish on cylinder liners, journal shafts and bushes. Misalignment can be caused by worn machine tools or operator error. It's wrong to assume that an engine's crankshaft-to-cylinder-bore-axis is correct, or that the camshaft bores are in alignment. Dowels may locate castings, like the split crankcases of some motorcycle engines, but it doesn't follow that main shaft bearing bores will be in precise alignment. It's good to consider the original manufacturing conditions, and how much a designer may have had to compromise from the ideal.

Blueprinting, like engine building in general, involves a modest amount of number crunching, and a builder's job is to check and verify specific numbers. For example, a 2000cc eight-valve single overhead camshaft engine has, amongst other components, 4 pistons; 4 wrist pins; 8 pin circlips; 4 ring sets; 4 con rods; 4 wrist pin bushes; 8 big end bolts, etc. Each individual component of a specific group – a wrist pin bush for instance – needs checking for alignment and fit in its con rod and mating wrist pin. This operation must be replicated for each bush. Measure individual components and consider their relationship to other components. To avoid confusion, split complex jobs into smaller operations – be methodical; check one set of components at a time before moving on to the next. For example, check the wrist pin bush-to-con rod fit in all the rods of a set before moving on to check the wrist pin clearance, rather than performing both operations on one rod at a time. Adopting such a method helps to minimise errors as it enables the mind to do complex tasks without having to retain large amounts of information: repetition simplifies work. It'll help if you use the inspection and build sheets presented in the glossary.

Nowadays blueprinting has come to refer to selective assembly with standard or non-standard parts. A 'grey area' exists when using non-standard parts – such as modern pistons made of high silicon alloy in an older engine whose pistons were a different composition, or altering castings or re-directing coolant flow – as the original blueprint specifications are invalid. This blurs the distinction between blueprinting and tuning.

The reason behind a so called 'dummy build' or 'mock-up' – temporarily building an engine prior to the final build – is to check specific measurements that are only verifiable on an assembled engine. Namely, the fit of certain engine castings, how machined surfaces contact each other, the interaction of gaskets of various thicknesses, and the movement of internal components. All such concerns need addressing so the result is an engine where internal components and castings fit together to best effect, thereby minimising stress and friction. This liberates horsepower and improves reliability. Best fit depends on application; two examples are:

1) A qualifying engine built for maximum power yet minimal use.
2) An endurance engine that has to produce good power for many racing hours.

Overall, the implication of checking and verifying is accuracy: leave nothing to chance. An unchecked or unmeasured component is an unknown; and is, therefore, a potential problem. Consequently, blueprinting could be defined as: selective assembly that increases horsepower and reliability.

DYNAMIC COMPRESSION

Do not fit different cams or raise compression without linking cam profile to dynamic compression. Matching cam profile increases engine harmony and optimises gas speed and combustion heat. A cylinder's dynamic compression ratio is the association between its combined, clearance and swept volumes, at the point of inlet valve closure, divided by the clearance volume. To put it another way, it is the compression existing in a running engine. The point of inlet valve closure largely determines dynamic compression. The inlet valve closes after bottom dead centre (ABDC), yet the piston has already begun to move up its cylinder. Effectively, this shortens the stroke as part of the charge has escaped out of the open inlet valve pushed out by the rising piston; in theory, reducing compression.

Dynamic compression is expressed as:

$$DCR = \frac{(SVI + CV)}{CV}$$

DCR = Dynamic compression ratio
SVI = Swept volume, at point of inlet valve closure
CV = Clearance volume

Dynamic compression is not the figure quoted by manufacturers; they quote static compression (see Chapter 6, 'Static compression'). Static compression, for purposes

of calculation, uses the whole of an engine's stroke: piston movement from bottom dead centre to top dead centre. Problems may arise when fitting a 'sports' profile camshaft without altering the compression. Sports cam profiles have greater duration (see Chapter 3, 'Duration'). Duration, properly sequenced, optimises gas wave inertia (see Chapter 9, 'Extract and ram effect') at higher engine speed, making engines more responsive. But, duration lowers dynamic compression, as the intake valve closes later. If compression is not raised to compensate, the result is an under-compressed charge and power-loss. On the other hand, retaining standard cams but raising compression leads to over-compression and possibly, detonation. The answer is to raise power output by increasing compression matched to cam design, specifically the point of inlet closing. This maintains or increases dynamic compression from standard levels, but always linking it to

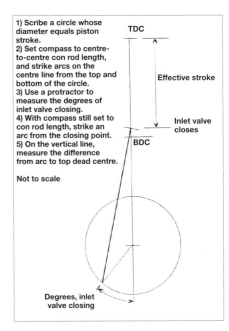

1) Scribe a circle whose diameter equals piston stroke.
2) Set compass to centre-to-centre con rod length, and strike arcs on the centre line from the top and bottom of the circle.
3) Use a protractor to measure the degrees of inlet valve closing.
4) With compass still set to con rod length, strike an arc from the closing point.
5) On the vertical line, measure the difference from arc to top dead centre.

Not to scale

TDC

Effective stroke

Inlet valve closes

BDC

Degrees, inlet valve closing

Fig 1-2: Convert degrees of inlet valve closing to linear measurement.

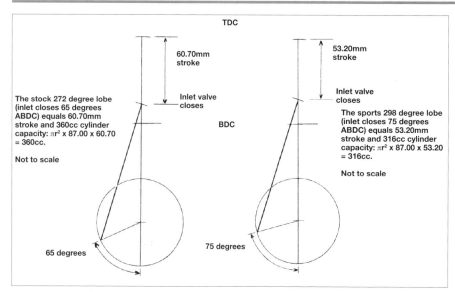

Fig 1-3: A sports cam can lower the dynamic compression.
With the stock cam, the dynamic compression in an 87.00mm x 75.70mm cylinder is
7.48:1 (left). Fitting a sports cam (right) lowers it to 6.69:1.

cam profile. To determine an engine's dynamic compression, first compute the effective stroke by converting degrees of inlet valve closing to linear measurement.

Imagine a single cylinder engine whose dimensions were:

Bore = 87.00mm
Stroke = 75.70mm
Con rod length, centre-to-centre = 120.00mm
Clearance volume = 55.50cc

The stock cam is 272 degrees duration (inlet closing at 65 degrees ABDC), but a sports cam is available at 298 degrees duration (inlet closing at 75 degrees ABDC). Convert the closing degrees to linear measurement for both lobes and work out the two swept volumes (see Chapter 6, 'Swept volume'). With this information, use the formula listed above to compute the engine's dynamic compression with each cam. The diagrams show that fitting the 298

degrees sports cam actually reduces compression. Therefore, to optimise high-speed performance, fit the 298 degrees cam but restore compression to the stock level by reducing the clearance volume 6.74cc. In most cases, this would be done by skimming the head or block, or by fitting a domed piston. On naturally-aspirated motors, for the sake of reliability, do not exceed a dynamic compression ratio of 8.0:1 for 2-valve engines, or 8.5:1 for 4-valve engines.

COMPONENT STRESS

When an engine is under stress – when cylinder pressure and piston speed increase – the chance of parts failing also increases. Wholly rigid structures do not exist. All components flex to some degree, yet in well-constructed assemblies this is a manageable amount.

Included in the appraisal of an engine (its suitability for a particular purpose) must be an assessment of its general robustness and strength. Will it be strong enough to do the job?

It may have potential weaknesses – for example, a heavy flywheel that could shake loose at high rpm; gears, sprockets or rotors secured by narrow section nuts; or poor quantity fasteners that impart flexibility into bolted joints – such parts may fracture. Designers sometimes use a 10-to-1 safety factor above yield strength when deciding component design.

A part's material (an alloy's constituents) largely governs its strength when in service. When a part fractures the fatigue fracture usually emanates from a surface crack. Exceptions are due to conditions like slag particles, porosity or brittleness. In such cases a crack can start under a component's surface. However, all cracks, whether starting internally or externally, develop at a stressed area: 'a stress concentration' that spreads during cyclic loading until reaching critical size, whereupon fracture takes place. Without a stress concentration, there would not be a fatigue failure. A stress concentration can result from normal use over a long period (old worn out parts), stress beyond design limits (overstressed components) or from a defect in design or surface damage. The internal surface of a tube or hollow component, like a wrist pin, is also a potential point of failure. Fatigue cracks can develop due to problems with heat treatment. Most engine building is concerned with modification rather than redesigning components. From this perspective, investigate two causes of stress when assembling a performance engine:

1) Surface finish-asperity, marks, scratches or burrs.
2) Loose-fitting component parts that *should* fit tightly together.

It's best to examine these two causes separately.

Surface finish

Highly-stressed components usually have a high-quality surface finish. 'Stress raisers' cause stress concentrations. These may be surface inclusions that cause sudden contour changes like burrs, sharp edges or tool marks or scratches. Gouges or dents, like a centre punch indentation, or score marks left by electric engravers, key ways, sharp-edged 90 degrees shoulders, and splines abruptly terminating at root diameter; these all interrupt surface flow and are potential stress raisers. There is a limit to what can be done without redesigning components. Nonetheless, remove inclusions and sharp edges; all the while aiming for the smoothest scratch-free finish on all components as this lessens the chance of failure. Depending on the part and resources, use a sharp triangular-pointed scraper, a fine file, fine abrasive paper, a fine flop wheel or polishing mop or a carborundum stone.

In the same way, remove any sharp edges on components left after casting or machining like casting flash, sharp edges adjacent to mating surfaces or burrs around holes.

To help avoid failure, handle parts carefully to avoid bruising or nicking. Where a mark cannot be removed, on a valve spring, for instance then the only remedy is replacement. A mark on any stressed component becomes more threatening when at a right angle to the component's route of stress. That means marks on a valve stem or a con rod that run along their lengths are less dangerous than those going across the beam. Removing marks on a con rod is not lightening, but stress relieving. Therefore, take off the minimum material to achieve a smooth finish. Forged 'I' section con rods are notorious for marks travelling across their beams. On un-dressed rods, a distinctive line around 5.00mm wide is usually visible

Fig 1-4 table

Good design	Questionable design	Bad design
Ground, polished surface. Low risk of stress raisers	Tool marks left after machining. Med risk of stress raisers	Rough, irregular surface. High risk of stress raisers and fracture
Large radius aids surface flow and reduces localised stress	Undercut fillet interrupts surface flow	Square shoulder causes stress concentration
Rolled thread, waisted shank dia. Thread area un-stressed	Rolled thread, nominal shank dia. Risk of fracture on stressed area	Screw cut thread. Risk of fracture at undercut
Radiused, waisted pulley & shaft. Low risk of fretting	Radiused, undercut pulley located on un-stressed area of waisted shaft. Med risk of fretting	Pulley located on stressed area of shaft. High risk of fretting

Fig 1-4: Surface finish and changes of contour.

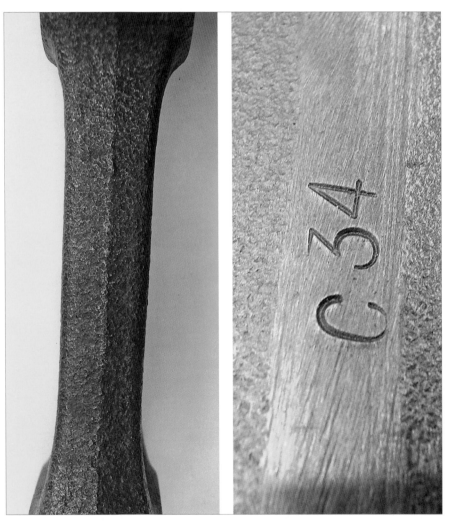

Plate 1-1: Stress raisers.
The marks on the beam of the left con rod, and stamp indentations on the right, interrupt surface flow. Both marks can lead to a stress raiser.

Plate 1-2: The removal of stress raisers. A smoothed, shot blasted con rod beam. Blasting compresses the surface so there's less chance of a stress raiser.

Plate 1-3: Loose assemblies. Both these bolts have been moving; shown by the discolouration on the left bolt, and the polished mark on the right. Eventually they may have fractured.

along the length. This excess material is 'flash,' residue from the forging process. Remove marks on the flash line using a flap wheel or by draw filing along the length. Follow this by light sanding to produce a scratch-free surface (equivalent to that of 800-grit abrasive paper). Polishing to a mirror finish used to be routine, and it certainly does no harm, but now quality rods are shot blasted (see Chapter 6, 'Shot blasting').

Loose-fitting components

Another source of stress raisers are parts that were designed to fit tightly together, yet which work loose. For example, a flywheel, a front pulley, or a sprocket or crankshaft-mounted alternator rotor, these are stiff

assemblies. Another example is the inner or outer surfaces of a bearing race that might be slipping on its mating shaft or moving in its bearing housing. A further source of looseness, often seen on older or long-stroke engines, is big end or main bearing shells not firmly nipped together, but moving in their bearing eyes. Then there are fasteners: bolts, nuts and screws that come loose or stretch and become un-tensioned. Looseness of the above-mentioned parts commonly falls under two general headings: fretting and galling.

Fretting, is the initial stage that a theoretically rigid joint, goes through when it starts to loosen. Fretting can be detected by the presence of polished areas where parts fit together. On shafts or the backs of bearing shells,

in bearing housings, on bearing races or as polished or rust deposits under the heads of fasteners. These 'telltales' indicate that parts have not been securely clamped together, or have lost their fit.

Galling, is the next stage, and is the result of severe fretting disturbing oxide films. Damage occurs to mating surfaces due to abrasive action as oxides continually form and tear away micro-amounts of parent material. This leads to a worsening of the fit, and greater looseness that produces a stress riser. Good examples are a loose front pulley wearing into a crankshaft nose, which might eventually shear off, or big end bearings moving and ultimately rotating in their con rod eyes.

Woodruff, and deep-set parallel

keys, like dowels on a flywheel boss, only locate components, they are not designed to transmit load. However, it is not uncommon to find keys and dowels that show signs of fretting. In mechanical applications, load transmission is by tapers, splines, and close parallel fits secured by fasteners in tension. Prevention and repair for these and the other mentioned problems are numerous. Better fitting keys, lapped tapers, de-burred splines, and upgraded bolts and nuts help eliminate fretting by increasing joint rigidity.

Secure marginally loose bearings or close parallel joints with Loctite 640 or Loctite 648. Both products are good at temperatures between 150C and 200C. In serious cases, bore-out housings and fit bronze or steel bearing sleeves, allowing an interference of 0.025mm per millimetre of outside diameter. Split bearings – main bearing and big ends – need 'capping' to restore their fit. To do this, use a belt sander to remove a minimal amount (usually around 0.05mm/0.002in) from the bearing cap abutments, then align hone the complete assembly to nominal size (see Chapter 5, 'Main saddles and caps'). In the case of fasteners, they are best upgraded and fitted with hardened washers.

BOLTS, SCREWS AND STUDS

Almost all bolts used on modern engines have rolled threads: threads formed, preferably after heat treatment, by cold rolling between thread dies. Rolled thread is stronger than machine or die-cut thread. Cut thread, no matter how well done, leaves machine marks that may lead to fracture. Use rolled thread fasteners wherever possible, but note that having custom threads rolled is expensive. On older engines or unusual thread sizes, such as 11.00mm, over-the-counter parts may be unavailable.

As a result, having a limited run of fourteen or twenty-eight die-box-cut head studs made is not ideal; but it will work. When having studs and nuts custom made, specify a superior grade of high tensile steel for the studs than for the nuts, thus ensuring that the nut strips before the stud.

The reason for upgrading fasteners is to achieve tighter, more reliable clamping. Although high-grade fasteners look 'professional,' an important point may be overlooked: if torque is not increased there is no more clamping load. This places an under-tightened, high-strength fastener in a dangerous condition as fastener reliability increases when tightened (stretched) to a specific amount. During cyclic loading an under-tightened fastener lengthens and shortens, which can lead to fracture. On the other hand, the stretch on a correctly tightened fastener prevents movement. As a result, when clamped to the same amount, under-tightened, high-strength fasteners are more liable to fatigue than bolts made of softer material.

High-grade fasteners, compared to lower grade, have superior recommended torque levels. Yet if parent thread, rather than fastener strength determines the maximum torque, high-grade fasteners will always be under stretched, and consequently susceptible to failure. For example, if an upgraded 25ft/lb fastener screws into an aluminium front cover but the parent thread strips at 20ft/lb, the fastener can only be tightened to the parent thread's limits. Hence, it will be under stretched and more liable to fracture than the original lower grade bolt. The situation is similar to welding a 7.00mm thick bracket to an exhaust pipe whose wall thickness is 0.80mm – the bracket is only as strong as the parent metal, which, in this case, is 0.80mm thick. In most instances, parent thread and not the fastener strength determines the maximum torque. To overcome this problem, match fastener length to thread hole depth by increasing the bolt length. It could be argued that using 180,000psi bolts to secure a front cover or carburettor base flange is an

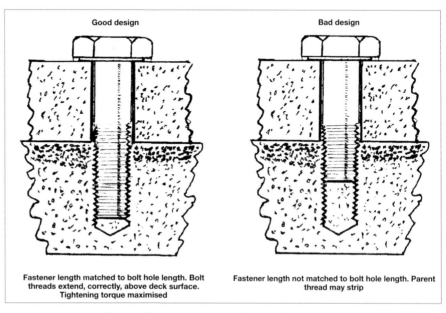

Good design | Bad design

Fastener length matched to bolt hole length. Bolt threads extend, correctly, above deck surface. Tightening torque maximised

Fastener length not matched to bolt hole length. Parent thread may strip

Fig 1-5: Match fastener length to bolt hole depth.

Plate 1-4: Bolts and screws.
For most uses, replace 8.8-grade bolts with stronger 12.9-grade cap screws.

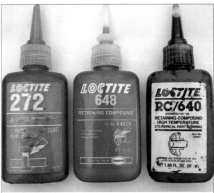

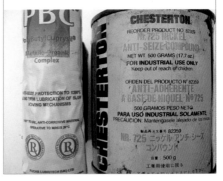

Plate 1-5: Retaining and anti-size compounds.
Use Loctite to retain fastenings, bearings and lip seals. Apply an anti-size compound to fasteners screwing into aluminium or on exhausts.

unnecessary waste of resources as the parent thread will probably strip long before the bolt is correctly stressed.

The usual standard of general fastening on most production engines is SAE 8.8 grade. These can easily be replaced with cap screws (internal hexagon headed), which are usually referred to as Allen or Unbrako screws. These are SAE 12.9 grade and good for everything except big end bolts. One disadvantage of cap screws is their smaller head size compared to hexagon-headed bolts. On heavily loaded applications, for example clamping a motorcycle final drive sprocket to its

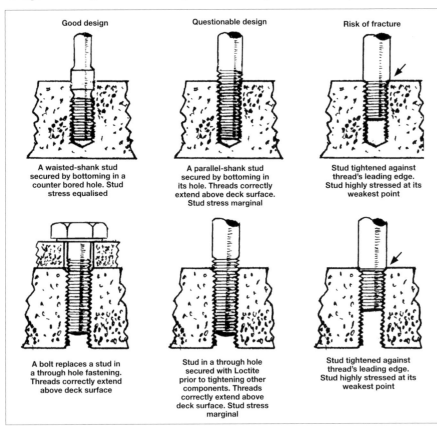

Good design

Questionable design

Risk of fracture

A waisted-shank stud secured by bottoming in a counter bored hole. Stud stress equalised

A parallel-shank stud secured by bottoming in its hole. Threads correctly extend above deck surface. Stud stress marginal

Stud tightened against thread's leading edge. Stud highly stressed at its weakest point

A bolt replaces a stud in a through hole fastening. Threads correctly extend above deck surface

Stud in a through hole secured with Loctite prior to tightening other components. Threads correctly extend above deck surface. Stud stress marginal

Stud tightened against thread's leading edge. Stud highly stressed at its weakest point

Fig 1-6: Locating critical studs.
Highly stressed studs can sheer or work loose if not correctly located.

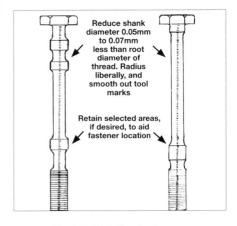

Reduce shank diameter 0.05mm to 0.07mm less than root diameter of thread. Radius liberally, and smooth out tool marks

Retain selected areas, if desired, to aid fastener location

Fig 1-7: Waisting fasteners.
Reducing the shank diameter distributes the stress of tension throughout the length of a fastener thereby increasing its fatigue resistance.

hub, or as head bolts, use hardened washers under the screw heads to increase clamping pressure. Do not use soft washers like turned-and-chamfered washers, as the screws will work loose when the screw heads dig into the soft material. Military specification bolts – 'AN' and 'NAS' – are widely available but quite expensive, they have minimum tensile strengths, respectively, of 125,000psi and 160,000psi.

Non-critical studs, such as those securing a sump pan or cam cover, are usually locked in their holes by tightening until the thread ends on the stud-shank. This stresses the area around the hole that, on soft castings, can lead to cracking or a circular burr. Such a burr or series of burrs on a mating surface can lead to the adjacent surface standing proud, and consequently allowing a leak. To fix this problem, remove the studs, de-burr the holes with a 90 degrees rose or countersink, and replace them with bolts or cap screws. Failing that, apply a drop of Loctite 272 to the thread of each stud and hand tighten them in their holes. That way, the studs will be locked in their holes without stressing the casting.

The threads of some studs are not deeply cut, which makes them hard to turn when screwing them into place. The purpose of this is to stop a stud and nut coming off together on disassembly, and to ensure maximum stud-to-parent thread interference on critical studs. One commonly finds this cut of thread on cylinder head, main bearing, and carburettor studs, but in reality, depending on a designer, they can be found anywhere on an engine. Do not Loctite this type of stud as this can lead to breakage. It's best to oil or apply anti-seize compound to their threads, then tighten them to ensure full thread engagement.

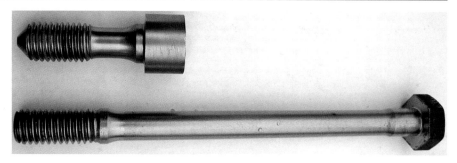

Plate 1-6: Waisted fasteners.
Removing material from the shanks of these two fasteners improves their fatigue resistance. The process is called waisting.

Critical studs, for example, studs securing a flywheel boss, a main bearing, or a cylinder head, must fit into blind holes, and should be locked by 'bottoming.' In other words, the studs will be fastened in their holes by the bottom of the stud contacting the bottom of the hole. Ideally, secure all studs in this way, as it reduces casting and stud stress around the last thread before the shank.

Where, due to design, critical fasteners do not fit into blind holes, such as some flywheel bosses, replace the studs with bolts. Furthermore, improve the resilience of critical studs, bolts and screws by waisting. This shifts the stress centre from the root of the thread and helps to reduce breakage by equalising the stretch. Waist a fastener on a lathe or centreless grinder by reducing the shank diameter, over most of its length, to 0.05mm/0.002in less than the root diameter. When turning on a lathe, use a round-nosed cutting tool. After turning, polish out the tool marks with abrasive cloth. For purposes of location, selected areas of the shank can be retained.

When bolts secure cylinder heads or main bearing caps on highly stressed engines, replace them with studs. The stress on a stud is exerted along one axis. A bolt has to twist while being tightened: it reacts to two different forces. Tightening-to-yield or torque-to-yield bolts could be considered as a production-type fastener that enables the moderately skilled to clamp components tighter with less risk of thread damage. These bolts are tightened to a predetermined torque then turned through a set amount measured with a protractor. This method stretches the bolt to within 2 per cent of its yield point, which elongates the threads – discard this type of bolt after each use. Replacing torque-to-yield bolts with cap screws is an excellent option.

NUTS AND WASHERS

Replace non-safety nuts with Nylocs or other shake-proof nuts. A Nyloc is a nut that contains an integral nylon insert which grips the mating thread; this prevents the nut vibrating loose. Nylocs can be reused several times before they become ineffective, and are good for most uses with the exception of exhaust or turbo applications. For areas of high heat, use deformed nuts like Aerotite, Jet Nuts or Binx. These grip due to distorted segments that press on a thread – they can also be reused. Of the three, many would suggest that Jet Nuts (also known as 'K-Nuts') are exceptional due to their narrow height and great strength which permits fitting shorter bolts, thus saving weight.

Plate 1-7: Different types of self-locking nut.
From the left: Jet nut, Aerotite, Stover, Binx and Nyloc. Of the five, Nyloc is the only one that cannot be used on exhaust applications as it has a nylon insert.

Compared to older designs, modern engines do not have that many washers, and the days of flat washer plus spring washer are long gone. Unless you're trying to duplicate visible authenticity, discard spring washers in favour of Loctite or Belleville washers – coned-shaped and smooth surfaced – or Schnorr washers, which are also cone-shaped but serrated: they are both made of hardened steel. The latter readily fit under cap screw heads when fitting into a counter bore, and do not unduly mark soft castings. Use hardened washers on heavily loaded areas. Use soft aluminium washers on carburettor unions, or with care, annealed copper will work. Use copper washers on oil and water banjo fittings, with or without a smear of sealant. On banjo joints, Dowty washers are effective; they are made of hard aluminium and have an internal rubber seal that has to fit precisely to the abutting faces. They are excellent where the components have precision

Plate 1-8: Different types of washer.
From the left: turned-and-chamfered (soft), Schnorr (hardened), Bellville (hardened), flat washer (hardened), wavy (hardened).

faces, yet they can be used only once. A further option for some sealing applications like water or exhaust or oil plugs is the crushable washer. These are either copper or aluminium and contain a crushable medium that conforms to surface irregularities.

THE WORKSHOP

A workshop usually represents some form of compromise, human nature being what it is the yearning for that extra tool or machine or more space is common. The comment is sometimes heard: 'If I need a tool once, I buy it!' Such a stance may help to keep an economy running, but from a mechanic's point of view it has tenuous validity. Extensive tool collections are no substitute for knowledge. A collection of tools, like a library of canonical texts, is only as good as the mind that utilises their potential. With care and planning good work can often be done with a few tools of the correct type in a one-car garage or shed. Specialist tools that may only be used once or twice, like large micrometers or bore gauges, can be rented.

For the assembly area, if space allows, allocate a smooth-surfaced bench fitted with a 4-inch vice: do not use this for cutting or filing. To prevent marking components remove the sharp serrations on the vice jaws by surface grinding. Basic hand tools, like sockets, will be required, as will a dial test indicator (DTI), a 6-inch or 10-inch vernier, and a

Plate 1-9: Special hand tools.
Different torque wrenches and pliers. From the left the pliers are: to remove valve stem oil seals, to install or remove piston rings, safety wire pliers, and two types of insulated pliers.

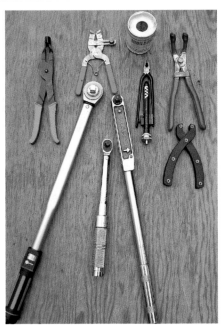

Plate 1-10: Custom made tools.
Tools for some engines have to be custom made. The examples are: valve stem oil seal installers, a camshaft rotator, installed height gauges, valve position punches, headstands, and a valve spring depressor.

0- to 1-inch micrometer – a cast iron or granite surface plate, or even a thick flat steel plate is invaluable. Engine stands,

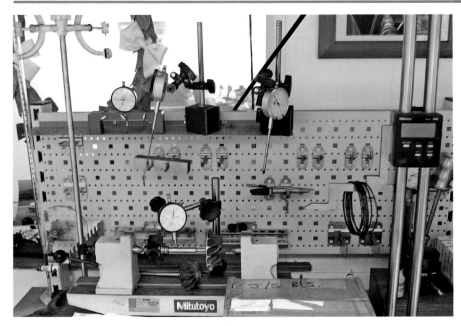

Plate 1-11: A specialist measuring station.
Comprising: a selection of dial test indicators, a bridge gauge, a burette and stand, slip gauges, a vernier height gauge, and a centre-to-centre stand to check turbo shafts.

jigs or fixtures particular to an engine can usually be made without too much trouble. Work, like crankshaft grinding or cylinder boring, that requires specialist equipment will be subcontracted, but be specific, and give written instructions to the machine shop. An engineering handbook is a good source of information when making or modifying components. Editions like *Zeus Precision* and Bosch's *The Automotive Handbook* are readily available.

CRYOGENIC TEMPERING

Cryogenic tempering benefits the racer and the restorer. It toughens components by making them stronger, more resistant to wear, and it improves their dimensional stability. Improved dimensional stability means that the assembled fit of parts is more likely to be maintained when in service. There will be less bore or crankcase distortion, for example. Aluminium or steel-alloy

parts, from crankcases to gear shafts, can be treated. The process involves Austenite and Martensite, which exist in heat-treated alloys as carbon and iron. Austenite is soft and brittle; it can lead to loss of hardness, strength and dimensional stability. Martensite is harder and more stable. Cryogenic tempering consists of the controlled freezing of components and 'soak' at temperatures of -79 degrees C or lower. At such temperatures, Austenite is unstable and transforms into harder, Martensite. In real terms this means that if a cylinder head had overheated, and was thought to be soft as it kept blowing gaskets, or a crankcase distorted as its main bearing axis was out of alignment, these kinds of components can have their strength improved by cryogenic tempering. Therefore, it follows that new or used parts with no obvious defects may also be made more durable and dimensionally stable. For example, in the late 1980s the cylinder of a Husqvarna desert racer

was cryogenically tempered before a particular race. The cylinder bore was inspected after the event, and only light abrasions could be detected, yet on previous occasions it needed re-sleeving.

On the other hand, the original parts on a rare or exclusive machine can be strengthened as the durability imparted by cryogenic tempering helps to guard against cracking and fracture. With original parts, a vehicle's provenance can be maintained.

As cryogenic tempering is specialist, it is important to plan the treatment in advance. Treatment may only be done on certain days, for instance.

CERAMIC TREATMENT

Ceramic treatment generally falls into two categories: 'wear coatings' and 'thermal barriers.' Wear coatings are particularly good for loaded components, like the cam lobes on pushrod engines or sparsely lubricated 2-stroke cylinder liners. Hard ceramic coatings dampen the rubbing action caused by mating components when in motion; this helps to reduce stress and prolong life. They also help reduce detonation. Some other parts that can be treated are piston rings, pistons, wrist pins and valves.

Thermal barriers applied to piston crowns and (or) combustion chambers may reduce combustion temperature as the ceramic acts as an insulator and reflective layer. This enables an engine to be fine tuned to optimise turbo boost, and fuel and ignition settings: this could result in more power. Like cryogenic tempering, ceramic treatments are specialist, so it's best to contact a company that performs such services to discuss particular needs. Two reputable companies are listed in 'Useful Addresses'; no doubt others exist.

Chapter 2
Disassembly & inspection

DISASSEMBLY PREPARATIONS

Before disassembling an engine allocate space to store the various components. This is important, because, depending on an engine's size and complexity, disassembly may take hours or days. From observation, many seem to have a natural tendency to rush; to 'teardown' an engine in an almost literal sense of the word. Such an approach suggests, implicitly, a lack of concern or awareness: parts can be broken or damaged, and observations or readings missed.

The word 'feel,' in an engineering sense, describes a person's dexterity; their subjective awareness or ability to judge necessary effort when working with precision components. With this in mind, caution and patience are important when evaluating a problem; for example, trying to remove a part that appears stubbornly fixed – take a moment and consider the difficulty. Is the force being used trying to remove the part sufficient to cause

damage? Are there screws, circlips or pins that need removing but have gone unnoticed? The disassembly of complex parts may sometimes be aided by considering how they were made and assembled. Be careful when handling parts as surfaces can be bruised and locally compressed if they are banged about; this leads to surface tensions that may result in fracture. When removing parts or assessing the relationship certain parts have to each other, such as the backlash of a gear, it's worth considering that a part may have been incorrectly assembled. Just because something comes out in a certain way does not mean it should go back in the same position. On some engines; pistons, rings, con rods or thrust bearings can be installed back-to-front or upside down and yet the engine may run with seemingly little concern. For the purpose of discussion, it's assumed that the engine is out of the vehicle, and oil and coolant have been drained.

Keep a notepad and camera to hand to record vital information; do not rely on memory alone. Some unheated workshops may become damp at night; so store records away from humidity. Keep all the old gaskets and seals in a safe place until the engine is finished and tested – sometimes the telltale signs on old gaskets can aid the discovery of such things as a crack in a casting. Do not touch or scrape gasket surfaces or the tops of pistons or combustion chambers before a thorough inspection, as this may alter or obscure a telltale.

Plate 2-1: Look for telltales. Do not scrape the top of a piston before an initial inspection as it may destroy a telltale.

Some contend that an engine should not be cleaned before disassembly as water from power washers or other cleaning fluids may enter fuel or ignition systems. However, when an engine is clean, it's easier to strip, and debris is less likely to fall into open fuel pipes or distributors. Before cleaning, to protect fuel and electrical systems, wrap them in plastic.

Universal engine stands aren't expensive, and it's even fairly straightforward to have something custom made. Mounting an engine on a stand makes work easier, and looks more presentable if any 'visitors' come round for a look.

Before disassembly make notes and photograph complex items, such as the routing of pipes, harnesses or linkages, the location of plug wires or a distributor's position – don't rush or errors may be made. Confidence increases with experience, and experience comes from doing. By working slowly, expertise and knowledge are gained without causing damage.

FIND ROTATION AND FIRING ORDER

The crankshaft of a 4-stroke engine can rotate clockwise or anticlockwise. Ostensibly, the internal components remain the same for either direction, as only the camshaft and ignition (excepting fuel injection timing) need to be altered. When a manufacturer's literature is not available, check the rotation before removal, by either cranking the starter or putting the gearbox in second gear and rolling the machine forward, thereby noting the rotation of the crankshaft. Another way is to look at the tooth chamfer on the flywheel ring gear, or the abrasions made by the starter gear – these are telltales to rotation.

If none of these options are possible, try fitting a compression gauge to a cylinder and turn the crankshaft while noting the reading. Rising pressure on a gauge when a piston moves up to TDC indicates the correct rotation. Some ignition, or fuel distributors or magnetos have a directional arrow on their casings: you can work out the rotation direction from these. If none of these options work for you, remove the cam or valve covers and turn the crankshaft in the most likely direction, observing the valves on a particular cylinder in relation to the piston through 720 degrees. They will follow the sequence shown in Fig 1-1. Stop approximately 10 degrees BTDC on the firing stroke, in which case the ignition rotor or trigger should to be timed to deliver a spark to the cylinder. Most car engines have clockwise rotation (when viewed from the crankshaft pulley), whereas some racing engines run the other way.

With the rotation known, it won't be difficult to find number 1 cylinder. In an engine with cylinders arranged in a row, number 1 will either be the cylinder closest to the pulley or at the other end near the flywheel. On a banked engine, like a V12 or horizontally opposed Flat-12, number 1 is usually the cylinder closest to the pulley on either the port or the starboard bank. Screw a compression gauge into the selected cylinder and turn the engine in the direction of rotation until the needle on the gauge begins to rise; it is approaching TDC on its firing stroke. Remove the gauge and shine a strong light down the cylinder bore, slowly turn the crankshaft observing the piston as it travels upwards, stopping when it's at TDC. The ignition rotor should be pointing to the distributor post for that cylinder. Using number 1 cylinder as a datum, an engine's firing order can be ascertained by observing the valve opening and closing points in relation to piston position – although on a 12-cylinder engine this can be rather laborious.

RECORD SETTINGS

When planning to change the camshafts or the pistons on a production engine, a handbook is probably available that states the timing and compression ratio, so there is little point verifying common knowledge. The matter is different when it comes to competition engines: treat most literature with scepticism. This is because an engine built for a certain race or to a competitive specification can be altered to suit prevailing conditions. On a race motor, it is sensible to record the ignition timing before going any further.

On all engines proceed as follows. Remove plug wires, cables, harnesses and any ancillary or fragile components. Depending on engine design, next remove the cam covers and (or) sump. Some people don't like to turn an engine upside down to gain easy access to the sump bolts – they contend that debris will fall into the cylinder bores. Arguably, of greater importance is the metallic residue and pieces of gasket or sealing material that may be lost: these are an indicator to the condition of the engine and the standard of previous assembly. With the cam cover or covers removed, record the valve timing and valve clearances, if thought necessary (see Chapter 3, 'Setting timing').

CAMSHAFT DRIVE

On a pushrod engine remove and store the rockers, pushrods and cam followers in order of disassembly. Usually, it's possible to withdraw a camshaft without too much effort; although on some motorcycle engines the crankcases must be split to gain access. On an overhead camshaft engine, check the numbering system, if any, on the cam bearing caps. These are usually stamped numerically or alphabetically and have a corresponding mark adjacent to their head casting. Stamp or etch unmarked cam caps.

For the sake of good working

**Plate 2-2: Mark components.
To avoid mixing components, stamp or
etch parts when they are removed.**

practice, wherever possible remove a camshaft drive with the engine at TDC firing stroke number 1 cylinder. The exceptions are where a timing chain has a removable link low down in the run and access is difficult or when an engine is damaged or hard to rotate.

The next step depends on an engine's drive system. When cams are gear driven they are removed first. Chain or timing belt drives are common on modern engines, and for these systems, rotate the crankshaft to gain access to the tensioner, and then lock up the camshafts. Locking overhead camshafts is a worthy safeguard to stop sudden rotation. Naturally-aspirated, two-valve engines in any state of tune are most at risk from unlocked camshafts. The reason is clear: when loosening the tension of a chain or belt, a camshaft can rotate by the action of valve spring pressure, and a valve might be bent by hitting a piston. The simplest way to lock a camshaft is to insert a piece of paper, 0.50mm/0.020in thick, under a single cam bearing cap and gently retighten. Surprisingly, it doesn't require much force to stop a camshaft rotating.

With the chain or timing belt disconnected, remove the camshafts and heads, either separately or as a unit. Place cylinder heads on their sides on a bench, or with their valves uppermost.

Putting a cylinder head with open valves face down on any flat surface, like a workbench, usually results in bent valves. It's sloppy practice to place even a bare head (one stripped of all hardware) face down on its machined surface as it will get scratched. Before going any further, measure the stroke, and, if necessary, record the compression ratio (see Chapter 6, 'Static compression').

CON RODS

Turn the engine upside down, or look at the con rods from the underside, and record the number stamped or etched on each big end eye. Also note whether the number points to port or starboard. For example, the rod numbers on an in-line engine are usually on the same side, and in a V-banked engine, the numbers on the port rods will point towards port, and the starboard to starboard. On some engines, the big end eye is slightly offset in relation to the wrist pin; in which case the rod numbers may switch.

Start at number 1 cylinder and rotate the engine to Bottom Dead Centre. On most engines, two rod and piston assemblies can be removed at one time. A length of hardwood, approximately 1in x 18in makes an excellent tool to push out pistons. After each extraction, double check the position of the rod number against existing notes – some rods are numbered on both sides: continue until all are removed.

CRANKSHAFT

If the front pulley is still attached and an impact wrench is available, this is the only time it could be used – impact wrenches impart no sense of feel and can easily damage components. It's better to lock the crankshaft; wedging the flywheel teeth, the flywheel bolts or by a suitable piece of aluminium or hardwood placed between a crankshaft's counter weight and the crankcase. Make a note

of the numbers on the main bearing caps. If cross-bolts are fitted, remove them before undoing the main bearing nuts, then remove the crankshaft and note the thrust washer position.

CYLINDER HEAD

Two cylinder head checks need to be made before cleaning and inspection, but they are only relevant for overhead camshaft and race engines:

1) Measure the valve shim thickness
2) Measure the valve spring height

Measure the old shims with a micrometer and compare their thickness to the range available. A typical manufacturer's shim range could be graduated from 0.90mm/0.354in to 2.770mm/0.106in. If the shims removed from an engine were 0.95mm, this is one size bigger than the thinnest shim, which indicates that the valves have sunk. If these valves were lapped, they would sink even more. As a result, the thinnest shim, 0.90mm, would be too thick to set the running clearance. The valves and seats need to be replaced. If the shim thickness had not been checked during teardown, this problem would only be apparent on assembly. Checks to spring heights only apply to competition or tuned engines where the available data on valve spring pressure is sparse or unreliable. The reason for measuring spring height is to determine spring pressure. For the procedure, refer to (Chapter 4, 'Installed height').

CLEANING

Parts should be cleaned at least 3 times:

1) To enable inspection and machining
2) To remove debris before a test build
3) Prior to the final build

Before cleaning the castings and

Plate 2-3: Measure valve shims.
Valves wear and seats recess, measure the position of the valves to ensure they fall within the manufacturer's tolerance, otherwise future work may be wasted.

Plate 2-4: Clean oil galleries.
Cleaning galleries with solvent and compressed air is not enough. Scrub galleries and drillings in the head, block and crankshaft to remove solid deposits.

crankshaft, remove all gallery and cross-drilling plugs and scrub through with a sized-brush. Pay particular care to remove debris and solid material as it only takes a small solid particle, a piece of gasket or a lump of silicone, for example, to wedge open an oil pressure relief valve. Improperly cleaned galleries may contain loosened debris that becomes disturbed and mixes with fresh lubricant on engine start-up. This can cause severe damage to a rebuilt engine. The piston cooling oil jets (squirters) can be overlooked when rebuilding a turbo engine. These may be jammed open by debris, reducing oil pressure and leading to rapid engine destruction.

Cleaning can be done in several ways, and is dependent on resources. Carbon deposits on cylinder heads, valves or pistons are the worst to shift. Clean them by immersion in a decarbonising or carburettor cleaner. This is available in 25-litre drums. Disassemble close fitting components like wrist pins to reduce the risk of parts binding together with varnish.

Caustic cleaning is another method carried out commercially: ferrous parts are submerged in a tank containing caustic soda, water and brighteners. For the enthusiast, cleaning on a small scale with caustic soda crystals is an excellent alternative to carburettor

cleaner. Many hardware shops sell soda crystals, whose use is often overlooked in favour of commercial cleaners. Crystals are priced economically, being about 2 per cent of the cost of a 25-litre drum of de-carboniser. The use of caustic soda as a cleaner of automotive parts used to be common when decarbonising was almost considered part of routine maintenance, and properly used, crystals are effective as a cleaner of carbon.

However, soda turns aluminium parts a matt grey, a patina that can only be removed by bead blasting or covered by painting. A caustic solution that is too strong can erode aluminium components, rendering them useless. Mix a mild solution, for example 2 per cent, in a plastic container (100 millilitres of crystals to 5 litres of cold water). Other ways to clean parts are by pressure washing in a hot washer tank, or a strong soapy solution, or with solvents like kerosene, Varsol or Jiser. Whatever method is used, it's important to scrub parts clean of debris, as flushing with solvents does not remove heavy deposits.

A razor blade knife is excellent for removing old gasket material as it does not scratch machined surfaces. For cleaning around studding, use a medium-bristle wire brush and abrasive pads,

such as Scotchbrite. Go over mating surfaces with a brass-bristle brush then a rubbing block covered in 350-grit abrasive followed by a fine carborundum stone, such as a slip stone. When free of oil and grease, castings and gears may be bead blasted in a dry or wet sandblaster (vapour blaster). Before blasting, block off all waterway and oil gallery holes. A good product for this job is 'Plug-It': a pliable material that can be moulded to shape and fitted over oil holes, yet it does not break apart or clog galleries. Plastic blanking caps, or (at a push) masking tape may also be used.

The finish on bead blasted or un-polished aluminium castings like motorcycle crankcases or finned cylinders is second to none. Removing the grit and dust detritus is a problem, however, as repeated scrubbing and washing with hot soapy water is necessary. If one's relationship can stand it, a power shower is reasonably effective at washing off sandblasting debris. High-pressure compressed air is insufficient to clean blind-threaded holes of all blasting debris. Run a thread chaser, coated with graphite or white grease, down every hole. Clean the chaser and repeat until clean, then wash the hole and dry with compressed air. A plug tap of the correct thread makes an excellent chaser when blunted by running it through a nut filled with valve grinding paste.

Bead blasted aluminium castings can be stained with clean oil during a dummy build. To remove stains, immerse the stained part in boiling soapy water for five minutes. A commercial-sized cooking pot works well, or a spotlessly clean 25-litre open-topped drum. Although be careful the heat does not disturb the interference of assembled parts like bearings or bushes. Do not clean delicate parts, like carburettors by vapour blasting as grit residue can never be wholly removed but will flow into drillings

Plate 2-5: Making a chaser tap.
Use a chaser tap to clean thread holes without damaging the parent thread. When a chaser isn't available, blunt a plug tap by coating it with grinding paste and running it several times through a sacrificial nut.

Plate 2-6: Clean components.
A stiff-bristle brush and abrasive pads are useful for cleaning parts. Clean mating surfaces with an abrasive-covered rubbing block or a carborundum stone.

Plate 2-7: Removing gaskets.
A razor blade knife is a good way to remove old gaskets without marking surfaces.

and cause no end of trouble. Paint thinner, is a reasonably effective cleaner for carburettors, but ultrasonic cleaning is best. Clock and watch repairers use this type of system where parts are submerged in a trichoethylene or a detergent-filled tank then subjected to cyclic sound waves that create bursting bubbles that dislodge contaminants.

CRACK TESTING

Crack test all major internal components and engine castings. Clean and dry any component or casting before testing. Check ferrous parts by Magnaflux testing. This is particularly effective at identifying cracks just below the surface; for example, on a polished component where the opening of a crack might have been burred over. Magnafluxing requires specialist equipment usually only found in engine rebuild or engineering shops.

Another process readily available to the amateur or professional is 'dye penetrant.' Modern dye penetrants have parallels to the old crack testing method. This was to swab or immerse a component in warm kerosene and after drying, sprinkle it with powered chalk or paint it with whitewash. Once left to 'develop,' any crack would be visible as a wet line formed by kerosene squeezed

Plate 2-8: Dye penetrant crack detector.
Use dye penetrant on ferrous and non-ferrous parts. A crack appears as a stain on the white surface of the developer.

out between adjacent surfaces. Such a crack would appear as a stain in the medium. A modern dye penetrant is no more than two aerosol cans, a coloured penetrant in place of kerosene, and a developer in place of chalk. Penetrant is spayed on the piece to be tested then washed or cleaned off before being coated with developer. Developer turns the work off-white. Any crack will show up as a coloured line on the white surface. Use this easy cost-effective method on ferrous and non-ferrous components. Common brands are 'Checkmor' and 'Spotcheck.'

Crack testing is not a universal remedy that restores over-stressed or outdated parts to useful service: all the most observant eye can do is to detect a surface flaw. A pessimist could point out that it is possible for a much used or stressed part, which has just passed a crack test, to fail soon after in service. Crack testing does not examine a component's inner structure. The parts being referred to are con rods and crankshafts; and in a drive train; first motion, and drive shafts. X-raying these components is a way to check for internal flaws or irregularities, but at the end of an X-ray test one may end up with little more than an expensive bill and old components. Consequently, unless originality is important, it is safer to replace or upgrade highly stressed parts.

STRESS RELIEVING

Old castings subject to severe or prolonged use, or those repaired by welding, can accumulate stress irregularities that may lead to a lack of strength, distortion or cracking. Hydrogen embrittlement can be caused by welding, cold working or pickling during cleaning processes. Stress-relieve components by removing and smoothing any sharp edges and then give them an extended heat soak in an oven. Heat soaking promotes the escape of hydrogen and helps restore ductility. When heating a component, solidly support it to avoid distortion. After soak, turn off the oven and let the component cool in the oven to ambient temperature. The actual temperature and length of soak depends on the material and its size. Generally speaking, for a cast aluminium crankcase, ten to twelve hours at 177 degrees C/350 degrees F would be enough; slightly less for a cylinder head.

RESIDUAL MAGNETISM

Internal components can become partially magnetised by certain types of cyclic action, for example when bearing shells turn in a big end eye. Magnafluxed parts not fully demagnetised may also retain a small magnetic field, which will attract metal debris and hasten bearing wear. These are both examples of residual magnetism. Check components for magnetism with a magnetic field indicator (these are modestly priced). The rougher detection method is to touch a component with a lightweight metallic object, like a scriber or small screwdriver, and feel the 'pull.'

Plate 2-9: Check for magnetism.
Magnetised parts will attract metal debris and hasten bearing wear. Check for magnetism with a gauss meter.

PAINTING

Although this chapter is concerned with disassembly, painting parts is something that needs planning. Paint engine parts individually before assembly, not the engine as a completed unit after build. Aesthetically, an engine built of individually painted parts is pleasing to the eye and easy to disassemble as paint has not adhered to fasteners, as would be the case if it had been painted as a unit. When painting, clean splashes quickly; there is no need for masking tape. Paint the exterior of a cast iron block otherwise it will be akin to a giant rust stain and poor looking piece of work. Paint all un-machined exterior surfaces before fitting core and gallery plugs, which, for appearance sake, are best unpainted as they're plated.

Concerning aluminium blocks, there is the option to paint or not; although aluminium oxidises, the rate of deterioration is slow and less obvious than cast iron. A clean aluminium surface stains quite easily, as mentioned previously. Crankcases are not usually bead blasted (motorcycle cases excepted). But no matter how clean their exterior, they may still be stained. For best appearance, paint the exterior of motor vehicle aluminium castings with Simoniz Cellulose Brushing Silver, product number SIM34. This paint covers in one coat and will not burn off water-cooled cylinder heads. After an engine has run for an hour or two, the paint patina changes and takes on the colour of an un-painted bead blasted aluminium surface. The patina is so subtle that a viewer is hard pressed to state whether or not the casting is painted.

When an internal surface has been bead blasted it needs to be washed and scoured repeatedly, and even then its cleanliness will be suspect. Rub the internal surface of a clean, dry blasted casting with a finger and a dusty oxide appears. It's rather like an unpainted concrete floor that has been brushed and mopped many times – once dry, a dusty film can still be felt. Painting seals surfaces, not only curtailing dust but also acting as a sealer against porosity. Painting the internal surfaces of engines is widely used by commercial diesel, aero engine and motorsport companies. It is very useful for older castings or those made of magnesium or Electron. Brush paint all bare un-machined internal surfaces throughout an engine with an etch primer or an enamel as used by electric motor re-winders. In other words, apply only to sand-cast surfaces – do not paint die cast aluminium. This is identifiable by its bright shiny finish. Brush painting requires no masking-up; get rid of any spillage or spots with a spirit-dampened cloth, or, when dried, remove splashes with a razor blade knife. Common colours are pale yellow or dull red – in reality, the particular shade is immaterial. A cry is sometimes heard: 'It will flake off and block the oil strainers." From the observation of engines after many hours of use, this is not the case. Strainers are under a bigger threat from gasket particles and sealant debris like RTV rather than flakes of paint.

Plate 2-10: Paint the internal surfaces of castings.
A painted internal surface is a barrier against porosity and traps any microscopic particles: it helps engine cleanliness.

Chapter 3
Timing drives

BEVEL DRIVES

Bevel drives used to be quite common before the invention of timing belts and roller chain, and arguably were the accepted method of transferring crankshaft drive to an overhead camshaft. They are expensive to produce, require skilful assembly and are quite noisy. Bevels with straight cut teeth are stronger than those having a spiral pattern as load is taken along the whole of tooth length rather than a portion. But straight cut teeth are noisier in operation and wear quicker due to their more sudden tooth engagement. Straight cut bevels also demand very rigid bearing housings to support their shafts and maintain alignment. Spiral bevels are quieter due to their gradual tooth engagement – more teeth are in mesh at any given moment – and the lower sliding action of the teeth when meshing. Unless working on a very old engine, the spiral pattern is most commonly encountered. Bevel gears

come as a matched pair – a pinion gear and a ring gear. After machining, gear sets are lapped together with micro-fine abrasive to remove tooth imperfections that remain after manufacture. For this reason, do not mix gears but keep pinion and ring gear sets together. When checking clearances, assemble bevels dry – with no oil on their teeth. On final assembly, this type of design should have:

1) Zero end float on each gear: in other words, the gears have no axial movement
2) The required backlash between the teeth
3) Gear transmission in the middle of the ring gear's teeth: referred to as 'depth'

Bevel gear adjustment is usually by shim. These come in various thicknesses, thereby allowing a broad adjustment range, and look in this particular case like flat washers. It is

Plate 3-1: An open bevel drive. Each gear on an open bevel drive is unsupported on its outward face. Before the invention of timing belts and roller chain, bevel drives were the accepted method of driving overhead camshafts.

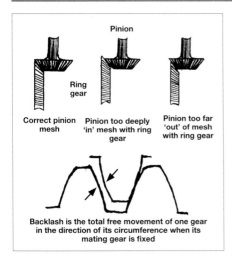

Fig 3-1: Bevel pinion mesh and tooth backlash.

Plate 3-2: Blueing a pinion gear. A blued pinion makes impressions on the teeth of a ring gear. Read the impressions then adjust the pinion depth.

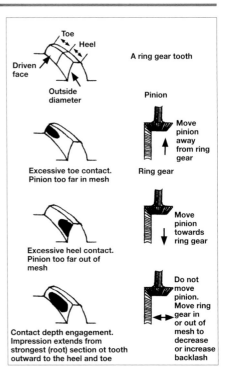

Fig 3-2: Bevel drives. Reading ring gear impressions made by Engineers' Blue. Correct engagement makes a drive stronger.

difficult to make specific statements about the method of eliminating end float as designs vary. Nonetheless, two adjustments are always the same on any open bevel arrangement:

1) Adding or subtracting shims behind a pinion gear alters the depth
2) Adding or subtracting shims behind a ring gear alters the backlash

Backlash, is defined as the total free movement of one gear in the direction of its circumference when its mating gear is fixed. The pinion gear is the smallest gear in a bevel set, so it's easy enough to spot, but if unsure, assemble the gears and note the backlash. Then remove a shim or two from behind one gear and reassemble. If the backlash is unchanged, and the gears do not appear to be meshing evenly on their outer and inner edges then the gear adjusted was the pinion. On the other hand, if play between the teeth has increased, then it was the ring gear.

Pinion depth

There are a number of different ways to assemble and adjust a pair of bevel gears; yet the following method yields accurate results and requires only a DTI, feeler gauges, and Engineers' Blue. Assemble the pinion so that is has zero end float: zero float, or a pre-load on the pinion shaft bearings is necessary to prevent the gears moving in-and-out of mesh when in service. Bearing pre-load is the amount of loading applied to bearings during assembly to take account of thermal expansion, wear, and flexing that occur in any design. Next, fit the ring gear – the end float on ring gear bearings is not critical at this stage, but the gears must mesh and turn when all the fasteners are tight. The object is to rotate the gears by turning the pinion shaft. The assembly may feel tight, but it is of little consequence. Nevertheless, if the gears are too tight to turn, adjust the shims on the ring gear to give some free play between the gear teeth.

When the ring gear can be rotated through 360 degrees by turning the pinion shaft, disassemble the ring gear to gain access to the pinion, and lightly coat the driving faces of the pinion teeth with Engineers' Blue. Reassemble, and rotate the ring gear through two revolutions in its normal direction of rotation. Disassemble the ring gear, and, under strong light, examine the impressions on the driven faces of its teeth, which ideally will be marked in the middle of each tooth. Clean off the impressions and add or remove shims to the pinion gear to make the engagement further in or out of mesh. Re-blue the pinion, and repeat the test until the desired result is obtained. Clean and dry both gears. The pinion gear can now be finally assembled, if required, remembering to apply the correct bearing pre-load.

The ring gear

Following on, the ring gear bearings need to be pre-loaded and the backlash

**Plate 3-3: Measuring backlash.
Measure ring gear backlash on the outside
diameter of a tooth.**

between the teeth measured. Most bevels used in engine applications are open pattern – supported from one side – and tightening the ring gear shaft pulls the whole assembly into line. To check the backlash, lock the pinion shaft and arrange a dial test indicator so its stylus rests on the outside diameter of a ring gear tooth. Always take measurements on the outside diameter of the ring gear. Due to some designs, access to the ring gear's outer diameter may be blocked by a casting or bracket. In such a case, made up a tool whose diameter corresponds to ring gear diameter with a flat on which the DTI's stylus can bear; then take measurements on this flat.

There's no golden rule governing the optimum backlash for gear sets. An assembly's design and thermal expansion affects the backlash between two running gears when under load and at full operating temperature. Nevertheless, one would not be too amiss assembling the cylinder head bevels on a water-cooled engine with an aluminium head to a backlash in the range of 0.038mm/0.0015in to 0.058mm/0.0022in, and iron heads to 0.05mm/0.002in to 0.063mm/0.0025in. Assemble an air-cooled engine on the low side of these tolerances. Concerning the lower drive coming off

the crankshaft, some designs mount a bevel gear directly on the crankshaft. Consequently, to take account of shaft flex, increase the clearance. If in doubt, run a larger clearance as it will not weaken a drive, but only make it noisier.

Timing adjustment: bevel drives

Timing is adjusted by vernier arrangement on the cam or by moving the camshaft gear on its shaft; the latter design is the hardest to adjust. To find out how many degrees correspond to each tooth on a camshaft gear, count the number of teeth and divide by 360. For example, for a gear with 28 teeth:

$$\frac{360}{28} = 12.8571$$

Each tooth corresponds to 12.8 degrees of camshaft rotation, but, as degree measurements are taken with a crankshaft mounted timing disc, and as crankshafts turn at twice camshaft speed, the figure is doubled. In that case, moving the camshaft gear one tooth (12.8 degrees) alters the valve timing by 25.7 degrees measured at the crankshaft. For simplicity, it's easier to refer to any adjustments using crankshaft degrees, and work backwards. In the example, any corrections less than 25.7 degrees (crankshaft degrees) would have to be made with an offset key. Such a key rotates the cam gear the required offset. These can be hand filed, but call for patience and skill, and, if more than one has to be made, it's easier, and perhaps more accurate, to have them machined. Using the figures above as an example, imagine that the valve timing is 9 degrees out from specification. It cannot be moved from its current position by 9 degrees as each tooth on the cam gear moves the timing 25.7 degrees. To work out the offset for a key, compute the degrees of cam gear rotation to achieve

9 degrees of crankshaft movement as follows:

$$\frac{9}{2} = 4.5 \text{ degrees}$$

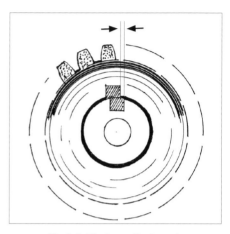

**Fig 3-3: Timing adjustment.
When moving a cam gear or sprocket a
single tooth is too coarse, an offset key
allows a smaller adjustment to valve
timing.**

Rotate the camshaft gear 4.5 degrees to achieve 9 degrees of crankshaft movement. To compute the key offset to move the gear 4.5 degrees use this formula:

$$\frac{(D \times F)}{A} \times E = O$$

Where:

O = Amount of offset
D = Diameter of shaft where cam gear sits
F = π (3.1416)
E = Desired valve timing figure
A = 360 (degrees in a circle)

For the example, the shaft size (D) is 15.00mm.

$$\frac{(15.00 \times 3.1416)}{360} \times 4.5 = 0.58\text{mm offset}$$

Improvements to bevel drives are limited, but anything that increases rigidity is beneficial as gear mesh is more consistent. Upgrade bearings to those with a higher manufacturing tolerance, or assemble bearing housings without gaskets using face-to-face joints. Replace brass shims with steel, or better yet, once a set of bevels is adjusted, have a single hardened distance piece made and swap it for the shim selection.

Spur drives

Spur gear drives are common in many older motorcycles, but in car engines they are usually only found in race motors. Gear drives are precise and expensive, and they make even more noise than bevels. They look complex yet, as the centre distances between gears is normally fixed, there is little chance of mismatching components. Examine gears for offset: gears should mesh on their full tooth width throughout a drive. Except on very old period engines, all gear trains have an odd number of teeth on one gear, which includes a hunting tooth. When gear sets take sudden loads or an unequal load during a revolution, a hunting tooth equalises tooth wear by ensuring the same series of teeth are not in constant mesh. For the engine builder, this means when rotating a timed engine the timing marks will not align until several further revolutions – this is no cause for concern.

Valve adjustment on spur drives is by vernier, or multiple key ways staggered to the tooth pattern. Timing gears are machined from stampings or billets. It's useful to drill the solid section of a gear. Although this reduces weight, power gains will be insignificant. Of more importance is the improved shock-loading that results from drilling. Instead of shock being transferred through a

Plate 3-4: The vernier hole pattern on a camshaft.
The series of un-symmetrically-spaced holes permit broad timing adjustment: a cam wheel can be pegged at various locations.

Plate 3-5: A drilled, de-burred spur gear. A drilled gear can withstand greater shock. This reduces the chance of tooth or key breakage. To minimise stress raisers, smooth the drilled holes' sharp edges to a contour.

rigid blank the spaces made by the holes dampen the load. Drilling is most easily done on a vertical milling machine equipped with a rotary table, but with care a pedestal drill is adequate. Ream holes after drilling or run them through with fine emery cloth on a lap. To avoid stress raisers, countersink or radius the sharp edge on each hole.

Chain drives

Chain drives can consist of a single, or up to three separate chains that transfer crankshaft drive to the camshafts. Roller chains can be single, double or triple row, and fitted with a split link or of endless construction. An endless chain eliminates a potential fault – the spring clip working off the split link. Therefore, they are a good upgrade. To get a rough indication of chain wear, arrange the side plates uppermost and gently bend either end watching for curvature, which should not exceed 10 degrees. This is not a measurable indicator of wear, but merely shows the sum of all link clearances. To measure chain wear accurately, stretch it over twenty links and use this formula:

$$\text{Percentage stretch} = \frac{M - (X \times P)}{(X \times P)}$$

M = Measured length
X = Number of pitches
P = Pitch

If 20 links of new 8.00mm pitch chain measures 160.00mm, yet the same number of pitches on a used chain is 164.80mm, there is a 3 per cent difference. The chain is worn by 3 per cent:

$$\frac{164.80 - (20 \times 8)}{160} = 0.03$$

(times 100 = 3 percent)

Replace a chain whose wear exceeds 1.5 per cent.

It's easy to overlook idler and tension sprockets. These are often bushed, which with loading can crack or lose their fit. Most chain drives have fibre guides or dampers that support chain run; these stop the chain from clattering and cutting into the front

Plate 3-6: Estimating chain wear.
Bending a chain is a rough indicator of wear. The curvature should not exceed 10
degrees. For a more accurate method, see the text.

cover. After some service, the fibre material can become grooved by chain action so they resemble marks like tramlines: this wear presents little problem. Dampers do not need renewing until their wear is to a depth of 50 to 60 per cent of their total thickness. Use a flat-linked, rather than a scalloped-link chain to avoid damaging the fibre. Upgrade sprockets by increasing the chain rows, such as replacing a single row to a double row. The design of a chain's run should also be examined, especially any long unsupported stretches and the wrap around smaller sprockets. Under severe conditions a standard design can give problems – a chain jumping a sprocket or excess slack cutting into a case. To correct these problems, fit additional guides backed with a fibre material like Tufnol.

Fixed valve timing is common on most production engines, and is set by aligning dots or incised marks on sprockets. Sports engines are sometimes fitted with slotted camshaft sprockets that allow adjustment, and more sophisticated designs use vernier. Less common are un-keyed camshaft sprockets retained by taper fit. This latter design is excellent, so long as the angle of taper is not acute. Always lap a taper, even one that seems in perfect condition. Dilute very fine carborundum paste with oil; apply a few spots to the shaft, and rotate the sprocket back-and-forth, turning 180 degrees every five seconds, and then continue lapping. Finish with metal polish and check the fit with Engineers' Blue.

Belt drives

An argument could be made that toothed belt (synchronous belt) cam drives came about in production engines because they were cheaper than chain drives. Whether lower prices were passed on to consumers is debatable as the cost of periodic belt changes must be taken into account. On the other hand, the cost of a toothed belt on a competition engine is not much of a concern. Tooth profile has changed since synchronous belts first appeared in the 1970s, from a trapezoidal straight-sided tooth to a curvilinear rounded style. Most are 9.5mm pitch, but some very early designs used 8.0mm. Some of the later rounded style can run on the early type pulleys. An engine with stronger than standard valve springs places greater load on its timing belt, in such a case the routine service interval for belt replacement must be discarded and the belt changed more frequently.

Toothed timing belts are an effective means of drive when installed on a well-designed system having tight turns around pulleys and good bracing by flanged idler pulleys. They are also excellent for externally driven pumps and superchargers. Maintaining belt tension on engines converted for competition use can be a problem, especially when the flywheel and/or the crankshaft have been lightened. Less weight makes an engine more throttle-responsive (it speeds up and slows down quicker). When in a low gear, if the throttle is shut quickly after a period of hard acceleration, or if the driver is using severe on-off throttle, a belt can become slack on the period of overrun and jump a pulley. When this takes place, the belt always jumps the crankshaft pulley as this is the smallest in the drive, and it, compared to the other pulleys, has the fewest teeth in contact.

To increase belt wrap around a crankshaft pulley it is sometimes not too difficult to fit an extra idler. As the idler will be in a fixed position, it may be possible to drill into the front cover and secure it with a stud or cap screw. Any moderately-sized idler will do the job, but given a choice always select one with flanged faces as this prevents a belt tracking fore-and-aft on its pulleys. Such a modification may render the original toothed belt too short. To compute the new length, work out the circumference of each pulley (3.1416 × diameter) and divide by 2. Add the circumference dimensions to the centre-to-centre distances between each pulley, allowing a little extra for the arc of the tensioner. Industrial suppliers are good places to buy a replacement belt as synchronous drives are common in industry.

There is much spoken of timing belt tensioning, and rightly so, as any manufacturer must give a specific tension figure. No universal tension gauge exists, so readings depend on the specific tensioning tool, the distance between pulleys, and belt width. Race or sport engines tend to have short runs, so tensioning without a gauge can be difficult. Nonetheless, kits can be bought with different adaptors enabling a variety of engines to be checked.

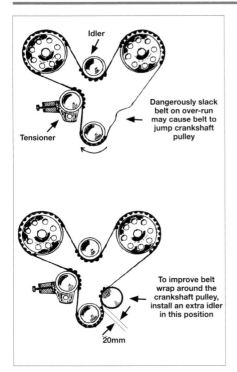

Fig 3-4: Improving timing belt drives. Raising the engine's state-of-tune or lightening the flywheel improves the throttle response, but the belt can become slack on overrun.

Any company building engines cannot tension a timing belt without setting and recording its value: anything less would be negligent. Yet from the standpoint of a privateer racer repairing his/her engine, or someone building an engine for their own use; in that case, the responsibility is to oneself.

What if a gauge cannot be rented or borrowed or if the drive has been modified? Will a cardinal sin be committed if a belt's tension is not measured, but rather, evaluated subjectively? The knowledgeable will probably answer; no. A problem arises, though, as subjective evaluation is unquantifiable. In other words, 'correct' belt tension for one person might be different for another. Nevertheless, one finds that the average belt tension

is not excessive on gauge-tensioned belts; tautness is little more than the elimination of slack on a belt's longest run. In some cases this equates to around 6.00mm of slackness. Belt tension must be enough to ensure good meshing and anything more is needless load that consumes power. Although it may shock a purist, the following is an effective method of gauging tension. Hold a belt between finger and thumb on its longest unsupported run (crankshaft to camshaft), and adjust the tension so the belt can just be twisted 90 degrees.

Manual tensioners

Timing chain or belt tension can be adjusted manually or hydraulically. Manual tensioners operate using a screw, a ratchet or an eccentric to tighten or release tension. On a manual system, the engine builder sets the amount of tension. Normally, screw adjusters are external: on the outside of an engine. Adjust the external screw to set the chain tension with the engine running, as this optimises power. A chain that is too tight not only loads bearings but it robs engine power. Follow this procedure – it's the same for all engines. Run the engine for a few minutes after the initial start-up, and then slow its speed to around 1000rpm, if possible. Slacken the tensioner screw 90 degrees at a time until the chain is heard to rattle. From this point tighten the screw 90 degrees to 180 degrees of a turn – the difference is due to the thread pitch on the screw.

Hydraulic tensioners

Hydraulic tensioners are usually equipped with a manual or ratchet device to set preload. This device maintains minimum chain or belt tension when there is no oil pressure, such as, when an engine starts. A problem can arise with hydraulic tensioners due to fluctuations

in oil pressure. On a rally car engine, for instance, when a driver is aggressively on-and-off the gas pedal or when a high compression engine is shutdown and the crankshaft momentarily rotates against normal rotation. Such a situation may lead to inconsistent oil pressure and not enough tension. Jumped timing and bent valves can be the result. For the sake of reliability, replace or convert an hydraulic tensioner to manual. Occasionally, a tensioner can be modified by fitting a collar or clamp around its piston that limits retraction once the oil pressure reduces.

CAMSHAFTS

Camshafts are made either from cold chilled cast iron or machined from a solid billet. Either can be hollow or solid throughout their length or for a partial length, and any openings in their ends can be unplugged or plugged. These differences depend on whether each camshaft journal is pressure-fed with oil from a head drilling or from a single journal then via a hollow camshaft having plugged ends. For example, in an overhead camshaft engine, a hollow

Plate 3-7: Camshaft manufacture. A billet camshaft (left), is machined from an alloy-steel. A cast camshaft, right, is cast in cold chilled cast iron. A billet camshaft is strongest.

unplugged (or solid) camshaft will have an oil feed in the head to each cam bearing. On the other hand, when a hollow camshaft is plugged, oil is fed to one cam bearing then through an oil groove into the shaft's hollow centre. From there it escapes through holes drilled in the shaft's bearing journals, thereby lubricating the cam bearings.

In quantity, cast camshafts are cheaper to make. After grinding and heat-treating their straightness and indexing between cam lobes is checked. They can be identified by their dark brown or blackish colour between the lobes, rough-cast finish, and fettling marks, left after grinding off casting flash. In theory, a billet camshaft could be machined from a cast iron blank, but alloy steel is the common material. Billet camshafts are found in many racing engines as they lend themselves to one off or limited production runs. They can be identified by machining marks between the cam lobes. If given an option, always select billet shafts as they are stronger.

Cam profiles

Most cam profiles are symmetric, which means that a cam's opening and closing ramps are identical. The rate of rise measured from the base circle to the precise midway point of maximum lift is mirrored by the closing ramp. In contrast, an asymmetric profile has different opening and closing. An asymmetric profile, depending on valve gear design, may have a conventional opening curve and a more rapid closing, or a slower rate of final closing. Engines with desmodronic valve operation may use the former and pushrod engines the latter. Asymmetric profiles may be used to enhance power, but they are also fitted to high performance pushrod engines in an effort to ease valve-train stress, or, as in the case of the 1950s

Plate 3-8: Types of cam lobes.
The opening and closing ramps on a symmetric cam (left), are identical. An asymmetric cam has different opening and closing ramps (right). The drilled lobe is a desmodronic closing cam.

superbike, the 1000cc Vincent, to facilitate cam follower geometry. Set asymmetric cam timing by using the valve opening and closing points.

There are many different cam profiles, made to suit varying engine uses, and, to avoid confusion, or buying the wrong cam, it's best to seek the advice of a specialist familiar with a particular engine. Anyone who wants to increase engine power needs to be careful that low-speed drivability is not sacrificed for top end performance (see Chapter 1, 'Dynamic compression'). If in doubt, it's best to exercise caution and to follow proven formulae – cam profiles that are known to work.

Re-profiled cams

Re-profiled cams are an excellent 'go-faster' option for production engines where performance camshafts are unavailable or expensive. On some overhead cam engines such a camshaft can be changed without removing the cylinder head. Re-profiling consists of grinding material off a cam's base circle: this raises valve lift by the amount removed. Duration can be increased if

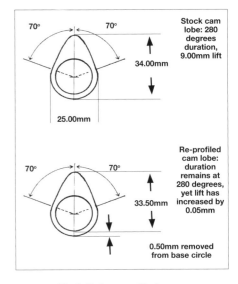

Fig 3-5: A re-profiled cam.
Re-profiled cams are an excellent 'go-faster' option for production engines, where performance camshafts are unavailable.

the grinding goes beyond the original opening and closing points, but for production engines this is not advisable. To do the grind, a cam-grinding machine is required, so it's a specialist job. However, a number of companies can undertake the work, which is not expensive. Depending on the amount removed, cams may need to be re-hardened after grinding as most case hardening on cams is around 0.88mm/0.035in to 1.16mm/0.040in deep, and, if broken through, rapid wear will follow.

Engines fitted with hydraulic tappets will need converting to solid, but this does not present too much of a problem. Remove the hydraulic piston by striking the tappet very sharply on the end-grain of a stout piece of timber. Once the piston is loose, pull it out along with the shuttle valve. Clean thoroughly, and replace the piston with a piece of silver steel (drill rod) the same diameter as the discarded hydraulic piston. This will be the shim. Its length is equal to the distance from the valve tip to the cam base circle, minus tappet thickness and running clearance. The cam grinding company will supply the running clearances. Make up a few test pieces then assemble the tappets and camshaft, measuring the clearances with a feeler gauge. Add or subtract the measured amounts to the individual test pieces to obtain the desired lengths. A drill grinder or lathe is easiest to cut the distance pieces, but silver steel can be hacksawed or filed, or fitted in the chuck of an electric drill and reduced in length with a carborundum stone.

Try to achieve a bright finish on the ends of the distance pieces, as they will work-harden over time, and a high quality finish speeds the process. A work-hardened surface is a compacted oxide layer (a glaze) formed on a rubbing surface when exposed to high temperature sliding action in an oxygen atmosphere: the glazed layer protects against wear. Silver steel is medium-carbon steel available in round or flat stock, and, before heat treatment, is quite soft. Hardening is unnecessary for tappet shims up to 12.00mm diameter.

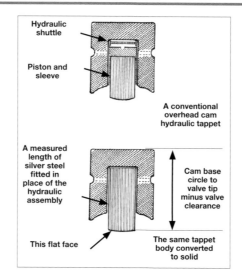

Fig 3-6: Hydraulic tappet conversion to solid. Re-profiling cam lobes will make hydraulic tappets obsolete. One remedy is to discard the hydraulic assembly and substitute it with a carbon steel distance-piece.

Larger diameter shims that fit on top of buckets have to bear a cam lobe's rotary impact, and so must be hardened. When a part needs to be hardened, heat it to 815 degrees C (blood red) and quench it in oil. A hardened shim must be tempered to reduce brittleness by heating for one hour at 140 degrees C. Silver steel can be bought through many engineering shops or from the steel suppliers listed in 'Useful Addresses.'

Cam specifications

Cam profiles are usually specified by power application, such as street use, rally, race or levels of tune, such as Stage 1, 2 or 3. Other information could be:

• Valve opening and closing points (in crankshaft degrees)
• Lobe lift
• Duration
• Lobe centre angle
• Lobe separation angle (single camshaft engines)

Along with the above there could also be suggestions about valve spring poundage. To help clarify some of these terms, it is useful to examine an engine's valve timing, and the timing of a Ferrari 330 has been chosen by way of illustration. This is a 1960s vehicle that had a V12, single overhead camshaft engine with two valves per cylinder. The valve opening and closing points show the engine could operate over a broad range yet had sports performance. The figures are:

27 degrees/65 degrees 74 degrees/16 degrees

This equates to:

Intake opens	27 degrees (BTDC)
Intake closes	65 degrees (ABDC)
Exhaust opens	74 degrees (BBDC)
Exhaust closes	16 degrees (ATDC)

The lobe centre angle, duration and overlap can be found with just these figures.

Opening and closing points

To ease valve gear stress, cam profiles have quietening ramps to limit valve movement during initial opening, and final closing. These are periods of very gradual valve movement. Engines that have more flexibility in their valve trains, for example pushrod engines, have longer quietening ramps than stiffer overhead cam designs. It should be noted that some manufacturers (especially US) list valve opening and closing degrees not at the point a valve physically begins to open or close, but at pre-determined points of lift, for instance 0.006in or 0.050in. The Ferrari's timing is measured at the physical point of opening and closing, 27/65 74/16.

```
ENGINE FORD 351C -- 400M


                        INTAKE    EXHAUST
VALVE ADJUSTMENT    HYD HYD
GROSS VALVE LIFT     .49 .494
DURATION AT
 .006  TAPPET LIFT  268        268
VALVE TIMING    OPEN      CLOSE
AT .006 INT      28 BTDC    60 ABDC
        EXH      68 BBDC    20 ATDC
THESE SPECS ARE FOR CAM INSTALLED
AT 106  INTAKE CENTER LINE
                  INTAKE    EXHAUST
DURATION AT .050   218        218
LOBE LIFT          .2853     .2853
LOBE SEPARATION    110


VALVE SPRING SPECS FURNISHED
WITH SPRINGS
```

Fig 3-7: Cam specs.
A typical specification sheet for a pushrod V8 engine. Listed are the duration figures at 0.006-inches and 0.050-inches of lift.

Duration

A cam's duration is the amount of time, measured in crankshaft degrees that a valve remains open during one 4-stroke cycle of 720 degrees. The intake and exhaust durations of an engine may be identical, but to optimise pressure waves, usually they are different. When choosing camshafts, most people focus on inlet duration, assuming that the exhaust duration is matched: broadly speaking this follows. A cam with high duration means a valve remains open for longer. High duration is associated with top end power. Therefore, comparing the durations of various cams is an easy way to evaluate their application. When calculating any duration, add 180 degrees to any reckoning as this is half the revolution of any intake or exhaust cycle.

Calculate duration thus:

Inlet: 27 + 65 + 180 = 272 degrees duration
Exhaust: 74 + 16 + 180 = 270 degrees duration

Lobe centre angle

Using the lobe centre angle as a reference point to time an engine is only applicable when its cams are symmetrical. The lobe centre of a symmetrical cam is the midway point of maximum lift. When a cam reaches maximum lift it does not immediately start to decline, but can hold a valve open for several degrees of crankshaft rotation. It is useful to use the exact midway point as a reference when setting valve timing.

Calculate the lobe centre angle thus:

Inlet:

$$\frac{Duration}{2} - Opening\ figure$$

$$\frac{272}{2} - 27 = 109$$

Exhaust:

$$\frac{Exhaust\ duration}{2} - Closing\ figure$$

$$\frac{270}{2} - 16 = 119$$

Overlap

Valve overlap is the period towards the end of the exhaust stroke and the beginning of induction. At this time, both intake and exhaust valves are open and the piston is near TDC. The exhaust valve is closing and the inlet valve is opening. On a naturally-aspirated engine that has a relatively short stroke, overlap is useful as it exploits exhaust gas inertia to draw in a new charge. It is most effective in the higher rev range when gas speed through the ports harmonises. The trade-off at low-speed is poor drivability due to reduced vacuum – slow moving gasses have little inertia, this delays the exhaust flow, pushing some of the new charge out of the intake. This condition is referred to either as reversion or standoff. Broadly

speaking, when calculating an engine's power characteristics, the amount of overlap is a rough but useful guide.

Calculate valve overlap thus:

Inlet opening + exhaust closing

27 + 16 = 43 degrees Overlap

An overlap of 43 degrees is small by modern standards. To indicate how cylinder head design has improved, the 500cc Manx Norton that won the 1950 Isle of Man Senior race had 115 degrees of overlap, yet a production 900cc Ducati SS from the 1970s had 121 degrees.

There is mixed opinion concerning the use of overlap on pressure-charged engines. On modern engines, some contend that around 30 degrees to 45 degrees is adequate, or even too much when the boost exceeds 25psi to 30psi. They contend that cylinder pressure at the end of the exhaust stroke is higher than intake pressure, and this causes reversion. Their argument may have validity on a short-stroke engine, and perhaps the exhaust valve closing a few degrees BTDC and the intake opening 15 degrees to 35 degrees ATDC might be appropriate. When the exhaust valve closes near TDC the descending piston reduces cylinder pressure, and therefore the chance of reversion.

On a final note, during overlap the valve heads on a 2-valve cylinder with a hemispherical chamber are close. Valves running in short guides (30.00mm) need a minimum valve head clearance of 0.77mm/0.030in to prevent clipping.

Cam graphing

With a DTI, it's possible to measure the lobes of an unknown camshaft to determine lift, duration and symmetry. Transfer this information to a sheet

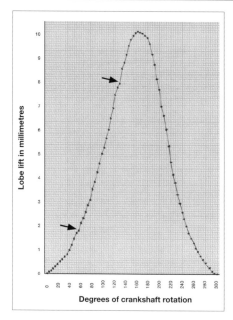

Fig 3-8: A cam graph.
Measured at 4 degree intervals, the 75 plots of a 300 degree asymmetric cam. There are two polydyne corrections on the opening ramp (arrows), which attempt to compensate for the kinetic energy inherent in the design's geometry.

Plate 3-9: Graphing a cam.
It's possible to measure the lobe, or lobes, of an unknown camshaft to find the lift, duration and symmetry. Measure a camshaft in its housing or whilst mounted in a lathe.

of graph paper, scaled in crankshaft degrees and units of lift. To measure a lobe, place the camshaft in a lathe or suspend it on v-blocks. Mount a timing disc on one end, and arrange a fixed pointer and DTI. Zero the DTI's stylus on a lobe's base circle. Rotate the shaft to the point of initial rise, and zero the timing disc. Record the rise at two-degree intervals all the way up to full lift, and down the other flank to the base circle. Two-degrees on a disc equates to four-degrees at the crankshaft. Alternatively, perform this operation with the camshaft resting in its cylinder head or engine block.

Variable valve timing

Any cam profile is a compromise between an engine's low and high-speed demand. A production engine needs to be docile in commuter traffic yet responsive on open roads. Variable valve timing (VVT) came about as a way to achieve this goal, boost horsepower, and improve emissions. A VVT system can either alter the timing on an intake camshaft or both camshafts. On some systems, valve lift may also be changed. VVT systems usually run a modest valve overlap at low to medium engine speed that increases at higher rpm. It could be argued that although designers may have made power gains, one of the primary reasons for VVT's invention was tighter US emissions standards. Having said that, the power-producing benefits of VVT on pressure-charged engines can be significant. When seeking power increases, specific suggestion whether or not to retain VVT is not possible as it depends on several factors. To mention only three: the type of system; engine use and the effect, if any, on emissions.

TOP DEAD CENTRE

Find 'true' top dead centre before setting the valve timing. On a short stroke engine a piston is at TDC for approximately 3 degrees to 5 degrees of crankshaft rotation. The centre point of this dwell is true TDC. There are two methods to find true TDC: dead-stop, or with a DTI. When setting cams for the first time the dead-stop method is easiest, though it's a little time consuming as a metal stop must be made. Number 1 cylinder is usually datum. Do not move the timing disc once TDC is established.

Reading a disc on an overhead camshaft V-banked engine can be confusing. For example, a 60 degrees V12 engine has two banks of cylinders (A and B) arranged at 60 degrees. TDC on number 1 cylinder A-bank (timing disc reads 0 degrees) is the first to fire. Sixty degrees later the next cylinder fires – but on B-bank (timing disc reads 60 degrees). So when aligning the cams on B-bank, 60 degrees equals the TDC datum. To reduce confusion, mark zero (0) underneath the 60 degrees figure. Then count, rather than read-off degrees from the timing disc when setting the timing on B-bank.

Find TDC: The dead-stop method

Make a stop that prevents the piston moving beyond TDC. Mount a large diameter timing disc to one end of the crankshaft, and a robust pointer to the casing. Sharpen the end of the pointer with a file. Rotate the crankshaft clockwise until prevented by the stop; align the timing disc to zero. Rotate the crankshaft in the opposite direction until the piston contacts the stop. Note the difference, and then half the amount. If the reading was 40 degrees, rotate the disc so the pointer reads 20 degrees. Now turn the engine clockwise and note the reading, which should be 20 degrees. Repeat the procedure until the pointer registers an equal amount either side of TDC. True TDC

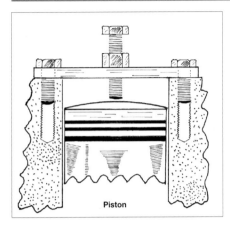

Fig 3-9: An example of the dead stop method of locating TDC.

will be equidistant between the two points. Remove the stop and turn the crankshaft to 0 degrees.

Find TDC: The dial test indicator method

Rotate the crankshaft clockwise so number 1 piston is a few millimetres down its bore. Place the stylus of a DTI centrally on the piston crown. Bring the piston up to TDC and note when the needle on the DTI stops rising. Zero the DTI and read the degrees on the timing disc, such as 3 degrees BTDC. Continue rotating clockwise until the needle just begins to fall – the piston is moving down. Read the disc; for example 1 degrees ATDC. True TDC will be in the middle of these two readings. Rotate the disc to that point then repeat the whole operation. This time when the needle stops rising, or falls, the degree reading either side of zero should be the same; in this example, 2 degrees BTDC and 2 degrees ATDC.

TO SET TIMING

'Degreeing' or 'dialling in' are colloquialisms describing the same operation – setting the valve timing; i.e. synchronising the camshaft to the rotation of the crankshaft. Most production engines have fixed valve timing, where reference marks like dots or incisions on sprockets, gears or timing belts are aligned. Do not use these marks on modified engines, as the best performance comes after degreeing. The procedure differs depending on engine design. On a straight four- or six-cylinder engine, the timing need only be set on number 1 cylinder. On a V-banked, or horizontally-opposed overhead camshaft engine, set on number 1 then move to the next firing cylinder: this will be on the opposite bank. On a single cam pushrod engine of any configuration, set the timing on number 1 cylinder.

Use one of the following to set the timing:

1) The valve opening and closing points
2) The lobe centre angle

Set timing: opening and closing points

Cam grinds can have small inaccuracies. For this reason, opening-and-closing-point-degreeing is not ideal. It has two other disadvantages:

1) The running clearance needs to be set before degreeing. Setting the clearance on an assembled engine that is not in time can cause a problem: it is easy to bend a valve.
2) Some European engine makers have a checking clearance as well as a running clearance. It is possible to have figures like 0.50mm checking clearance, and 0.25mm running clearance. As a result, adjust the clearance to 0.50mm to set the timing, then reset it to 0.25mm to run the engine: this is time consuming.

Find out whether the timing figures represent physical opening and closing, or valve position at a specified lift. In either case, arrange a DTI so its stylus contacts a valve bucket edge, a valve cap, or with care, a rocker arm. Rotate the crankshaft in the direction of its running rotation until the valve just opens (or to the fixed lift, if using such a figure). Read the timing disc. Continue turning in the same direction past full lift until the valve just closes (or to the fixed point). Compare the readings with the stated figures and adjust as necessary.

Set timing: Lobe centre angle

Setting to the lobe centre angle has two advantages:

1) Timing disc readings are unaffected by valve clearance. Whether the clearance is zero or 0.50mm during degreeing, when the timing is set and the running clearance adjusted, the timing is unaltered.
2) When experimenting with valve timing it is easier to compare a single figure – a lobe centre angle – than a series of opening and closing points. To use the Ferrari figures as an illustration: if its timing were advanced 5 degrees the points would change from 27 degrees/65 degrees 74 degrees/16 degrees to 32 degrees/60 degrees 69 degrees/21 degrees. In comparison, the lobe centre angle would change from 109 degrees inlet/119 degrees exhaust to 104 degrees inlet/114 degrees exhaust.

Do not use the valve opening and closing points when setting to the lobe centre angle. The figures 109 degrees inlet and 119 degrees exhaust, represent the inlet and exhaust cams' midway point of maximum lift. This takes place 109 degrees after and 119 degrees before TDC. To clarify further: every 4-stroke cycle consists of 720 degrees of crankshaft rotation. The piston is at TDC

Plate 3-10: Set timing.
On some engines, measure off the cam follower (right). When this is not possible measure off the valve; either on the rocker arm (left), or on the valve bucket.

twice: once at the start of the power stroke and the other at the end of the exhaust stroke. Use the second TDC position to reference lobe centre angles. It is reached after a cylinder fires and its piston has travelled down the bore to BDC and up to TDC on the exhaust stroke. So, from this TDC 0 degrees point, if the crankshaft were turned against normal rotation until the timing pointer indicated 119 degrees this is the point where the exhaust cam will be fully open (119 degrees BTDC). Return to TDC 0 degrees then move with rotation to 109 degrees, this is where the intake cam will be fully open (109 degrees ATDC).

Take 0.50mm/0.20in measurements from each side of a cam to find its centre point. Rest the stylus on a valve bucket or spring cap while turning in the normal direction of rotation. The exception is a pushrod engine: due to valve train flexibility, take readings from a cam follower. On all engines proceed as follows. Start from TDC firing stroke number 1 cylinder then rotate until the intake valve is just before full lift. Set up a DTI, and then continue to turn until the DTI's needle no longer climbs; this indicates full lift. Zero the DTI, and then rotate the crankshaft in the opposite direction, against normal rotation, until the needle registers a fall of 1.00mm/0.40in. After that, turn in the normal direction of rotation, stopping when the needle indicates 0.50mm/0.20in. Record the reading on the timing disc – the number of degrees from TDC. Whilst watching the DTI, continue turning in the same direction past zero until the needle begins to fall, stopping at 0.50mm/0.20in: take a second reading. Add the two readings together and divide by two: the result is the lobe centre angle. For example, if the first reading was 65

degrees and the second 160 degrees the lobe centre angle would be 112.5 degrees.

$$\frac{(65+160)}{2} = 112.5$$

If the Ferrari's timing were being set, 112.5 degrees would make it 3.5 degrees retarded. To advance an intake cam, turn it in its normal direction of rotation, and an exhaust cam, against rotation. Set the exhaust timing in the same way. The generally repeated notion is that advanced timing improves low and midrange torque, while retarded timing improves high rpm power. In reality, few engines would show an increase in horsepower with retarded timing; 115 degrees, and intake and exhaust figures around 102 degrees and 104 degrees are common on tuned engines.

Chapter 4
Cylinder head

MATERIALS

Aluminium alloy has mostly replaced cast iron as a material for cylinder heads, because it's lighter and is a better conductor of heat. Better conduction equals greater thermal stability – even heating, and less chance of a 'hot spot.' The camshafts and valve buckets of older aluminium head engines typically ran in bearing inserts made of either white metal, bronze, or austenitic cast iron. In the 1960s, some manufacturers increased the silicon content in their casting alloy to 5 to 7 per cent. Alumasil alloy enabled camshafts and other moving parts to run directly on machined aluminium surfaces. When re-machining Alumasil, such as when boring the cam bearings on a warped head, after the final cut, dull the mirror finish. Use 120 grit abrasive paper. Dulling creates valleys which trap oil; without dulling a surface can run dry, and will shear and break away, which can lead to seizure.

INSPECTION AND STRAIGHTENING

Check heads for distortion on the head gasket face and cam bearing saddles. Clean the face and place a straight edge or two-foot rule on its length. Shine a light behind and use feeler gauges to check for warp. Inspect cam saddles in a similar way, but beware of false readings, as one is measuring along the length of a series of semi-circles. Another way is to lay one of the camshafts – of known straightness – in the saddles and try to rock it up-and-down. It is not unusual to find skimmed heads whose cam bearings are out of alignment. An engine will run with a 0.25mm/0.10in cam misalignment but it is a frictional loss.

On engines having more than one head, compare their thicknesses as only one head may have been repaired in the past. It's a good idea to measure the combustion chamber volumes on the end cylinders of a head: unequal volumes indicate taper.

The remedy for a warped head is to make it straight by skimming the gasket surface, and capping and re-machining the cam bearings. Alternatively, a head can be heated and straightened in an oven. A domestic oven is adequate as straightening temperature is 260 degrees Centigrade. To straighten, a two inch thick steel plate or a braced cast iron plate is needed. Bolt the head to the plate using the two central stud holes, and shim it at each end by 50 per cent of the total warp. If a head were warped 0.25mm/0.010in, place a 0.13mm/ 0.005in shim under each end. Put the head in a pre-heated oven for six hours at 260 degrees C. Retighten the bolts after three hours. On cooling, remove the head from the plate and recheck; with patience, an accuracy of 0.05mm to 0.08mm is obtainable.

When an engine has badly overheated, its aluminium head can become soft because the alloy is annealed. Annealing due to overheating mostly takes place on the exhaust side, sometimes extending to the fire ring. Annealing leads to head gasket failure as clamping pressure in the block-to-gasket-to-head sandwich is weak. The hardness of an aluminium head must not be less than 24 to 25 Rockwell A (HRA). Hardness is easily checked at a quality machine shop. An annealed head needs heat treating or replacing; although cryogenic tempering may also be effective (see Chapter 1, 'Cryogenic tempering').

CRACK TESTING AND REPAIR

There are three types of head leaks:

1) A combustion crack that could run, for instance, from the exhaust valve seat to the spark plug hole
2) A crack into the water jacket
3) A leak from a porous casting

1) Combustion cracks are mostly limited to the areas that get hottest in service: the exhaust valve seats. 2) Check for coolant and oil leaks by pressure testing a head with water.
3) Porosity can be due to a casting flaw or oxidation and can take place in a water jacket or an oil gallery. When this happens, coolant can leak into the cylinder, or externally or oil can mix with coolant.

Some people like to use hot, rather than cold water, arguing that it simulates an engine's running condition. But the heat of hot water may close some cracks; so cold water is best for most testing. Before checking, remove the valves and oil gallery plugs, and clean off carbon. Tighten the camshaft fasteners as this loads a head similar to when it is fitted. Cap the water openings but equip one with a metal valve stem from an inner tube or a magnesium wheel. A blanking plate is needed to

cap the waterways normally sealed by the head gasket. If there is only one or two heads to test, a quicker way than making a blanking plate is to use the old head gaskets and reassemble the heads to the bare engine block. Fill the system with water from the highest opening and vent air from the water jacket. Fit the cap with the valve stem then pressurise the system to 30psi. Check for leaks, and if there are none, increase the pressure to 50psi. Maintain pressure with a gauge-equipped foot pump. Look for leaks in the combustion chamber and oil galleries. **Warning!** Wear safety glasses, as temporary plugs can sometimes pop off.

Repair water jacket cracks by cold pinning or welding. The former is known by the cognomen as the 'Boiler-Makers Stitch.' This is a series of overlapping threaded inserts, or brass screws, fitted along the line of a crack. Stitching and welding are quite specialist and should be entrusted to an engine repair shop.

The enthusiast can seal non-combustion chamber cracks with a two-part metal epoxy. This is available for aluminium or cast iron and manufactured by companies like ICI, Belzona or Devcon. Use this procedure: draw an accurate line along the length of a crack with a felt-tipped pen. Extend the line 10 to 12mm on each end. Grind or v-out the length to a depth of around 10mm, although this depends on casting thickness, and apply the epoxy. If the epoxy has a tendency to run, apply masking tape to the casting's exterior: when hardened, grind or file off the excess.

For non-combustion chamber repairs to porous castings, use Araldite or the US equivalent, JB Weld. Thin the medium to a runny consistency with trichoethylene; although paint thinner also works. Cover the casting's exterior with masking tape to prevent leakage,

and arrange the inside in some way so the cement has time to seep into the casting. Alternatively, use a commercial sealer like Seal-All or Fluid Weld; although in essence these use a similar process.

HEAD FASTENERS

Where possible, replace bolts with studs, as, arguably, this improves clamping pressure. If replacement is not possible, waist the bolts as this equalises their stretch (see Chapter 1, 'Fasteners'). In all cases, fit hardened washers under fastener heads or they will dig in and lessen clamping force.

Dowels often locate cylinder heads. When heads or decks are machined, a long dowel can prevent proper tightening. Measure each dowel's length, and the depth of its corresponding hole in the deck and head. Add the two depths together, and the crushed head gasket thickness. The dowel length must not be greater than the combined hole and gasket dimension.

PORTING

The type of work an engine will do should govern the size of its ports. Will it be roadraced or rallied, or used on track days, or de-tuned to lower the torque point? A roadrace engine could spend most of its time in the upper 25 per cent of its speed range, whereas a rally car engine operates over a broader spread of power. A road engine also used on track days must have a greater spread of power: it will spend time idling at traffic lights and in go-slows in the city, as well as at speed on the track. Altering the size of ports changes the air speed, and this influences the delivery of power. Air velocity increases when sucked into a restriction like an inlet tract. For injected and carburettored engines, high velocity air can be exploited when it contacts a fuel stream, as fast-moving air quickens atomization.

Due to mechanical limitations, the valve and port sizes on old, slow-revving engines were restricted to stop over speeding. At high velocity the air-flow choked when it tried to pass through a small port, and power fell off. The ports on such an engine could be enlarged and it may rev harder. But what about the valve size? Big ports and small valves mean the valve size is the restriction. The answer is to increase port size linked to valve size: large ports and valves for top end power, and smaller-sized ports and valves for midrange power.

The following four points may be useful – but view them as a guide. When building an engine for top end power aim for the gas speed figures, for a road car, go slightly lower. The units of measurement are metres/second (m/s).

1) When valve lift is 28 per cent of port size, the port limits the flow
2) When valve lift is 25 per cent of valve head diameter, maximum flow takes place
3) For 2-valve engines, a mean gas speed of 80m/s
4) For 4-valve engines, a mean gas speed of 90m/s

Old racing engines sometimes had a mirror-like finish on their intake ports. Now it is common knowledge that a polished surface de-atomizes a charge, especially at low gas speeds. Whatever a port's finish, though, there's never complete atomization as fuel in droplet form (wet flow) is present. Wet flow gathers in boundary air that clings to the port walls. It cools combustion, and so reduces power. The type of inlet port finish produced by 320- to 400-grit abrasive paper is usually found on modern racing engines. To tailor ports,

some shops dimple inlet tracts, or grind grooves in the port floor just upstream of the valve seat. These grooves can be around 4.00mm wide by 3.00mm deep. The idea behind the 320-grit finish, dimpling and grooving is to create vortices to agitate boundary air. This lessens wet flow by drawing it into the air-stream. Less wet flow means that the mixture can be leaned. The idea is similar to grooving or gluing restrictors in the runners of a multi-branch plenum: it balances the mixtures of individual cylinders.

A more restrained solution than grooving is to create a series of small vortices rather than a single incision. Score marks scratched in the port floor just before the valve seat, or the port wall before a radius, help stimulate gas agility. They must be in the same direction as the port offset, so as not to impair swirl, and end approximately 8.00mm to 10.00mm before the seat or radius. Scratch grooves at 1.50mm to 2.00mm intervals for a length of 25.00mm to 30.00mm at around a 35 degree angle. Make them with a grooving tool fashioned from a length of 5.00mm drill rod whose square-sided point must rest against a template of the desired curvature. Of course, such score marks may not be necessary for all engines; however it can be effective. When performed on a Porsche 911SC engine built for a North American endurance race, the agitation created by the grooving reduced wet flow and enabled the fuel metering to be leaned.

It's sometimes the case that enlarged ports need to be reduced, for example, a head with roadrace-size ports destined for a rally engine. All is not lost, though, as intake ports can be reshaped with a two-part epoxy. The type used for crack repair is effective; although a little difficult to use in tight places. User-friendly epoxies

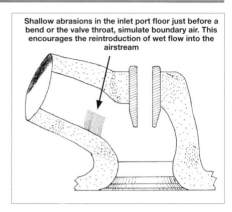

Fig 4-1: Intake port grooving.

are Belzona's 'Super Metal 1111' and Goodson's 'Port Reshaping Epoxy.' Both are long-lasting if their mixing instructions are followed, and are a cost-effective alternative to welding. Remove the valve guides before applying the epoxy, and substitute greased wooden dowels. When the epoxy has set, remove the dowels before shaping

Plate 4-1: Reshaping an inlet port. Do not scrap the head when the ports are too big, reshape them with a two-part epoxy.

**Plate 4-2: Indicating callipers.
Use a pair of indicating callipers to
measure the wall thickness. This avoids
breaking through the casting.**

the port. To avoid breaking through
when doing this type of work, a pair of
indicating callipers is useful to check
casting thickness. Exhaust ports, due
to their high heat, cannot be re-worked
with epoxy and must be welded.

VALVES AND GUIDES

Check valves for the following:
straightness, indenting of the stem's
tip, burring around the valve lock
groove, and wear on the stem. Valves
sometimes get bent in service; not only
due to over-revving, but often a worn
guide can make the valve head hit the
seat at an offset. There are special tools
to check straightness, but a lathe or
quality electric drill works just as well.
It's possible to reface a valve that has a
slight bend: 0.10mm/0.004in or similar.
The problem then is that the margin on
one valve will be less than that of the
others: this can lead to compression
imbalance. If you decide to face a valve,
be sure to face the other valves by the
same amount.

Smooth any burring around the lock
groove with a carborundum stone. Valve
tips can be indented by rocker adjusting
screws. Rather than scrapping valves,
regrind the ends on a valve grinder or
drill sharpener. The same goes for valve
stem wear; grind out imperfections on
a centreless grinder: a machine found
at precision engineers. A set of worn

valves, for instance, could have their
8.00mm stems reduced to 7.90mm.
Then fit new guides, and hone to size.
From an engineering point of view, such
a repair is 100 per cent effective, and
when valves are expensive ...

Valves on older engines were made
of silicon-chromium steel (Silchrome 1).
On naturally-aspirated engines, replace
these with valves made of nickel-based
alloy (Nimonic Alloy). This retains its
hardness (67-70 HRA) at temperatures
up to 800 degrees C. Pressure-charged
engines, due to their higher combustion
temperatures, need sodium or stainless
valves. Sodium valves have hollow
stems partially filled with metallic
sodium powder. The powder changes

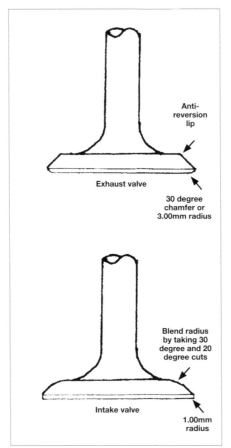

Fig 4-2: Valve modification.

**Plate 4-3: Aluminium-bronze valve guides.
Replace cast iron guides with aluminium-
bronze guides. For any given temperature
rise, aluminium-bronze expands more than
cast iron. This helps to cool the valves and
maintain fit in the head.**

into a liquid at 97.8 degrees C, whose
movement helps cooling. To identify
a Nimonic valve use a magnet, as the
valve head is virtually non-magnetic. The
stem, though, will be magnetic as it's
made of a lesser grade material, friction-
welded to the head.

The inlet air-flow can be smoothed
by cutting back intake valves on a lathe:
make a 30 degree cut just behind the 45
degree seat. Exhaust valves must not
be cut back, in fact, some come with
a raised area just behind the seat, the
purpose of which is to hinder exhaust
backflow at low lift; these should be
retained.

Replace cast iron guides with those
made of silicon aluminium-bronze, or
a material like Hidural 5, which, in the
past, was used to make valve seats.
Aluminium-bronze has a better heat
transfer than cast iron, so it will aid
valve cooling. In addition, cast iron's
coefficient of thermal expansion is
0.000011in, yet aluminium-bronze is
0.000018in – it expands quicker. This is
an important point, because when an
engine is being pushed hard it gets hot,
and a guide may loosen in the head. This
can result in two major troubles:

1) The guide and spring cap can make

contact. This may lead to a bent valve due to piston-to-valve contact
2) Oil can seep into the combustion chamber between the loose guide and its retaining hole and lead to a smoky exhaust

However, as aluminium-bronze expands at a rapid rate, guides are less likely to loosen. In aluminium heads the normal interference for guides that have 7.00mm or 8.00mm valve stems is around 0.076mm/0.003in to 0.10mm/0.004in. However, if stated, follow manufacturer specifications, as too tight an interference can crack the head. This is important on a ported head, as they usually have less material to support the guides. To achieve the desired fit, oversized guides are available from some manufacturers, or they can be made on a lathe with little trouble. Knurling also increases the outside diameter of a guide by approximately 0.015mm. Lightly dot punching a guide in a close pattern does the same job, and is an acceptable cure for a single loose guide.

For the amateur without specialist equipment a problem arises: how to measure the valve guide hole in the head? A pin gauge is sometimes too big to fit inside, and some bores tend to be scored where guides have been replaced previously: scoring may lead to a false reading. One way to overcome the problem is to notice a guide's fit when knocking it out. Use a suitable steel drift and 1lb hammer. The job calls for a bit of mechanical feel, but loose guides can be detected without much difficulty. On removal, note the diameter of a loose guide and add the necessary increase in outside diameter to its replacement. Knock out valve guides from a cold unheated head (20 degrees C ambient temperature) as heating a cast iron head fitted with

bronze guides increases their fit, and although aluminium alloys expand faster than bronze, heating them for removal is unnecessary.

To fit new guides, place them overnight in a freezer. The following day heat the head in a pre-heated oven for one hour at 120 degrees C/250 degrees F. At that temperature a guide with 0.10mm interference will go into place with strong finger pressure. When an oven is not available a head can be immersed in a tank of boiling water. The valve guides will fit just the same, but they may require slightly more hand pressure due to the lower temperature of the head. As an added protection, some engine builders like to coat guides, just before installation, with a sealer like Fluid Weld to help guard against the possibility of oil running between a guide and its hole. On the face of it, this is unnecessary as, with the right interference, oil cannot pass between two tight-fitting, non-porous surfaces – nonetheless it is added protection.

SPRING CAPS AND LOCKS

Valve locks, also known as collets, should be checked for burring and galling on their outer and inner faces. Their invention is claimed, way-back-when, by the JAP Engine Company. When assembling locks, their ends must not touch otherwise they will not be tight. To check them, place the spring cap on a valve stem, fit the locks, and pull and twist the cap. The locks must grip the stem without their ends touching. The end gap should be in the region of 0.75mm to 1.00mm. The exception, sometimes used on production engines, is passive valve rotation: identifiable by two or more lock grooves. On this system, the ends of locks touch to allow the valve to rotate. For performance work replace such

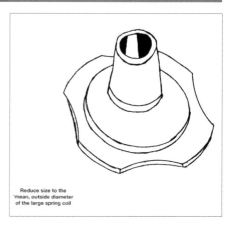

Reduce size to the 'mean, outside diameter of the large spring coil

Fig 4-3: A lightened valve spring cap. If a valve cap weighed 8 grams, reducing each cap's weight by 1 gram on a 16-valve engine would be a 12.5 per cent decrease in overall weight.

valves and caps with the conventional kind. When seat pressures are raised 40 per cent or more above standard, fit uprated locks and valves as the raised pressure can destroy non-hardened locks or elongate valve stem grooves.

Any reduction in valve gear weight that does not compromise rigidity is beneficial. The weight of spring caps can be reduced by scalloping or turning off their outside diameter. Limit this modification to valves having nose pressures of around 170lb or less. Reduce the outside diameter of the caps to the mean size necessary for full spring contact. A cap can also be scalloped on a milling machine equipped with a rotary table. However, with patience and care, grinding can achieve the same result. In each case, polish the scallops to a dull burnish to reduce the risk of creating a stress point. Lightweight caps made of hard alloy or titanium are available for many engines; although some claim their service life is short. This is not meant to imply that alloy or titanium caps should not be used, on the contrary, they are a good idea, but rather, follow the advice of a reputable manufacturer.

VALVE SEATS

Modern engines (1970s onward) were often fitted with hardened valve seats made of austenitic iron; this was to cope with the effects of lead-free gasoline. Before this seats were made of silicon aluminium-bronze: Hidural-5. Current fuels lack the lubricating properties of lead and the absence results in valve seat recession. This takes place when oxide particles form on an open valve face, fuse with the seat on closure, and are torn away when the valve re-opens. In reality, seat recession is a slow process but it affects an engine's compression ratio as well as a valve's ability to seal. Theoretically, if the 42.00mm and 40.00mm valves in the cylinder of a two-valve engine were each recessed 0.50mm, this would affect a compression ratio by 13.20cc.

With a knowledgeable operator, a valve seat cutting machine like a Sunnen or Van Norman is very accurate, but there are disadvantages. When building a custom motor the ideal valve position may only be found during mock-up (see Chapter 10, 'Engine assembly: mock-up'). Questions need to be answered like: How deep do the valves need to be to avoid piston-to-valve contact, or to arrive at the chosen compression ratio? A machine operator will machine to an explicit dimension, but if the dimension is unknown ...

Blending valve seats, therefore, is one of the last jobs to be done. Another concern is the expense: to have valve seats replaced and machined is costly. But it is a job within the limits of a competent person who has basic hand tools, a valve seat grinder, and a domestic oven and refrigerator – though no doubt there are machine shops that will claim otherwise. A three- or five-angle seat can be blended with a hand-held grinder. For the amateur or small shop, a hand-held electric grinder is

Plate 4-4: A hand-held valve seat grinder. The diamond dresser is on the left. Use different diameters and angles of stones to make a three- or five-angle seat.

excellent for machining seats. Suitable grinders appear fairly regularly on internet auction sites, selling for modest amounts.

To replace valve seats, first remove the old ones: at times, this can be trying, especially when sized 40.00mm or above. One method is to drill a small hole (around 3.00mm in size) into the old seat. Then pull it out with a seal puller or a Roll Head pry bar, or to use the hole as an anchor point for a drift, and give it a hammer blow. On the other hand, any overhang will help removal. Machine shops may choose to machine out old inserts until they are wafer-thin, and the shell is easily withdrawn. With the seats removed, and the ambient temperature at 20 degrees C, measure the diameter of the valve seat recess with a telescopic gauge and micrometer. Also check the depth, as the intake and exhaust seats can differ – exhaust being thicker to increase fit and heat transfer. Work out the interference according to a manufacturer's specifications, or use the following suggested seat interferences:

• Cast iron heads 0.019mm per millimetre of outside diameter
• Aluminium alloy heads 0.025mm per millimetre of outside diameter (air-cooled engines 0.027mm)

Buy new seats from engine reconditioning shops. Fitting is similar to the procedure for valve guides. The seats are frozen overnight but the oven temperature is hotter, 180 degrees C/360 degrees F. Before fitting, carefully remove any small burrs from around the seat recesses and scour them with an abrasive pad (Scotchbrite, for example). Fit the valve guides before the seats; they are a register for the mushroom-shaped fitting tool needed to square a seat into its recess. This is important with larger diameter seats, as they're more likely to twist on entry. For most bike or car engines, typical seat interference is around 0.076.00mm/0.003in to 0.152.00mm/0.006in; the difference is due to seat diameter and head material. As the valve seat interference is tighter than for guides, the seats may need to be lightly driven in. To avoid confusion, in case the inserts are a different size, fit all the exhaust, or all the inlet seats, rather than a combustion chamber at a time. Try and work smoothly rather than quickly – there is nothing wrong with fitting a few seats and then re-heating the head. Keep heat-proof gloves, a hammer, drifts, and an ice bucket for the valve inserts at hand before starting work.

To grind a multi-angle seat, begin with a 'face cut.' This will be where the valve's 45 degree face seals on the seat. Although the valve's angle is 45 degrees, adjust the seat angle to 44 degrees as a 1 degree interference speeds sealing. Do not remove more seat material than necessary as this leads to a recessed

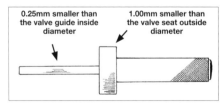

Fig 4-4: A valve seat punch.

valve, which will obstruct the gas flow. Conversely, a valve protruding off a seat can aggravate combustion temperature. Incorrect valve depth, either recessed or protruding, can upset valve train geometry, which may hasten guide wear or lead to valve train unreliability. Concerns like valve shim thickness also govern valve depth. Ask the question: where does the valve fall in the shim range after machining a face cut? Much the same importance applies to heads fitted with hydraulic buckets. Seats are usually machined to suit one of the three thickest shims in any range. If a shim range were from 0.90mm to 2.75mm, ideally, machine the seats so that fitting a 2.75mm shim gives the correct tappet clearance. In contrast, if the compression ratio is the deciding factor, measure the combustion chamber volume to find the best depth. Either way, when beginning, test-machine the seats on one combustion chamber then fit any valve gear to check the base valve depth. Once found, cut the other seats to the same depth. This ensures that all combustion chambers are uniform and have the same volume.

Having machined the valve depths on all the seats a three-angle seat may be made by grinding a 30 degree top cut and a 60 degree throat cut. A three-angle seat smoothes the abruptness of the 45 degree face, and thereby assists gas flow. The most reliable type of seat is a low abutment. This means the seat-to-valve abutment is low on the valve face rather than in its centre. A hot valve expands up its seat, and so on a running engine this places the abutment in the centre of the valve face. To create a low abutment face, set a pair of spring bow dividers to register 1.50mm less than the valve head diameter. Colour the 45 degree seat with a felt-tipped pen and take a light 30 degree top cut to check concentricity to the seat. Continue

machining until the lower diameter of the 30 degree cut equals the dimension of the dividers. Fit a 60 degree stone to the grinder and narrow the 45 degree seat by taking a series of light throat cuts. Seat widths of 1.50mm exhaust and 1.00mm inlet are typical for most engines. Blue the seat and check the valve face. This process constitutes a three-angle seat. The valve can now be ground or it may

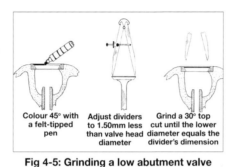

Fig 4-5: Grinding a low abutment valve seat.

Fig 4-6: Valve seat position. Maximise valve sealing by using low abutment seats.

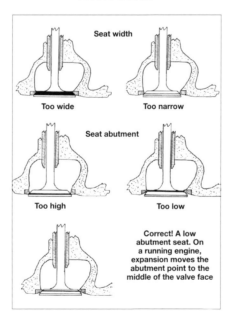

be found that grinding is unnecessary as the abutment is a perfect match.

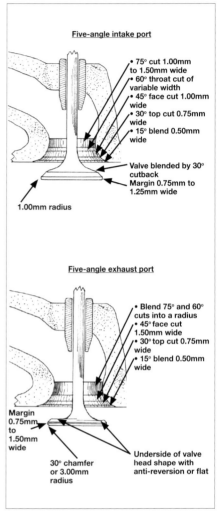

Fig 4-7: Ports and valves. A five-angle intake and exhaust seat and their valves.

A seat can be blended further by making two cuts of 75 degrees and 15 degrees; each about 0.50mm to 0.75mm in width. This is a five-angle seat. Smooth the two 60 degree and 75 degree cuts into an 8.00mm to 12.00mm radius. This type of seat cutting calls for more human intervention than the mechanical repetition of a commercial seat machine, but nonetheless the results can be very accurate. For information on valve lapping refer

Plate 4-5: Hairpin valve springs. Hairpin springs were used before coil springs could cope with big valve lifts. They are found on many older racing engines.

to Chapter 10, 'Cylinder head: final assembly.'

Lastly, if you decide to have the work done by a machine shop, avoid any business that removes all but the remaining 0.20mm from each side of an old seat, then shrinks a new insert into the space. From an engineering point of view the final interference may work. But aesthetically it is like extruded sealer from a gasket surface or paint runs – they offend the eye and are unprofessional: and few would have the arrogance to claim authorship.

HAIRPIN SPRINGS

Hairpin springs came about due the unreliability of coil springs when piston speeds and valve lifts increased. Velocette Motorcycles claimed their invention. The object was to keep spring coils away from hot cylinder head surfaces, and cope with big valve lifts: something beyond the capabilities of period coil springs. Though no longer used on modern machinery, they were standard equipment on authentic racing motorcycle engines and also used by car manufacturers like Ferrari and Maserati on some of their competition engines.

There is rubbing action to the upper arms where the ends of the hairpin contact the valve collar, which can wear the wire's diameter. This wear causes little problem and springs are still useable so long as the total diameter of the wire is not reduced by more than 20 per cent. Check spring pressure in the conventional way, but make a heavy weight jig to hold the lower arm of the spring and then an oblong-shaped pad to press on the upper arms. If performance and dependability is sought, converting an engine to coil springs is an option. In some cases, this entails little more than a modest amount of machining and the replacement of valves and guides.

COIL SPRINGS

To increase service life and dependability, all quality coil springs are shot peened; for this reason, never clean springs with abrasive pads or on a buffing wheel. Coil springs are available in single, double or triple coil. Their poundage can be single or dual rate. Identify dual rate springs by looking at the closeness of their uncompressed coils: a section will be closer wound than the other. When fitting, install the closer wound section towards the head.

Some engines due to their valve design are more susceptible to surging or harmonic vibration (pushrod engines). Springs for these engines often come with a tight fitting flat inner spring that presses on the outer coils. Although it should be said, that the inner coil of a double coil spring is sometimes a tight fit, and this provides a degree of damping.

A valve spring's job is to maintain cam-follower-to-cam-lobe contact throughout the motion of opening and closing. Valve spring poundage must match a valve train's demands; such as the damping force, the mass of the moving components, the result of mass

Plate 4-6: Test spring pressure. The spring tester (top), and the bathroom scales and drill press (bottom), do the same job: they check spring pressure. An engine is more reliable when every valve spring has the same pressure.

times acceleration on the system, and the system's rigidity. Broadly speaking, a lobe that has a steep rise and fall or a valve train with inherent flexibility,

Plate 4-7: A dual rate spring.
The two coils on the right side of the spring are closer wound: when they start to compress, the poundage increases. Fit dual rate springs with the closer coils towards the head.

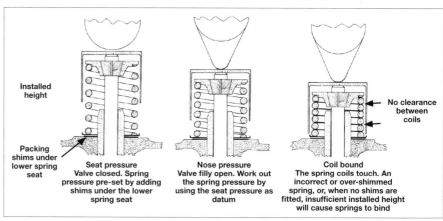

Fig 4-8: Valve spring pressures.

needs stronger springs. Calculating the spring poundage necessary to maintain follower contact is beyond the remit of this book; but even if it were it is a series of complex calculations. It is best to follow a manufacturer's recommendations, or if none are available, the advice of someone with experience of the particular engine. Arrive at a balance between adequate and excess spring poundage. Where there is inadequate poundage a valve may float, meaning that the follower loses contact with the cam. This prevents an engine reaching its maximum rpm due to reduced cylinder pressure. Excess poundage, in contrast, is a frictional loss and it can wear out valve train components. The spring poundage must be the same on each valve. There are two specific poundage measurements: seat poundage (valve closed), and nose poundage (valve fully open). Once seat poundage is set on new or unworn springs, the nose poundage will be consistent.

Another measurement, although nothing to do with poundage, is coil bind. A spring can compress until its coils touch: this is coil bind. A valve with a coil bound spring can ruin an engine as the spring's closed coils restrict valve movement. This may result in piston-to-valve contact. To check a spring's coil

Plate 4-8: Measuring coil bound length. Compress a spring in a smoothed-jawed vice until a 0.05mm/0.002in feeler gauge begins to tighten. Tighten the vice a fraction more then measure the distance between the jaws.

bound length, a smoothed-jawed vice will do the job just as well as a valve spring tester. Clamp a spring between the jaws until a 0.05mm/0.002in feeler gauge begins to 'nip,' tighten the vice a fraction more then measure the distance between the jaws. For safety's sake, check all the springs of any set. If there are any discrepancies in the range of 0.1mm to 0.15mm, add all the measurements and divided by the number of springs to get an average. Aluminium heads always have a steel washer, of some description, under the lower spring. This is the lower spring

cup. Take the washer's thickness into account when working out a spring's pressure.

CHECKING SPRINGS

Before measuring a spring's poundage, it's good practice to compress it a few times to get its molecules working. A situation may arise when spring sets need to be compared, or perhaps a manufacturer calls for springs with specific poundage per inch. Measure poundage by compressing the spring under test to some cardinal dimension, for example 1¾ inches, and read the poundage. Compress it a further ¼in, and take another reading. To find the spring poundage, multiply the difference by four. For example:

1¾in = 25 pounds
1½in = 100 pounds

The difference is 75 (75 pounds-per-¼ inch), which, multiplied by 4 = 300 pounds-per-inch (lb/in). Therefore, the spring rate is 300lb/in.

It's better to have a target seat or nose poundage than just to measure and see what comes about. Along with one of these, find out the valve lift, the running clearance, and the coil bind length. The following is Example A:

75lb	Seat poundage
290lb	Nose poundage
10.75mm	Valve lift (minus running clearance)
18.00mm	Coil bound length

If a lower spring cup is fitted, it's easier to do any checking with it placed under the spring, otherwise allow for it in calculation. Put the spring on the tester and compress it so the scale reads the target seat poundage, in this case 75lb. Measure the length of the spring: for the example, 31.00mm. As a result, fitting the spring in the head at a length of 31.00mm will pressurise it at 75lb. This dimension is the 'installed height.' From the 31.00mm length, compress the spring a further 10.75mm and note the poundage, e.g. 290lb: this is nose poundage. Just to double check, it's a good idea to continue compressing until reaching bind; although bind is more accurately calculated. So the result is:

75lb @ 31.00mm: the installed height
| 10.75mm | Valve lift (minus running clearance) |
| 18.00mm | Coil-bound length |

31.00	
10.75 –	
18.00 –	
02.25mm	Clearance before bind

Concerning minimum bind clearance, on direct contact overhead camshaft engines 1.00mm/0.040in is enough, but increase this to 1.60mm/0.063in for pushrod engines. Of course, the more clearance the better as this increases the safety margin and prolongs spring life. Avoid the bind checking method of setting the cam to full lift on an assembled engine and measuring the distance between the valve spring coils with a feeler gauge. This is not precise as spring coils move

Plate 4-9: Checking installed heights. Check the installed heights on an overhead cam, valve bucket engine with a thin-walled spacer.

under feeler gauge pressure, and, therefore, readings will only be reliable to +/- 0.25mm/0.010 inches.

INSTALLED HEIGHT

After lapping and blueing each valve, check the installed heights on the head. Assemble each valve with its spring cap and locks and, depending on access, measure the dimension with a DTI, a vernier calliper, or a telescopic gauge. On direct contact engines with recessed bucket bores there is poor access. In such a case, make up a thin-walled spacer around 25.00mm long to sit in place of the outer spring. Consequently, if the spacer were 25.00mm long, and the DTI registers 6.50mm of movement, the installed length would be 31.50mm. However, referring to Example A, to get

75lb the spring needs to be compressed to 31.00mm. The spring poundage would be less than 75lb if it were fitted at 31.50mm. The answer is to put a 0.50mm shim under the lower spring cup.

To avoid mixing up springs after they have been checked get a wooden board and fit it with wooden pegs or nails: one for each spring. Use the valve sheet from the rear of this book.

THE HEAD GASKET JOINT

Bear in mind that a head gasket seals three major systems: combustion gas, oil, and coolant. Of these three, the fire ring seal has the hardest job – the mean cylinder pressure on a naturally-aspirated engine, in no great state-of-tune, could be 180psi. The oil seal has to contend with engine oil pressure – this can be 120psi to 150psi on some engines when starting from cold. With a restrictor, the pressure on the coolant seal can be up to 45psi. When a fire ring leaks, combustion gas bleeds into the lower pressure systems or to atmosphere. In addition, when shutting down an engine, residual pressure (contained by the radiator cap) is greater than cylinder pressure. This may cause coolant to seep into a bore via the faulty fire ring.

Engines with iron blocks and aluminium heads are the most difficult to seal due to their unequal expansion rates. Over time, shearing action takes place that can ruin a gasket. To help the problem, surface finish is important; although the level of roughness depends on the kind of gasket. The five most common kinds of gasket are:

1) Teflon or graphite-faced
2) Composite
3) Deformed
4) Solid
5) Layered

1) Teflon or graphite-faced gaskets allow a degree of movement in the block-to-head sandwich. Graphite's conductivity helps heat transfer from the head to the block. They work best with a surface finish around 40- to 60-roughness average (RA). As a guide, the texture of an 80 RA finish can easily be felt with a fingernail.

2) The composite gasket is common on production engines. This has a stainless steel or steel core faced with composite fibres. It needs a smoother finish than a graphite gasket.

3) There are two kinds of deformed gasket: single and three-layer. Single layer is found on production engines and consists of a single soft steel sheet that has raised areas around its water, oil and combustion holes. The raised areas crush when tightened making a seal; they need a polished surface. A three-layer gasket may have deformed Teflon-coated outer sheets that sandwich a thicker flat sheet of stainless or soft steel. The deformities on this kind of gasket are not as big as those on a single-layer. They tolerate misalignment, and because of their smaller deformities, they can be reused.

4) The solid gasket was often found on 1950s and 1960s competition machinery. It is a single steel sheet around 2.00mm thick. It used to be sealed with gasket cement or thick aluminium paint.

5) The layered gasket is three or four steel sheets held together by the fire ring crimp. The soft layers distort when tightened and conform to surface irregularities, but enable the head and block to move without shear. Fit to smooth mating surfaces.

A three-layer deformed gasket is good for most performance engines, but, if available, use a layered gasket. This is superior due to its greater tolerance to temperature and misalignment. Use this kind on pressure-charged engines.

An engine may be old or unique, and so a commercial gasket might not be available. In such a case, make a single layer steel sheet gasket. Its thickness will be around 1.50mm to 2.25mm; the difference is due to compression requirements and valve geometry. Seal it to the oil and waterways with K & W Copper Coat, Loctite 510 or Hylomar. Even though most head gaskets are recommended to be fitted without sealant, coating a gasket with a spray-on sealer like Copper Coat is insurance against leakage.

Finding good quality gaskets for some engines can be a problem. The punched holes and fire ring crimp on some gaskets could be more precisely located. The fire ring can overhang the cylinder bore, which, if left, can be a detonation source (see Chapter 8, 'Pre-ignition and detonation'). To correct the problem, elongate the gasket's stud holes with a hole punch.

O-RINGS

Where only standard gaskets are available, one way to increase fire ring clamping is to fit O-rings. Do not use a layered gasket with O-rings, as the wire cannot embed itself into the outer layer. O-ringing consists of fitting a piece of wire in a machined groove underneath the fire ring. The groove is made shallow so the wire protrudes above the deck, thereby lifting up the gasket. This increases the fire ring pressure, which also holds the gasket in position reducing the chance of it leaking. Solid steel or copper wire is used

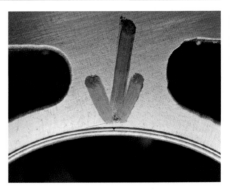

Plate 4-10: A head gasket O-ring. When only a standard gasket is available, one way to increase fire ring pressure is to O-ring the block. A solid wire in a machined groove protrudes above the deck, pressing on the fire ring.

(commonly MIG welding wire), of either 0.70mm/0.027in or 0.90mm/0.035in diameter. The protrusion can be half the wire diameter but when clamped tight, around 0.20mm/0.008in is ideal. To fit a wire in its groove, square one end with a carborundum stone, preform it into a rough circle and ease, rather than hammer, it in position. Cut to length, and square the other end. It is good practice to arrange the wire so that its ends join on the cooler, intake side of a block. A wet-liner engine can also be O-ringed by either fitting them to the liner land or to the head. The drawback with O-rings is the machined groove, if its depth in inconsistent, this alters the protrusion. A variation, favoured by some US tuners, is a 0.004in to 0.006in sized wire that rests on the deck underneath the fire ring. The wire is made to a specific bore diameter so not all sizes can be bought.

COOPER MECHANICAL JOINT

A further alteration is to use a regular gasket to seal the water and oil joints, but separate fire rings. Maserati used solid fire rings on its F1 winning, 1957 Tipo 250F. Solid steel rings are also found on large diesels that run over 4-bar boost; so the design is trustworthy. A variation is crushable fire rings that fit in a machined recess. Some claim that these were used first on the 1950s Vanwall F1 engine. The crush was approximately 0.60mm/0.025in: more than a regular gasket. Wet or dry liner blocks can be modified to accept crushable rings, which are usually called Elrings or Coopers' Rings. To modify a block, machine a recess of appropriate diameter and depth to suit the ring dimensions, and take it through into the cylinder bore. The limit to this modification is the difficulty in finding crushable rings of the correct size.

PYRAMID RINGS

It could be argued that a sturdier seal than a Coopers' Ring is a solid fire ring that fits in a recess. Solid rings cannot be bought commercially as they are only found on racing engines, such as Lancia's pressure-charged S4. They fit in a recess like Coopers' Rings, and are not a problem to make as only a lathe and a vertical mill is needed to make the rings and recess the block. It is within the scope of a modest machine shop. Recess the liner 2.00mm to 3.00mm deep, depending on the top ring's proximity to the deck, to a width of 3.00mm to 3.50mm. Turn rings out of austenitic iron (valve seat material) or Hidural 5. For high boost engines, or, where expense is unimportant, use Beryllium due to its fire retardant properties. Caution! The lung infection, Berylliosis must be mentioned here. It is caused by inhaling Beryllium dust when machining; so exercise caution.

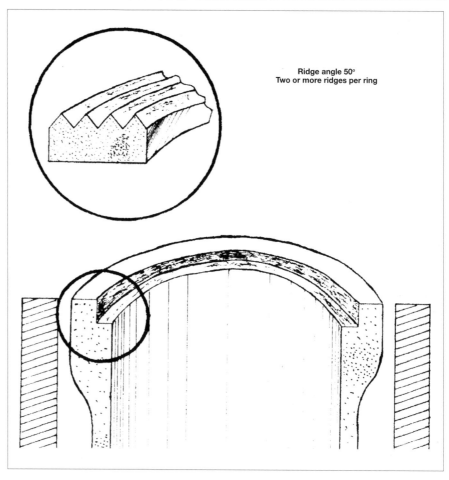

Ridge angle 50°
Two or more ridges per ring

Fig 4-9: A high integrity head joint.
A recessed liner and a solid fire ring. The peaks of the ridges contact the head's underside, making the seal.

Whatever material is used, shape the upper edges of rings into a 'W'- or 'A'-design. These pointed edges embed themselves into the head gasket face creating a bullet-proof joint. The easiest way to seal the oil and coolant passages is to use a regular head gasket and cut out areas a little bigger than the pyramid rings. The other way to seal the passages is to use Viton O-rings, but this entails a bit of machining. Either way, make sure the pyramid rings and the seal both have enough crush to make leak-free joints. Gasket crush needs to be around 0.30mm and pyramid ring crush in the head 0.10mm to 0.15mm.

Chapter 5
Crankcase & crankshaft

PLAN WORK

Stiffening a crankcase improves the alignment of shafts and pistons, which means they run truer and with less friction: this helps reliability and can raise horsepower. Parts that move in greater harmony can run closer to each other without damage. This allows certain assembly clearances to be reduced, notably the quench (see Chapter 6, 'Quench'). A close quench helps combustion by mixing a charge more efficiently. In addition, as parts are aligned better they may be able to rotate faster. A faster rotational speed is important considering that in any given time period, a faster-revving engine produces more horsepower than its slower-revving equivalent.

After inspecting the crankcase, make a list of jobs and a schedule. Decide what can be tackled alone, and by sub-contractors. Re-boring, re-sleeving, align-boring, repairing damaged threads, cryogenic treatment,

etc., needs to be planned. Work systematically – it's bad policy to finish-hone a block then weld a broken lug. Good record-keeping helps – make a note of what parts were sent for repair, and to whom, and the date they were returned – as does being able to sit quietly and think through processes then transfer the ideas to a master list. In simple form, this can be little more than a 'to do list,' where each job is crossed out and dated when it is completed.

DRY LINER BLOCKS

A dry liner block has parallel cylinder liners of high-grade cast iron that are located by an interference fit. The liners do not contact coolant but are surrounded by a water jacket. Dry liner blocks are closed deck, which means they have a full head gasket mating surface. The block gasket surface, the deck, is a similar shape to the head gasket surface. Dry liner blocks are usually made of cast iron, which makes

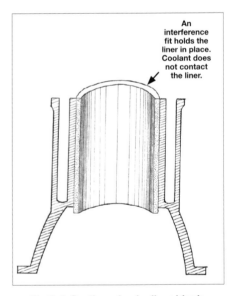

An interference fit holds the liner in place. Coolant does not contact the liner.

Fig 5-1: Section of a dry liner block.

the block and liner expansion rates much the same; thus maintaining liner fit on a running engine.

A different type of dry liner block is where the liner surface is Nikasil coated. In automotive applications this

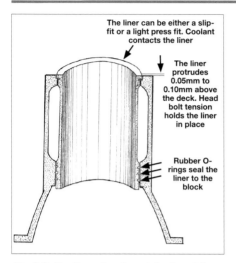

Fig 5-2: Section of a closed deck wet liner block.

Fig 5-2a: Section of an open deck wet liner block.

The unsupported upper liner can split on a modified engine. The lower flange retains the liner. Certain conditions can expand the upper and lower portions at different rates, leading to a leak.

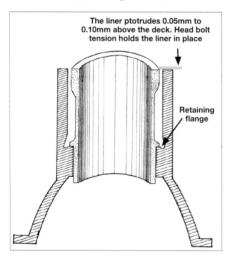

is found on aluminium block, racing or high performance engines. The cylinder bore, is part of the cast block as there is no inserted liner. The piston runs on a hard nickel-phosphorus plated finish, galvanically deposited on the aluminium surface. This has several advantages, most notably reduced weight, greater thermal conductivity, and expansion control as iron liners are eliminated. It's interesting to note that Nikasil coated bores are common in aluminium lawn mower engines.

WET LINER BLOCKS

On a wet liner block the liner is part of the water jacket as it is surrounded by coolant and seals the jacket on its upper and lower ends. Wet liner blocks are commonly cast in aluminium, and they can be either closed or open deck. A liner on a closed deck block is retained by a flanged top joint, which also acts as the fire ring abutment. It is sealed on its lower end by O-rings. On the other hand, a liner on an open deck block is flanged more than half-way down. This latter design is not as robust as a liner has less support, and under severe load may flex along its upper length and split. What is more, under certain conditions, for example, hard acceleration uphill followed by an off-throttle descent, there may be an issue maintaining head gasket integrity as a difference in expansion can occur between the liner flange and the fire ring. Of course, it is possible to strengthen such a system, but not without serious machining. On a closed deck wet liner engine, an expensive but useful modification is to replace iron liners with aluminium Nikasil treated liners. This is a valuable weight reduction and improves heat transfer. Such an arrangement was used on the Formula 1 Hart V10 engine.

Precautions, wet liner blocks

To ensure liner retention and fire ring seal, the liners on all wet liner engines must protrude above the deck face by around 0.05mm/0.002in to 0.10mm/0.004in. Protrusion may be measured with a feeler gauge and straight edge, although a DTI is more accurate. Take two readings, one from the port, and the other from the starboard side of the deck to the fire ring face. Add the two readings together and divide by two to get an average. This is important as older engines can suffer 'creep.' This condition is caused by the gradual extension of materials when placed under a constant load, and is made worse by high temperature. In real terms it can cause liners to recede or sink into a block, which lessens protrusion. The correct remedy is to fit new liners and then machine the protrusion accordingly. This is expensive; and where the existing liners are not badly worn modifying them to accept wire O-rings can be an effective repair.

As the exterior surface of a wet liner comes into contact with coolant, it forms part of the water jacket, and, as a consequence, has to be sealed to prevent water leakage. There are various types of liner seal: rubber-type O-rings, paper gaskets, or face-to-face joints with some form of sealant. The difference really depends on fit or tightness in the block, as, depending on design, a liner may be a light interference fit or a hand fit. When overhauling a closed deck block it's not necessary to remove unworn liners that have good protrusion. Nonetheless, pressure test any block with water to check for leaks. Seal a hand fit liner with a non-hardening sealer like K & W Coppercoat, Wellseal or Hylomar.

CRACK TESTING

Check old or suspect blocks with water (see Chapter 4, 'Crack testing and repair') and with a dye penetrant to areas unconnected with the water galleries. Water jacket cracks may occur that result in internal (into an engine) or external leaks. Use penetrant to examine non-coolant related highly stressed areas, for example between the cylinder bores, around head stud holes, and adjacent to main bearing saddles. It's possible for a crack in a main bearing saddle to extend into an oil gallery; and an engine may run well until up to temperature, after which the crack opens and oil pressure drops. Cracks around stressed members like main bearing saddles can sometimes be repaired by welding, but for other techniques see Chapter 4.

MAIN SADDLES AND CAPS

Before cleaning, examine the main bearings for signs of looseness. Fretting can take place in two separate areas, either singly or at the same time: between a bearing insert and its cap, and (or) between the cap abutments. In both instances, telltale polished spots or areas of dull lustre, indicate movement. Insert movement can be due to:

Plate 5-2: Two ways to reduce bearing fretting.
1) Measure the bearing crush (left). Assemble undamaged bearings in a housing and torque one side. Measure the gap under the other abutment with a feeler gauge (see text for dimensions).
2) Use a round-nosed chisel to peen the crankcase edges. This reduces the register, tightening the cap (right).

1) An oversized bearing housing
2) Not enough fastener torque – the bore size is correct but as the fasteners are loose, the assembly moves

To check for an oversized housing, measure the bearing crush. Assemble a set of undamaged bearings in a housing and fully torque one side. Depending on bearing diameter, the clearance under the other abutment should be between 0.0127mm/0.0005in to 0.05mm/0.002in. Measure this with a feeler gauge. To repair an oversized bearing housing, even if only one bearing were loose, remove a few thousands-of-an-inch from each main bearing cap abutment, reassemble and align hone the bearing housings: this procedure is called, capping.

Where the bearing crush is within limits yet the inserts show signs of movement, the fault lies in insufficient fastening. Loose fasteners are also the cause of movement between the cap and saddle abutment. Repairs include, replacing bolts with studs, or fitting waisted cap screws and increasing the torque 5ft/lb to 10ft/lb.

Old, un-modernised engines, may have locking tabs or castle nuts. Unless provenance is a concern, discard old fasteners in favour of hardened washers and aircraft quality nuts and studs. Clamping torque can loosen after a time when a nut digs into a soft locking tab, and torque can always be increased a minimum of 5ft/lb with quality rolled fasteners. It may also be possible to deepen the threaded section of fastener holes and fit longer studs, or improve the integrity of dowels or the cap register. Any caps that are not a snug fit should have their adjacent crankcase edges peened with a round-nosed cold chisel to increase their register.

Check the main bearing bore alignment, as a crankcase may have distorted, and then when in service the unnecessary friction will be a power drain. An easy way to check alignment without expensive measuring equipment is to fit all the bearings then thinly coat the main bearing journals with Engineers' Blue. Fit the shaft to the crankcase, but do not rotate.

Plate 5-1: Bearing fretting.
Check the backs of the bearing inserts, and the saddle and cap abutments for polished areas. These indicate bearing or cap movement.

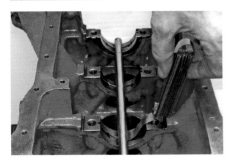

Plate 5-3: Two ways to check for crankcase distortion.
1) Lay the block on a solid surface. Place a ground rod in the saddles. Check for clearance with a feeler gauge (left).
2) Blue the main journals of a straight crankshaft. Fit the shaft and bearings, and then torque the fastenings. Rotate the crankshaft two revolutions, and remove. Each saddle insert must be blued on 70 per cent of its lower semicircle (right).

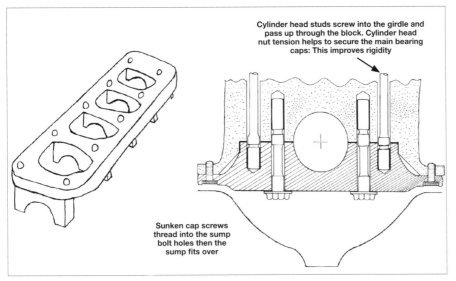

Cylinder head studs screw into the girdle and pass up through the block. Cylinder head nut tension helps to secure the main bearing caps: This improves rigidity

Sunken cap screws thread into the sump bolt holes then the sump fits over

Left. Fig 5-3: A main bearing bedplate.
A one-piece assembly increases crankcase rigidity. This can improve horsepower by reducing ring blow-by and crankshaft whip, thereby allowing a closer quench clearance. A variation of a bedplate, is to bolt a 10.00mm thick plate of hard alloy across the main bearing caps.

Right. Fig 5-3a: A main bearing girdle.
A girdle, is a one-piece main bearing cap assembly that also forms part of the sump.

Fully torque the main bearing fasteners, then, to avoid distortion, remove the block from its engine stand and place it evenly on its deck surface. Rotate the crankshaft through two revolutions, and then remove. The saddle bearing shells must show consistent blued evidence along 70 per cent of their lower semicircles. Because of bearing eccentricity, shells will rarely be marked for a few millimetres from either side of the bearing abutment.

Distortion can be due to poor design, or the extra stress resulting from raising an engine's power output. To improve rigidity, fit a cast sump, if available. Other modifications include machining a bedplate from steel or aluminium. This could be little more than a single robust plate secured to the main caps by its fasteners, or all main bearing caps made as a single assembly. A further stage is to make a girdle, as used on the Lancia S4 rally engine, which is similar to a bedplate, but also forms an integral section of the sump – or in dry sump engines, becomes the sump itself.

DE-BURRING

Check the thread condition on all screwed holes. Clean threads with a thread chaser or a blunted plug tap (see Chapter 2, 'Cleaning'). De-burr holes using a countersink rose. The deeply threaded holes of cylinder head studs are difficult to inspect and the probe of a fibre optic flashlight is helpful: these can be bought from specialist tool suppliers.

Remove sharp edges from castings, like pieces of flash or loose material, with a file or a grinder. Use a scraper or small file to blunt the sharp edges on either side of mating surfaces as this hinders the formation of stress raisers and hand injury. Machine any distorted surfaces. Correct minor blemishes by rubbing a surface on a thick sheet of plate glass, lightly oiled and spotted with fine grinding paste. Use consistent hand pressure and move the casting in a figure '8' motion to ensure accuracy. To check for flatness, lightly blue a surface plate and gently rub the casting's surface over the blue. High spots will be coated with Engineers' Blue.

OVERBORING

When intending to bore out a dry liner block to increase the swept volume, check the casting thickness around the

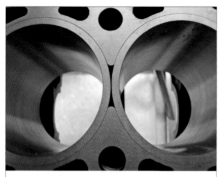

**Plate 5-4: An overbored block.
To avoid distortion on an overbored block, convert it to wet liner. The casting between the liners has been removed (top). Liners seal the water jacket (bottom).**

bores before machining. Make a pair of indicating callipers similar to those shown for porting in Chapter 4. They differ, though, from porting callipers in that their ends must be narrow enough to reach through the deck holes and into the water jacket. Alternatively, a hand-held ultrasonic thickness gauge will check a casting with greater accuracy. As the thrust faces of cylinder liners take the greatest load, the thickness of the casting in this area must be in the region of 4.60mm/0.181in to 5.00mm/0.196in. The space between cylinders is less highly stressed but removing material makes structures less rigid, and, when too thin, the cylinder walls may distort and lead to gas leaking past rings or a cracked casting. An alternative solution is to convert a dry liner block to wet liner.

BORING AND HONING

Always re-bore cylinders with a deck plate bolted to the block and all the main bearing caps fully tightened. A deck plate is a thick cast iron or steel plate, precision made to suit a type of engine. It is fitted, along with the head gasket and all fasteners to simulate cylinder head distortion: its aim then, is to reduce ring blow-by. Bore cylinders to 0.08mm/0.0031in to 0.09mm/0.0035in smaller than their finished diameter then progressively hone to final size with 280-grit then 500-grit stones. During this process, form a crosshatch pattern on the liners which is 20 to 30 degrees off the horizontal. Do this by moving the honer up-and-down the bore with an un-hurried synchronous movement. Lubricate the stones with a 50 per cent kerosene and 50 per cent mineral oil mixture. Crosshatching is necessary for oil retention and ring bed-in and is distinguished by peaks and valleys.

To save cost, do the honing with a hand-held honer that is driven by an electric drill. This is a job within the capabilities of any mechanically-minded person, but it's somewhat tedious. When finished with the 500-grit stones, the honing on a non-performance engine can be left at this point. In which case, the piston rings will rub the peaks off the cylinder walls but in the process shorten their life. This is the colloquially-termed 'breaking-in' period, which equates to around 600 road miles. For performance applications a 500-grit crosshatched finish is not acceptable. For best sealing, hone cylinders with 600-grit stones or, when unavailable, stones wrapped with 600-grit, or finer, wet-and-dry paper. Using such a fine grit produces a mirror-like finish that imitates the burnish of a fully broken-in cylinder surface yet still retains the oil retaining valleys of crosshatching. Such a technique has been used by builders

of performance engines for many years, but making such a fine finish is time consuming.

Plateau honing is a production technique now widely practised by motor manufacturers, and independent machine shops, that attempts to duplicate the finish of fine-grit hand honing, yet in a fraction of the time. It is claimed, with justification, that plateau honing largely eliminates new ring break-in. During plateau honing, fine-grit stones do make the final few passes on a bore, but for a limited time only. Given fine enough stones and sufficient time to do the job there's no reason why the finish of a plateau-honed liner could not be mirror-like. Ultimately, it comes down to time and money.

On a small bore single cylinder engine, or where time is not a factor, hand-honing is an option (model steam engineers use a similar procedure to lap piston bores to high precision). Cut an old piston in half and fit a firm spring over the wrist pin bosses then locate it on a suitable mandrel. When 60 per cent to 70 per cent of the final honing is complete, slide the hand-hone up and down the cylinder, partly rotating every other pass. Use a fine medium, such as 700-grit carborundum silicon carbide, thinned with light mineral oil, or a powdered siliceous rock like Turkey Stone, and then finish off the bore with metal polish. No matter what method is used, after honing, chamfer the sharp edge on a bore by 1.50mm/0.060in so that new rings easily enter without chipping. Where there is no access to a bore stone, a sharp bearing scraper works well, so long as chatter marks are smoothed out with an oil stone.

Sometimes there is talk of low tension rings. These are narrow rings that are around 1.00mm to 1.5mm wide. Narrow rings help to reduce ring flutter (an effect, on over-square engines,

Plate 5-5: Chamfering a liner.
After honing, chamfer the liner edge 1.50mm to help piston ring entry. Use a bearing scraper then smooth out marks with an oil stone.

associated with crankshaft speeds above 7500rpm), and frictional losses caused by rings rubbing against liner walls. In reality, to lessen friction, the builder of a performance engine who already has a set of pistons can only reduce the tension of the oil control ring. The process involves re-bending one end of the expander and trimming it with a file. For more on this subject (see Chapter 10, 'Fitting piston rings').

BLOCK GROUTING

Grouting is a means of increasing crankcase and liner stability, which is beneficial as all engines distort under load, and distortion contributes to piston ring blowby. However, only a dry liner block can be grouted. The process consists of filling the water jacket, to around 40 to 45 per cent of its capacity, with a hard-setting epoxy. This coats itself around the lower cylinders and increases their rigidity. It is very effective at helping to control distortion and can be performed on any dry liner block. It is almost a license to make horsepower, but unless a block is inherently weak, the results of grouting will be more apparent on pressure-charged engines as they're subject to greater cylinder pressure, and, consequently, distortion.

Grouting also reduces friction, as arguably the lower cylinder walls are unnecessarily cooled. As a result, raising

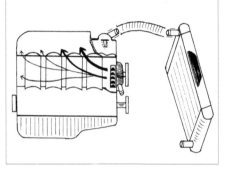

Fig 5-4: An un-grouted cylinder block.
Heat comes from the combustion chamber, but coolant reaches the lower liners first. They are over-cooled, and the chance of piston ring blow-by increases.

Fig 5-5: A grouted cylinder block.
Grouting strengthens a block and leads to a useful temperature rise in the liner's lower section. This reduces friction and ring blow-by. Pressure charged or heavy-crankshaft engines benefit most from grouting as they endure greater cylinder pressure and distortion.

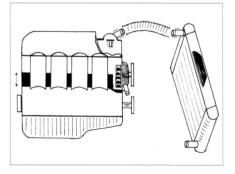

the lower liner temperature lessens the frictional losses credited to rings.

Some people seem intimidated by the prospect of converting part of a water jacket into a solid: they claim overheating will result. Grouting a block will not lead to overheating, but it will lead to a beneficial temperature rise in selected areas, specifically, the lower section of the liners. Cooling is not worsened as only the lower cylinder areas are covered, and of course heat is generated in the combustion chamber. In fact, this modification has been common knowledge within select North American racing circles since the 1960s. Furthermore, when carried out in conjunction with the cooling system changes to pressure and pump speed detailed in Chapter 7, performance improvements are guaranteed.

To grout a block, calculate 40 per cent of the water jacket. Work this out by measuring the depth from the deck to the bottom of the jacket. If the depth were 100mm: 40 per cent of 100mm is 40.00mm. Therefore, fill the block with grout until it is 60.00mm from the deck. Another way to work out the percentage is to fill the jacket to the deck with water, measuring the amount. Either way, once a block is measured clean out any rust or scale from the jacket by capping the lower openings, and soaking overnight with a 2 per cent caustic soda solution (100 millilitres to 5 litres of water). The next day flush the jacket with cold water. When the jacket is dry, blow it out with compressed air and then rinse it with brake cleaner or paint thinner. On designs where the water pump impeller fits inside the jacket, make up a wooden pattern to simulate the impeller intrusion, plus a reasonable amount for unimpeded water flow. Grease the pattern's inner surface to enable easy removal. Renew the core plugs and apply a thin layer of grease to their inner surfaces.

The water drains must not be forgotten, as otherwise these will be blocked by the grout. To overcome this, insert a small diameter plastic tube into each drain hole, and force a piece of strong wire down the tube from the deck. Adjust the tube's height so it protrudes about 10.00mm above the proposed fill level, and seal the opening around the drain with Play-Doh or silicone. On V-banked engines, each bank must be filled with a level deck, so only one bank can be filled at a time. Sometimes, it's necessary to arrange a dam to ensure that grout does not flow from the filled to the un-filled bank. Before filling, take the weight off heavy blocks that are bolted to engine stands, fully torque the main bearing caps, and make ready the cylinder head and an old head gasket: these will be fully tightened before the grout has firmed (about an hour, depending on viscosity). Fully tightening these components' fasteners, attempts to duplicate the stress of service.

Mix the epoxy in small batches to prevent it from firming. If necessary, dilute to a fluid consistency with trichoethylene or paint thinner so it can run through a funnel and between liners. Use a metal rod to agitate the epoxy in position between, and around liners to eliminate air bubbles and ensure good filling. When the epoxy reaches the desired level, fit the gasket and head and fully tighten. In the past, the two-part epoxy JB Weld has been used to good effect, but others have tried Plastic Steel Putty and Duragrout, which are manufactured by Devcon. Duragrout should be treated with caution, as it is appears to be nothing more than a concrete grout. Currently, Devcon's, Plastic Steel Liquid B is a great epoxy to grout a block. It does not need to be thinned, is rated up to 121 degrees C, is stable expansively and, what's more, the

Plate 5-6: Grouting a block. Seal the drain opening with silicone after inserting a plastic tube into the drain hole. Pour the grout into the block then agitate it with a metal rod to eliminate air bubbles.

cost of a 1kg can is comparable to ten packets of JB Weld. When completed, leave a block for several days to cure – this depends on ambient temperature and the epoxy's viscosity. All that remains is to trim the water drain tube and clean the drain plug threads with a hand tap.

OIL GALLERY AND CORE PLUGS

In production engines oil gallery drillings are often plugged with a ball bearing or a thin metal disc, staked in position. Potentially, these can work loose and it makes sense to replace them with screwed and lockwired plugs. Gallery holes are sometimes tapped in pipe thread: this is tapered. Correspondingly, the thread on pipe plugs is also tapered and a seal is made by the taper. As a result, when tapping a previously un-threaded gallery hole with non-pipe thread, the plug must have a head and sealing washer abutting a flat face.

Core plugs could be discarded in favour of threaded plugs but this is a bit of an overkill. A simpler solution is to stake new plugs in position by

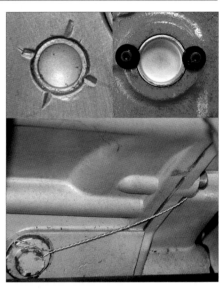

Plate 5-7: Gallery and core plugs. Stake, screw, or drill and lock wire plugs.

drilling and tapping two holes, one on either side of a plug and fitting them with fender washers. These overlap a plug's edge and prevent it moving. Alternatively, and perhaps neater-looking, is to fit a thin aluminium strip between the two holes. Screwed plugs and core plugs are made to be fitted dry, but it's a good idea to coat them with a sealer like Flange Sealer or Liquid Teflon.

TYPES OF CRANKSHAFTS

Crankshafts can be cast, forged or made from a billet (machined from a solid piece of alloy steel) and heat-treated to improve surface strength. Cast cranks are heat-treated by a process called Tuftriding, and forged or billet cranks by Nitriding. Both these processes do not make crankshafts stronger throughout, but it gives them a tough protective skin more resistant to abrasion, and therefore cracking. Cast crankshafts are the weakest of the three and should be upgraded wherever possible. Having said that, a well designed cast crank is usually adequate for a non-pressure-charged performance-enhanced road engine. Identify cast and forged crankshafts by their different width separation lines, which on cast cranks are around 1.00mm wide, and on forged, about 10.00mm.

On V8 engines, for example, crank pin configuration denotes whether the shaft is 'flat-plane' or 'two-plane'. American V8 engines are two-plane, yet some European manufacturers like Ferrari and Lotus employ flat-plane crankshafts as they have less rotating mass, which makes them more throttle-responsive and increases their rev limit. A flat-plane V8 crank is sometimes compared to two 4-cylinder cranks, as the crankpins for each bank are in line – on the same plane. When the front piston on bank A or B is at TDC so will the rear on the same bank, rotating the crankshaft 180 degrees, brings both middle pistons to TDC. Yet the pistons on a two-plane crank do not move with the same unison. Some configurations may have all the pistons on one bank slightly below the middle of the stroke while on the other; two may be at the top of the stroke and two towards the bottom. Crankshafts can be made to order, see the manufacturers listed in 'Useful Addresses'; although there are others.

CRANKSHAFT INSPECTION

When crack testing a crankshaft pay attention to areas around the big end and main journal oil holes, journal fillets, key ways or splines and the flywheel boss holes: these are areas of weakness or subject to high stress. Measure each bearing journal with a micrometer in four places: at either end (for taper), and at 90 degrees on the same circumference (for ovality). When journals are off by 0.0127mm/0.0005in, or greater, have them ground on a crankshaft grinder. When within specifications micro-lap

Plate 5-8: Measure journals for ovality and taper.
Measure each journal with a micrometer in four places: at either end (for taper), and at 90 degrees on the same circumference (for ovality). Correct journal irregularity of 0.0127mm or greater, by re-grinding.

journals to improve their surface finish. Use 1500-grade wet-and-dry paper lubricated with kerosene. Cut a piece of paper, approximately three-quarters journal width, and take-a-turn around it with a leather thong then simply pull it back-and-forth. This should also be done to new or reground journals.

Crankshafts can become bent, so check straightness, either between centres on a lathe or on suitable knife-edges. Another method, although it could be argued, potentially less accurate, is to assemble the crankshaft in its crankcase on the front and rear main bearings. Tighten the cap fasteners, and measure any deflection with a DTI whose stylus rests on the centre main journal. The ideal irregularity is zero but in reality heavily counterweighted shafts can sometimes be bent in service by 0.05mm/0.002in with seemingly little adverse effect (shafts flex when under load). Straighten a bent crankshaft by re-grinding or peening: a custom round-nose drift is hammered into the fillet on the low journal, settling shaft posture. Quality motor machine shops can do this job.

Crankshafts are cross-drilled between main and big end journals to supply big ends with lubricant. The gallery also acts an oil thrower as heavy particles are separated from the oil by centrifugal action. Solid material builds up in the gallery so it must be removed. On most production crankshafts the cross-drilling holes are plugged with a ball bearing or a pressed-in metal cap. Remove the plugs and scrub the drillings with a gallery brush as cleaning with solvent and compressed air will not dislodge debris. A useful modification is to thread the un-threaded holes and replace the metal caps with screwed plugs; although on Nitrided shafts this will not be possible due to their hardness. Sized aluminium plugs, Loctited in position are an alternative.

The clutch pilot bearing is sometimes overlooked, what with all the focus on seemingly more important matters. Bronze bushes frequently come loose, or split, and needle roller bearings run dry of lubricant. Sealed ball journal bearings are the most reliable, but, of course, check everything. Be wary of matching the crankshaft to a non-standard transmission as small diametrical differences to a pilot bearing or a flywheel boss may not be obvious until closely inspected.

LIGHTENING AND BALANCING

Crankshafts can be lightened but it's time consuming, and sometimes the benefits can be hardly worth the effort. A lighter shaft will not improve power, but will improve the engine's ability to accelerate and decelerate. Perhaps the biggest advantage of a lightened shaft is the reduced crankcase stress. Generally speaking, production crankshafts are unnecessarily heavy, and it's useful to reduce their weight. However, reducing the weight of even a heavy crankshaft by more than 20 per cent may negatively affect drivability. Lighten around the counter weights with care, as removing too much material can make shafts difficult to balance. Regardless of how much material is removed, remember to de-burr, knife-edge and smooth shafts.

To start, thickly wrap all journals and machined surfaces in thin metal sheet followed by taping: this is to avoid grinding wheel slip. Use an angle grinder to smooth rough surfaces and radius corners. To help reduce windage (see Chapter 7, 'Sump modifications and breathers') grind the trailing edge of counter weights to 45 degrees or a V-shape: this is knife-edging. After grinding, go over the whole surface with a flap wheel, first 80-grit then 120-grit. Although pleasing to the eye, polishing is unnecessary as the desired result is merely a smooth surface devoid of scratches.

Flat-plane crankshafts are easy to dynamically balance as they require no temporary counter-weighting to simulate the reciprocating weight of the pistons and con rods: just the rotating mass is balanced. In other words, although the

weight of individual rods and pistons are equalised, they do not impact on crankshaft balancing. For this reason, an industrial balancer (used to balance fan blades or armatures) is useful to balance a flat-plane crank. Balance a crankshaft in four stages:

1) The shaft, by itself
2) The shaft with the front pulley
3) The shaft with front pulley and flywheel
4) The shaft with the front pulley, flywheel and clutch cover

This way, if ever a front pulley or flywheel is changed the crankshaft's balance is unaffected. Depending on resources, static balancing is also a possibility. Two knife-edges are needed to support the shaft on its front and rear journals. The knife-edges must be solidly mounted, perfectly flat and true. Start the crankshaft moving with gentle hand pressure and any out of balance will show up as a tendency to come to rest in the same place, and heaviness to one side will cause tracking. To double-check this, swap the shaft end-to-end.

Two-plane crankshafts are not so easy to balance, as they require accurate counter-weighting during the balancing procedure. Firstly, the weights of all the pistons and rods are equalised, and then weighed. The amount of temporary balance for a particular engine – a known factor, the balance factor – is computed, and the necessary weights attached to the crankpins to replicate partial reciprocating weight. For more on this topic see Chapter 6, 'Balancing rods'. Balancing a two-plane crank requires specialist equipment and must be entrusted to a motor machine shop. It should also be noted that all work to the pistons, for example adjusting the quench or the valve pocket depth must be completed before

balancing. Finally, de-magnetise the shaft before assembly as grinding can set up magnetic fields.

FLYWHEEL AND CLUTCH

The purpose of a flywheel is to absorb excess energy on the power stroke as the crankshaft speed increases. This energy is then released during the following three strokes. As a large portion of the mass of any flywheel is at a big radius from its centreline, reducing its weight will drastically change a vehicle's driving characteristics. Lightening a flywheel will not alter an engine's idle, but it's worth repeating that it will alter a machine's ability to slow down: a vehicle will slow down quicker when the throttle is closed. This can adversely affect a machine's cornering characteristics, as shutting off the throttle can seem like applying the brakes. As a result, not enough speed is carried into a corner, necessitating very precise throttle control.

On mass-produced vehicles, cast iron is the common material for flywheels, but on sports or race machines, it is steel. A cast iron flywheel cannot be excessively lightened, as it is liable to become a weak structure and may explode. Therefore, remove material with care. To lighten, mount a flywheel on a lathe faceplate, and skim material from the inner face (non-clutch side) with a round-nose turning tool. Depending on diameter and thickness, turn-off material from the outer 55.00mm to 70.00mm of the face to a depth of around 5.00mm to 10.00mm, keeping well away from the flywheel boss. To finish, set the lathe speed to approximately 120rpm and polish out turning tool marks using a 120-grit flap wheel in a die grinder. Alternatively, slot it on a milling machine using a rotary table. Due to its large diameter, pay particular attention the balance of the flywheel. For example, a

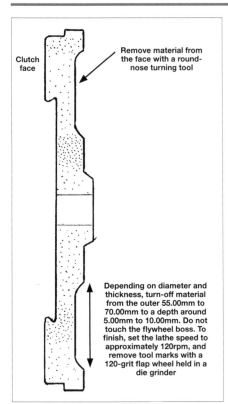

Clutch face

Remove material from the face with a round-nose turning tool

Depending on diameter and thickness, turn-off material from the outer 55.00mm to 70.00mm to a depth around 5.00mm to 10.00mm. Do not touch the flywheel boss. To finish, set the lathe speed to approximately 120rpm, and remove tool marks with a 120-grit flap wheel held in a die grinder

Fig 5-6: Section of a lightened flywheel. A vehicle will accelerate and decelerate quicker with a lighter flywheel.

disparity of 7 grams on a rotating part at a radius of 300mm causes a 186lb imbalance at 6000rpm. The following information may be useful when drilling holes in a flywheel.

Weights of materials per inch of depth:

Steel
⅜ diameter = 0.50oz/14.1 grams
⁷/₁₆ diameter = 0.68oz/19.2 grams
½ diameter = 0.88oz/24.9 grams

Cast iron
⅜ diameter = 0.45oz/12.7 grams
⁷/₁₆ diameter = 0.62oz/17.5 grams
½ diameter = 0.80oz/22.6 grams

A powerful, modified engine will benefit from a lighter, stronger clutch assembly, and such an assembly may have one or more plates. A minor change is to fit to a standard flywheel a clutch friction plate lined with hard-wearing organic material, and a more powerful pressure plate. This is an improvement over a stock clutch. The most common competition clutches have A-ring or Lug Drive covers used with cerametallic or sintered friction plates. Cerametallic paddle-plates have sintered friction material riveted in place. A 3-paddle plate resembles the shape of a 3-spoke wheel; each spoke carrying an area of sintered material. Friction plates can be bought with 3, 4 or 6 paddles, and used in single or twin-plate assemblies. A sintered friction plate, on the other hand, has a layer of friction material sintered onto its steel plate, and such an assembly is mainly intended for road racing. The most common size of both types is 184.00mm/7¼in.

For most road, track day and rally use, fit an A-ring cover with a single or twin-disc cerametallic paddle assembly. Cerametallic plates are similar to stock clutches in that they have controlled slippage. This means that they are progressive and have smooth engagement without judder. Pedal pressure is usually stronger but this depends on the spring rate and progression. A 3-paddle friction plate is suitable for most purposes. To use an A-ring cover on a stock flywheel, a recess will need to be turned to locate the housing's adaptor ring. To do this turn a spigot on the clutch side to suit the inside diameter of the adaptor ring, and drill six equally spaced 8.00mm fixing holes to attach the assembly. Arrange the fixing bolts to pass from the rear of the flywheel through to the clutch cover (from-the-driver-to-the-driven).

Multi-plate clutches can sometimes suffer clutch drag when the plates of a disengaged clutch rub together. This can slow gear changing, or, when stationary, make a machine creep forward as if the clutch were partially engaged. Shimming the clutch springs helps to equalise the pressure plate's axial run-out, which can reduce or eliminate clutch drag. Make (using a lathe) an assortment of shims 0.10mm/0.004in and 0.20mm/0.008in thick. The shims fit in the spring cups, so their outside diameter must equal spring nominal diameter. Assemble the clutch with a new spring set, and measure the axial play with a DTI. Fit shims under the springs that have less protrusion. The best run-out is zero, but due to the rubbing action of the pushrod on the pressure plate that is rarely attainable. A run-out between 0.25mm/ 0.010in to 0.35mm/0.014in will still result in smooth clutch operation.

Plate 5-9: Shimming a pressure plate. Shims equalise the springs on a pressure plate (top). Use a DTI to measure the axial run-out (bottom).

Chapter 6
Pistons & con rods

TYPES OF PISTON

Pistons are either cast or forged, and, although it's possible to machine them from solid, a forging is strongest. A forged structure is denser enabling greater heat transfer and reduced combustion temperature. Cast pistons are fitted to many production engines, so a useful upgrade is to replace them with forged items. To qualify that, cast pistons with solid skirts seem to perform well enough in naturally-aspirated engines of moderate performance. Cast pistons made using the hypereutectic process – solidified silicon particles at the eutectic point that form a hard skin – are available for many engines, but if replacing old pistons with new, it make sense to pay a little more and fit forged. To identify a forged or a cast piston look at its underside markings. A forging has a lightly-grained smooth finish, burnished a silvery-blue colour. By comparison, the same area on a cast piston is rough; it also displays lines or patterns, and is matt-silver in colour.

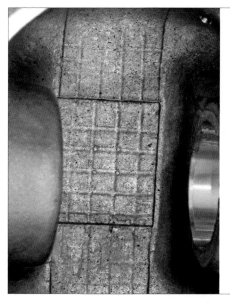

Plate 6-1: Cast and forged pistons.
Identify a piston by its markings under the crown: cast (left), and forged (right). Forged pistons are stronger than cast.

PISTON-TO-BORE CLEARANCE

Generally speaking, the silicon content in the composition of an alloy is a useful indicator of its expansion rate; and therefore this affects the piston-

Plate 6-2: Measuring a cylinder with a bore micrometer.
1) Measure the piston skirt 90 degrees from the wrist pin axis, approximately 10 millimetres from the edge of the skirt.
2) Set the bore micrometer to the piston skirt diameter, and zero the gauge.
3) Measure the bore in six places: top, middle and bottom – then 90 degrees to the first measurements.

to-bore clearance. As a result, a best bore clearance for engines does not exist as, amongst other concerns, the running clearance is dependent on piston alloy. Too small a piston-to-bore clearance causes pistons to run on their ring lands rather than their skirts, and too large a clearance will allow them to rock back and forth leading to poor ring sealing. Consequently, follow the piston manufacturer's advice.

Piston skirts are oval, the largest diameter being 90 degrees from the wrist pin axis and approximately 10 to 15 millimetres beneath: always measure piston diameter at this point with an outside micrometer. A bore micrometer is the best tool to measure a cylinder bore. To avoid confusion, set the bore micrometer to the piston skirt diameter and zero the gauge. If the skirt diameter were 86.00mm, set the outside micrometer to this dimension and use its

jaws to hold the bore micrometer pads apart then rotate the bezel on the dial gauge to zero. This way, when taking bore readings, the needle on the dial gauge will register + or - of the 86.00mm

Plate 6-3: Measuring a cylinder with a feeler gauge.
Although not as precise as a bore micrometer, feelers are reasonably accurate. Use several thin blades for greater accuracy as they conform to bore curvature.

dimension. When a bore micrometer is unavailable, an expanding pin gauge and the requisite size of outside micrometer are also effective. A further method (cruder but reasonably accurate) is to use a feeler gauge. Enter a piston in its bore, crown first, and measure the clearance with a feeler gauge resting on the skirt's large diameter. It's a simple matter to note the nip or feel when checking with different sized gauges. Use several thin blades for greater accuracy as they more readily conform to bore curvature. Keep a record of all measurements by using the bore sheet from the rear pages of this book.

MODIFICATIONS AND WHAT TO BUY

A piston can be modified with a view to improving an engine's power but generally speaking, alterations to an existing piston are few in number and are limited to lightening and the addition of coatings. Only drill lightening holes in a race motor piston as their working life is short. A modification that reduces weight without compromising stiffness is to waist the parallel bore of a wrist pin by tapering each end. The length of taper should be around 35 per cent of the total pin length, and taper towards each end to 20 per cent larger than the pin's internal diameter. Pins are hard to machine, and this job is best done on a lathe using a selection of rotary burrs, finished off with fine emery to reduce the risk of a stress raiser.

A slipper piston is a piston whose lower skirt is radiused so it clears the crankshaft counterweights at bottom dead centre. The pistons of almost all modern engines are of this type. Concerning a piston's skirt, a narrow skirt will shorten ring life quite considerably due to reduced piston stability. A generous or even a full skirt is most practical when its thrust faces

Plate 6-4: Lightening a piston.
A piston, lightened by drilling holes in its pin boss (left). To reduce weight, waist the parallel bore of a wrist pin by tapering each end (right).

Plate 6-5: Piston skirts.
A narrow skirt piston is less stable in a cylinder bore. This shortens ring life (left). Full skirts are more practical (centre and right). A skirt that extends further than 30.00mm from the wrist pin centre line adds weight but little more stability.

extend no further than 30.00mm from the wrist pin centreline. A skirt that extends further adds weight to the piston without appreciably increasing its stability, so reduce it. Concerning buying guidelines, a piston for a performance engine could have the following: two 2.00mm thick compression rings, and one 3.00mm thick oil control ring – this consists of an expander and two rails. Ideally the piston should come with a waisted pin whose ends have been chamfered 45 degrees, and retained by spring wire clips (without bent ears). To aid lubrication, a drilling should connect the oil ring groove to the wrist pin bore.

PISTON CROWN SHAPE
Combustion chamber design largely dictates piston crown shape. A reasonably high compression may be had when using a 4-valve-per-cylinder pent roof chamber and a flat-topped piston. On the other hand, using a flat-topped piston in an engine with a hemispherical or flattened spherical combustion chamber will result in low compression, as these chambers, by design, always have a large volume. They need a domed piston, as the intrusion of the dome reduces the clearance volume, and as a result raises the compression.

Flame travel can be obstructed by a dome's intrusion. This is why raising compression by fitting a high-domed piston can sometimes reduce power and cause complications, such as plug masking. This occurs when a sparkplug's electrode is so close to the crown that it prevents good combustion. This may lead to an engine making more midrange power but less top end, when gas speeds are fastest.

If pistons are high-domed, it's a good idea to measure, during mock-up, the height from the top of the crown to the combustion chamber ceiling. Six to seven millimetres is a typical dimension, which can be checked using Play-Doh. Plug masking can be a particular problem on high compression 2-valve engines. It can, though, be helped by machining a fire groove in the piston crown. This can take the form of a shallow channel across the crown, approximately 2.00mm to 2.50mm deep and 5.00mm wide, that links the intake and exhaust valve reliefs, or, where a cylinder has an offset sparkplug, a depression in the crown adjacent to the electrode. The depth of the depression depends on the desired compression ratio and crown thickness. A crown thickness of 3.80mm/0.150in to 6.30mm/0.250in is quite typical.

PISTON RINGS
The notion of low tension rings is really about ring thickness; as it follows that a 3.00mm thick ring will exert a greater parasitic drag than one only 2.00mm thick. This is why 2.00mm thick compression rings were previously

recommended. Concerning the oil control ring, some work can be done to reduce drag. The ends of the expander on a three-piece oil control ring butt together to force the ring face onto the bore surface. This parasitic drag can be reduced by bending and filing the expander ends. Reducing friction, without loss of power or reliability, is worthwhile, but to avoid oil smoke use a modest end gap. A gap of 0.08mm/ 0.003in can be tried; then again, others claim end gaps as large as 0.25mm/ 0.010in to 0.38mm/0.015in are desirable – the matter is subjective and open to interpretation. On one engine the oil ring drag was measured before and after bending the expander ends. The oil ring was fitted to a piston and pulled through a lightly oiled cylinder with a spring-scale. Once in motion, the pull on the scale was read. Back-to-back dyno tests were not carried out to examine the usefulness or otherwise of this single alteration; although the before and after measurements did show a reduced pull on the spring-scale. As a result, the effectiveness of this modification cannot be judged.

Where ring options exist, choose the most suitable type of ring for an application. For example, whether the engine is pressure-charged or not, or will be used in dusty areas. Grey cast iron piston rings perform well on most naturally-aspirated street engines as they bed in easily and tolerate bore imperfections. For longer life, or more dusty abrasive conditions, use plasma molly cast iron rings. These are molybdenum-coated, very hard, and self lubricating, which assists break-in. Ductile iron rings are very strong and resistant to breakage. They are suitable for pressure-charged engines as they withstand temperatures at which a cast iron ring might begin to scuff. The best choice concerning ring selection is to

use a combination, rather than rings of one particular type. A good combination for a naturally-aspirated engine is:

1) Plasma molly 1st ring
2) Cast iron 2nd ring

For pressure-charged engines:

1) Ductile iron 1st ring
2) Plasma molly 2nd ring

One-piece cast iron oil control rings have largely been replaced by three-piece assemblies, which is just as well as the former had a tendency to break. Three-piece assemblies consist of a central expander and two chrome-faced side rails: an arrangement that gives little trouble.

The best ring gap on a running engine is one that is close to zero when at a sustained full load. In plain language this means that when driving wide-open in top gear on an endless straight or on a dyno pulling maximum load, the ends of a ring are almost touching. Polished ring-ends are evidence of insufficient end gap, which is a very dangerous condition. Rings are usually pre-gapped, meaning the end gaps have been computed and machined during manufacture. The end gaps on File-to-Fit or File-Fit rings, on the other

hand, need to be set manually by the engine builder. Unlike pre-gapped rings, this type of ring is oversize for a given bore dimension, and when available, it enables accurate gaps to be set without selective assembly. A method to check ring gaps is described in Chapter 10, 'Fit piston rings.' Where specifications are unavailable or they appear excessively large use the figures in the accompanying chart.

VALVE DROP

Valve drop, is the clearance between a piston and a valve head. For an exhaust valve this is closest from 3 degrees to 5 degrees BTDC, and for an intake valve, from 3 degrees to 5 degrees ATDC. Clearly, if a valve is too close it may contact a piston and bend. What's more, even where there is enough clearance to avoid contact, on a well-built engine there will also be a little extra room. This is the safety margin in case of over-revving or missing a gear change. In reality, an exhaust valve will always be closer to a piston than an intake valve as it is still quite a way off its seat at TDC, and, when over-revving occurs, it's the exhaust valve (or valves) that invariably get bent.

Measure the valve drop after the timing is set. The valve running clearance also affects readings. If the

Ring material and engine type	Minimum end gap
Plasma or ductile iron, top ring	*Per millimetre of diameter*
Naturally-aspirated	0.0045mm
Pressure-charged	0.008mm
Air-cooled	0.0035mm
Ductile or cast iron, second ring	*Per millimetre of diameter*
Naturally-aspirated	0.003mm
Pressure-charged	0.005mm
Air-cooled	0.0025mm

Suggested end gaps.

manufacturer specified a minimum valve drop of 1.75mm/0.070in and a valve running clearance of 0.50mm/0.020in, but, during mock-up the clearances were 1.50mm/0.060in valve drop and 0.25mm/0.010in running clearance, then there isn't enough valve drop; so it needs to be increased by 0.25mm. To increase it, an inattentive engine builder may machine a piston relief or sink a valve. But during final assembly the running clearance would be reset: they would be increased by 0.25mm. In turn, this would alter the valve drop and bring it to specification (1.75mm/0.070in) without machining. Though, the inattentive builder, in the process of machining, would have lowered the compression ratio.

On pressure-charged engines valve drop is not usually a problem due to their low static compression, and even on some naturally-aspirated engines the drop is sometimes a generous 4.00mm/0.160in. A valve drop clearance of 1.80mm/0.070in for exhaust and 1.30mm/0.051in for inlet should ensure reliability on an overhead camshaft engine. Of course, it's possible to make clearances tighter, down to, say 0.70mm/0.027in, but all slackness must be eliminated from the timing drive, which means regular maintenance. On pushrod engines you would be wise to aim for a minimum valve drop of 2.80mm/0.110in.

QUENCH

Quench, also known as squish, is the process whereby a charge is squeezed between two narrow lands: one on the piston crown and the other on the combustion chamber. The quench land on a piston is a machined ring running around the crown's outer edge. Depending on combustion chamber design the land can be angled or flat and its size and shape correspond to those

Plate 6-6: Quench lands.
A quench land is a machined ring running around the crown's outer edge. This mirrors a similar shaped surface on the chamber. At TDC, the close surfaces expel the charge allowing a higher compression.

of a similar surface on the chamber. In a running engine these two surfaces are extremely close at TDC. Such proximity expels a charge and thereby aids mixing and combustion speed. Although Ricardo designed a side valve quench-type combustion chamber in the 1930s, some would claim Norton Motorcycles developed the idea for use on overhead valve engines. Norton's work with quench enabled the mid-1950s Manx Norton racing engine to run a higher compression without detonation. Generally speaking, the closest quench possible without piston-to-head contact is desirable, as the sudden movement of the charge lowers temperature. This helps to prevent charge pre-heating and the colliding flame fronts that cause detonation.

High compression is one of the causes of detonation, where cylinder pressure exceeds combustion chamber limitations. This can raise the temperature to a level where spontaneous combustion ignites the un-burnt charge. The resulting high velocity shockwave heats up the internal surfaces and can lead to piston, head gasket, or sparkplug damage. The pressure wave creates an audible sound, a ringing or pinging,

which reduces the cylinder oil film, and worsens overheating and piston ring wear. In the quest for more power, make every effort to run a close quench and a high compression consistent without detonation. Each change in ratio, say from 9.0:1 to 10.0:1, is equal to a 4-6 per cent increase in horsepower throughout an engine's entire power range.

To avoid confusion when working out the quench, number each piston with a felt-tipped pen on its forward-facing wrist pin boss – number 1 piston to rod number 1, etc. Then fit the piston and rod assemblies to the engine but omit the rings and circlips. Use the new crankshaft bearings intended for the final build and fully tighten the fasteners. There are two operations to carry out when measuring the quench on flat-topped pistons:

1) Measure the piston protrusion: Use a DTI to measure how far the piston protrudes above the deck by securing the DTI's magnetic base to a piece of ground-flat stock. Set the piston at TDC then zero the stylus on the deck. Take two measurements on the flat quench land, one on each side of the piston above the wrist pin axis. Add the readings together and divide by two to get an average. For example, if one reading is 0.15mm and the other 0.17mm: 0.15 + 0.17 = 0.32 ÷ 2 = 0.16; the average is 0.16mm
2) Measure the compressed head gasket thickness with a micrometer

As an illustration, the quench for a cylinder with 0.16mm piston protrusion and 0.82mm thick head gasket would be:

0.82mm compressed gasket
<u>0.16mm</u> - piston protrusion
= 0.66mm quench

Plate 6-7: Measuring a flat quench. Take two measurements on the quench land, one on each side over the wrist pin axis. If the piston protrudes above the deck, subtract the protrusion from the head gasket thickness. If the piston is below the deck, add the amount – the result is the quench clearance.

Yet if the same piston were recessed 0.16mm below the deck the quench changes to:

<u>0.16mm</u> + piston recession
= 0.98mm quench

Pistons and rods can be swapped from cylinder-to-cylinder in an attempt to equalise the readings, but ultimately, the only practical solution is to turn down the crowns on a lathe. An easy job, comparatively, for most machine shops (see Chapter 10 'Setting the quench').

An angled quench land cannot be measured with a DTI; it must be checked using Play-Doh, pre-flattened solder wire or lead wire. Strategically insert two pieces of the chosen medium

Plate 6-8: Measuring an angled quench. Place two pieces of lead wire on the quench land above the wrist pin axis. Fit the head and gasket, torque the fastenings and rotate the crankshaft 360 degrees. Measure the crushed wire with a micrometer – the result is the quench clearance.

on the quench land, above the wrist pin axis. Fit the head and gasket, torque the fasteners and rotate the crankshaft through 360 degrees. It is difficult to get a reading with Play-Doh that is more accurate than 0.01mm/0.004in. Lead wire is the most accurate, but it is rarely available, as a result use solder wire. Solder does not crush like pure lead as it contains tin; therefore, gently flatten the wire to within 0.26mm/0.010in of the expected reading. It should be noted that on some engines the angle of the piston-to-combustion chamber quench land is not consistent: it may be narrower towards the periphery. Consequently, the thinnest part equals the minimum clearance before contact.

CONVERTING A NON-QUENCH ENGINE

Older, pre-quench engines can be modified to incorporate quench design – these will be 2-valves-per-cylinder chambers. It may be possible to change the combustion chamber by welding-up the area on either side of the valves. This reduces the chamber volume which necessitates using a flatter-domed or

flat-topped piston. It is then a matter of finding the correct modern piston and machining the surfaces to suit.

OPTIMUM QUENCH

The optimum quench for any engine can only be found by back-to-back testing. For instance, if a cold engine were started and slowly warmed until it was pulling 90 per cent load, by such a time its castings and components would have expanded and be flexing under the load. As a result, a 0.56mm/0.022in quench, set on a 4-cylinder iron block engine, may have closed to an acceptable level, yet the same clearance on a two-plane, iron block V8 would result in piston-to-head contact. The major differences concern component rigidity and material. Under load, the inertia of moving components causes castings to flex.

Expansion is another factor; casting alloy like LM23 expands at twice the rate of cast iron. Therefore, an expanding aluminium block will greatly increase the quench. The difference between an assembled quench and a running quench is often referred to as 'rod stretch.' This is an erroneous phrase that implicitly shifts blame to one set of components while ignoring the impact of others. Nonetheless, the following are some suggested quench clearances that have been proven on performing engines. The figures are for engines that use steel con rods. An iron block 4- or 6-cylinder engine: 0.64mm/0.025in with the minimum about 0.46mm/0.018in (when the engine has an aluminium block, reduce these figures by 0.13mm/0.005in). An aluminium block V12 can run 0.59mm/0.023in without any problem, and set the quench on a two-plane, iron block V8 engine to around 0.89mm/0.035in.

SWEPT VOLUME

Measure the swept volume before

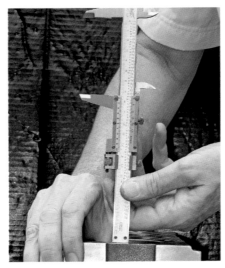

Plate 6-9: Measuring the stroke. Use a depth spike to measure the crown-to-deck distance at BDC. Take a similar reading at TDC. If the piston is below the deck, subtract the second reading, and if above, add it – the difference is the stroke.

checking the compression ratio, as manufacturers sometimes round up the stroke of engines to cardinal dimensions. Do not rely on what is stated in a service manual, but verify the data. To measure the stroke, position the piston at BDC, verified with a DTI, and use the depth spike of a vernier calliper to measure the crown-to-deck distance. Bring the piston to TDC, and take a similar measurement. The difference between the two is the stroke. For example:

> 75.90mm distance at BDC
> 00.20mm distance at TDC
> = 75.70mm = stroke

Next, measure the bore diameter. For the sake of example it is 87.00mm; therefore, the bore and stroke are 87.00mm x 75.70mm. To compute the swept volume use:

$$SV = \pi \times (R^2) \times L$$

SV = Swept volume
π = 3.1416
R = radius
L = length

When a calculator does not have a π button, half the diameter, in that case:

> 3.1416 x 43.50 x 43.50 x 75.70 = 450013.22 or 450cc

The cylinder's swept volume is 450cc.

COMPRESSION RATIO

A cylinder's static compression ratio is the association between its combined, clearance and swept volumes, divided by the clearance volume. To put it another way, the reduction in volume from swept volume to clearance volume expressed as a ratio. It is expressed as:

$$CR = \frac{(SV + CV)}{CV}$$

CR = Compression ratio
SV = Swept volume
CV = Clearance volume

As mentioned previously, raising the compression increases an engine's horsepower, which is due to improved volumetric efficiency. Although, when the compression is greater than the limitations of a combustion chamber it will cause detonation. In such a case, it would be better to have a narrower quench and a lower compression than a higher compression and wider quench. The following is an example that illustrates the link between compression and quench. In the late 1980s, a client raced an Alfa GTV6 in a local championship. After suffering piston-to-valve contact caused by loose fitting guides, the owner re-assembled the engine. He fitted over-bored slip-fit liners and custom high-dome pistons to

achieve the same compression ratio as on the previous build. After a four-hour break-in on the company dynamometer it was load tested at its previous settings, yet it made less power and detonated in the upper 500rpm. On examination the quench was found to be 0.28mm larger than on the previous build.

The easiest way to raise compression is to fit different pistons. Replacement pistons are often available (or can be made) with a greater compression height. This is the dimension measured from the wrist pin centreline to the quench land. A larger compression height will raise the compression and reduce the quench as a piston sits further up its cylinder. Skimming the deck or head surface is another option but on overhead camshaft engines with non-vernier pulleys, skimming alters the valve timing as the set distance between the crankshaft and camshaft changes. Even on engines that have vernier pulleys, skimming will have the effect of lengthening the toothed belt, which may compromise a drive's tension.

The clearance volume must be known to compute the compression ratio, and it can only be measured accurately with the cylinder head removed. The procedure where the piston is at TDC, and an assembled cylinder is arranged plug-hole-uppermost, and then a fluid is run into the plug hole, is not reliable. Leakage may occur past piston rings that cannot be established or disproved – there is no way of knowing if it has, or has not taken place. There are three operations in the recommended method to measure the clearance volume:

1) Measure the volume on top of the piston
2) Measure the volume of the combustion chamber

3) Measure the volume of the cylinder head gasket

Measure the volume on top of the piston

Two special tools are needed: a blanking plate and a burette. The blanking plate must be big enough to seal the top of the cylinder; make it out of Plexiglas (Perspex) that is between 3.00mm to 5.00mm thick. Drill and countersink the plate's centre to accept the burette tip, and add eight to ten randomly scattered vent holes. When the time comes, seal the plate to the cylinder with light grease. Use a zero-to-50cc burette, or larger, to fill the cylinder with a fluid medium like kerosene, Varsol, or Jizer. To prevent the medium leaking past the piston, fit it with two old rings, or, if unavailable, one new compression ring. Fit the piston to the requisite cylinder then coat it lightly with grease and position the piston at TDC, measured with a DTI. Use a spirit level to set-up the deck so it is horizontal. A flat-topped piston that does not protrude beyond the deck is the easiest to check. When ready to measure, let in the fluid from the burette – try to do this quickly to minimise potential leakage time – and read off the amount when all the air has been expelled. Immediately check the underside of the piston for leakage. As the piston does not protrude beyond the deck add the result to the combustion chamber and head gasket volumes.

Domed or flat-topped pistons that jut above the deck can be said to 'intrude' into the combustion chamber. Measure the amount of intrusion and subtract it from the combustion chamber and head gasket volumes. There are two ways to measure an intrusion:

A) Descend the piston
B) Use a sized measuring ring

Plate 6-10: Measuring the clearance volume – engine block.
Grease and position the piston at TDC. Level the block, and fit a blanking plate (top). Let in the fluid quickly from the burette to minimise leakage (bottom). Read the amount when the air has been expelled.

Descend the piston

From TDC (measured with a DTI) descend the piston a minimum measured amount so the top of the dome is just below deck height. Fit the flat blanking plate and measure the volume as before. To calculate the intrusion, subtract the measured volume from the theoretical volume. If a piston in an 87.00mm bore was descended 21.00mm from TDC and 93.00cc were found to fill the cylinder. Work out the theoretical volume of a cylinder 87.00mm in diameter by 21.00mm long. Use:

$$V = \pi \times R^2 \times L$$

V = Volume
π = 3.1416
R = Radius
L = Length

3.1416 x 43.50 x 43.50 x 21.00 = 124838.54 or 124.83cc

Subtract the measured volume from the theoretical volume:

124.83 - 093.00 = 031.83cc intrusion

The piston dome intrudes into the chamber by 31.83cc.

Use a sized measuring ring

A sized measuring ring is a Plexiglas or alloy ring, of known volume, that fits over the piston crown at TDC. Fit the ring with a blanking plate on top and measure the volume. The difference between the ring's volume and the measured volume is the intrusion.

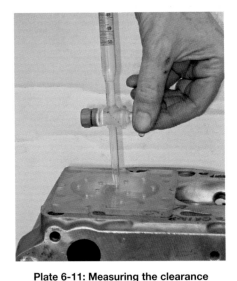

Plate 6-11: Measuring the clearance volume – cylinder head.
Level the head and fit a greased blanking plate, then let in the fluid. After the reading check the ports, as leakage cancels a test.

Measure the volume of the combustion chamber

To do this, arrange the head perfectly level, lightly grease the valves (if not fitted with springs) and attach a blanking plate. The combustion chamber volume for the example is 83.69cc.

Measure the cylinder head gasket volume

Work out the compressed head gasket volume as its space is part of the clearance volume. Measure the gasket bore as diameters don't always conform to bore size; for instance an engine with an 87.00mm bore may have a gasket of 88.00mm internal diameter. Measure the gasket thickness with a micrometer and work out the volume using the same cylinder formula as before.

$$V = \pi \times R^2 \times L$$

For instance, the volume of a gasket 88.00mm diameter by 0.60mm thick is 3.64cc:

3.1416 x 44.00 x 44.00 x 0.60 = 3649.28 or 3.64cc

Measure the volume of an irregular-shaped gasket with fluid: run in the medium when the gasket is sandwiched between a flat greased surface and a blanking plate. Bring the volume figures together:

83.69cc combustion chamber
31.83cc intrusion
03.64cc head gasket

Therefore:

83.69 - 31.83 = 51.86

51.86 + 03.64 = 55.50cc clearance volume

Consequently, using the formula:

$$CR = \frac{(SV + CV)}{CV}$$

$$\frac{(450 + 55.5)}{55.5} = 9.1:1$$

When altering the compression to a desired ratio the valves may need to be sunk or the head surface skimmed to a certain depth. Rather than using the haphazard method of randomly machining then measuring the result, calculate the clearance volume for a desired ratio. This way, for example, the precise effect of sinking two 20.00mm valves by 0.30mm will be known before machining – use ($V = \pi \times R^2 \times L$).

To compute the clearance volume for a specific ratio use:

$$CV = \frac{SV}{CR - 1}$$

CV = clearance volume
SV = swept volume
CR - 1 = compression ratio minus 1

Using the previous figures as an illustration, if a compression ratio of 9.1:1 is sought on a cylinder of 450cc swept volume but the clearance volume is unknown:

$$\frac{450}{8.1} = 55.50cc \text{ clearance volume}$$

BALANCING PISTONS

Equalise piston weighs to within 1 gram or less. Weighing can be done on a balance beam scale or a 0.50-gram tolerance digital scale. The weight difference between piston rings and pin circlips of the same set is negligible; therefore, only equalise piston and wrist pin weights.

Weigh pistons and pins separately; write the particular weight on each one with a felt-tipped pen, and graduate

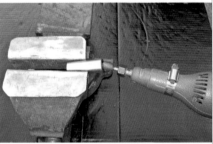

Plate 6-12: Balancing pistons. Equalise the combined piston and wrist pin weight to 1 gram or less. Match a light piston with a heavy pin, and vice versa. Remove piston material from the sides of the wrist pin boss (top). Because alloy is light, it's easier to remove weight from the wrist pin with a rotary burr (middle).

Plate 6-13: Polishing a piston crown. Polish piston crowns to a brilliant shine. A polished surface absorbs less heat, and converts more combustion heat into energy.

them according to weight on a large uncluttered workspace. Try to match a light piston with a heavy pin, and vice versa. The lightest piston and pin combination is datum, and the job is to bring all the other combinations to within 1-gram of this datum. Because alloy is light, reducing a piston's weight by 0.5 gram means the removal of a large amount of material. It is often easier to remove weight from the heavier wrist pin by using a rotary burr. Nonetheless, when removing material from a piston do so from the sides of the wrist pin boss or even the lower skirt if it is not already thin. This can be done with a rotary burr or a mushroom-headed cutter on a milling machine. Do not touch a pin's lower boss as it must have a minimum thickness of 4.00mm.

When finished machining, weigh each piston with its chosen pin to double check the results. Weigh a set of rings and circlips and add this to the weight of each piston and pin assembly. Make a note of the weight

range, for example 'piston weights with pins, circlips and rings: x-grams to x-grams'. As a final touch, polish the piston crowns with a mop and rouge to a brilliant shine. Such a polished surface reduces carbon, absorbs less heat and converts more combustion heat into energy.

CON RODS

Con rods made from steel-alloy stretch less and have a longer working life than those of aluminium alloy. Steel-alloy

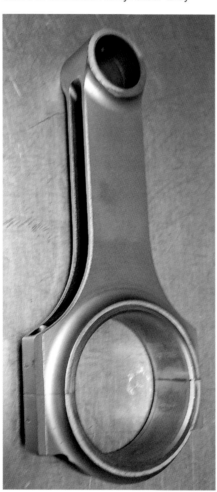

Plate 6-14: An H-section con rod. This section is very strong. As its surface is compressed, there is less chance of forming a stress raiser.

Plate 6-15: Remove sharp edges. Radius the sharp edges around rod bolt holes to reduce stress.

rods have two types of cross-section 'I' or 'H'-section. I-section rods are found on most production engines but if needs demand they can be replaced with the stronger, H-section. Custom rods can be made to order by some of the manufacturers listed in the section, Useful Addresses. To guard against denting and bruising, treat con rods carefully. They are highly stressed components, and a dent can create a stress raiser that may lead to a stress concentration, and fracture.

Some production rods have an ugly square-sided lump on the little and big end eyes. These are balancing pads, which, in the pursuit of lightness, can be ground off – so long as all rod weights are equalised. Aside from that, it's not advisable to remove any more material than necessary, other than smoothing the flanks of an I-section rod (see Chapter 1, 'Surface finish'), and to radius the sharp edges around rod bolt holes.

A mirror-like finish over the whole rod used to be fairly standard on racing equipment. This is best done by using rouge and a 3000rpm polishing mop. Others might propose shot blasting the polished surface to optimise surface compaction. It's difficult to dispute such

Plate 6-16: Con rod bearing tabs. Assemble bearing tabs on one side. When fitting new un-numbered rods of symmetrical design to an in-line engine, position the tabs on the thrust side of rotation, and facing outwards on a V-engine.

a proposition, but to save costs, it could be argued that blasting is not strictly necessary for non-racing, naturally-aspirated engines – the robust engine of the Abarth-designed super-and turbo-charged Lancia S4 was equipped with I-section rods that had a forged finish.

Rods are usually numbered on one side, for example number 1, on rod and cap. In which case, assemble with the numbers facing together. It will be noted that the bearing shell retaining tabs also face together: on one side – they must always face the same side. Solely for good practice, when fitting new un-numbered rods of symmetrical design in an in-line engine, position the tabs on the thrust side of rotation, and facing outwards on a V-banked motor.

SHOT BLASTING

Shot blasting (shot peening) is a process which compresses a component's surface, and thereby forms a tough skin that discourages stress concentrations. It could be viewed as a form of work hardening where a tough boundary surface forms a barrier. Shot blasting increases component life and allows higher levels of loading. Although the finish of a shot blasted surface may look similar to that of a surface after bead blasting, shot blasting is not the same as bead blasting. Shot blasting is performed using sized round steel shot under controlled conditions that are concerned with the size and speed of shot, the nozzle size, the exposure time and the skill of the operator. The cost-effective answer is to de-burr and polish quality I-section rods or, if they are not up to the job, buy new H-section rods. Do not waste money shot blasting old parts.

WRIST PIN AND BIG END EYES

Wrist pin bushes are sometimes overlooked when an engine is torn down. Wrist pin-to-bush fit is precise, but the clearance can be accurately measured with not much more than a DTI and hand dexterity.

Assemble a dry pin and bush, and clamp the pin between soft jaws. Arrange a stylus to bear on the rod eye and pull-and-push the rod. Movement on the dial gauge will show any play. It is not just checking fit, bushes crack, come loose, or become hammered. Some bushes are wound from stamped flat sheet, and, not being solid, can rotate and block off the oil supply hole. Discard wound bushes in favour of solid turned bushes. Due to chatter, it's not possible to size a bush to its pin with a reamer. A pin may seem to have a nice solid fit in a reamed bush, but the bush's surface will be covered in imperfections – high spots – that will quickly wear off and lead to a loose pin. Ream bushed to within 0.10mm to 0.15mm of their finished size, and hone to fit with a three-legged hone (a brake hone), reversing the con rod after a few passes to avoid taper. Most oil holes are already chamfered to reduce stress and present a large oil collection area (make sure this is the case) and lastly, check the oil hole alignment.

Big end eyes only need attention if they have become oval or subject to fretting. Where looseness is suspected, but not shown by fret marks, check the bearing-crush by using the procedure described in this chapter. The fit of ring or solid dowels and big end bolts must be snug. Avoid any slackness, as this encourages movement that may lead to fretting. When a cap is difficult to remove, it may be elongated. Such damage can be due to fretting, a spun bearing, or fatigue. In such cases, replace the rod.

BIG END BOLTS

Inspect big end bolts for abrasions, cuts, or stretching in the thread area, which indicate over tightening or long service. Replace damaged bolts or uprate fasteners to those made of chrome molybdenum alloy steel that has a minimum tensile strength of 180,000psi. Without sufficient clamping pressure, bolts may loosen or movement can occur between the cap and the rod that will inevitably lead to failure.

Arguably, tightening big end bolts with a torque wrench is adequate for most moderately stressed engines, even though there is some variation due to thread and collar friction, the type of assembly lubricant, and torque wrench inaccuracy. Moreover, thread and collar surfaces impact on each other, flattening out microscopic irregularities that result from the manufacturing processes. In poor quality materials this can lead to collar or thread embedding – in essence it works loose.

The best way to prevent movement is to use top quality bolts that have been tightened to a measured stretch (see Chapter 10, 'Big end clearance'). A stretch gauge is a micrometer with pointed jaws; use it to measure bolt length before and after tightening. Information on the recommended elongation accompanies quality bolts. When the elongation is unspecified, tighten bolts with a torque wrench. Such specialist fasteners are available from motorsport suppliers or directly from companies like SPS Technologies, Coastal Fabrication, or Automotive Racing Products – find their contact details in Useful Addresses.

BALANCING RODS

It's useful to consider a con rod having two distinctive weights: rotary weight and reciprocating weight. Rotary weight is that which revolves around the crank pin – the big end eye – and reciprocating weight is the weight of the wrist pin eye and upper rod. This is an important distinction because a situation could arise where two con rods might have the same total weight yet un-equal rotary or reciprocating weights. When working on a set of con rods, matching the big end and all the wrist pin weights usually brings the total weight of each rod to within 1 gram.

Weigh rods end-to-end to check their rotary and reciprocating weights. There are specialist scales to weigh con rod eyes but a 'triple beam balance scale' can be modified to do the same job. Remove the weighing table, and make up a dummy crank pin and wrist pin. Support them on a fabricated carriage that fits on the fixed, and the weighing end of the scales. A piece of aluminium bar turned to within 1.00mm of the eye's inside diameter and fitted internally with a pair of small ball journal bearing is ideal.

Follow the example given in Sheet 3 of the inspection and build sheets located in the rear of this book. Copy this sheet or start with a large sheet of paper and write down headings and rod numbers. Weigh and record the weight of each eye. Scan the figures for discrepancies – individual rods are sometimes replaced and their section and weight can be different to others of an engine set. For each particular eye, the lightest wrist pin or big end weight is datum. Reduce the weight of each wrist pin or big end eye to within 0.5 gram, + or – of datum. Balance all the wrist pin eyes first before moving on to the big ends.

A bench grinder or sanding belt are ideal for removing material from around the respective upper or lower portion of the eyes. Reduce the weight a little at a time and recheck. When the

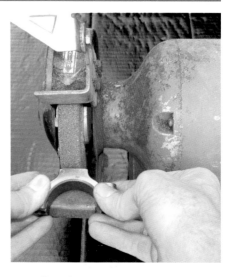

Plate 6-17: Balancing con rods. Grind off the balancing pads from the caps, and equalise the big end weights. Remove grinding marks with an emery wheel.

weight is close to the datum, remove the remainder with an emery wheel to sand out any stress raising grinding marks. After equalising the eye weights, check the total weight of each rod as this is a means of error-checking. Finally, dismantle and scrub the rods to remove any remnants of grinding material.

Chapter 7
Cooling & lubrication

SYSTEMS EXPLAINED

A well-modified cooling or lubrication system can make a real contribution to power and reliability, but, unlike fitting pistons or cams, in many cases modifications to these circuits cost very little. On all but the most sophisticated engine there is usually something that can be done to improve things.

Improvements to any machine are usually the result of understanding. Although it may be possible to fix a broken machine without grasping its intricacies, in the main success would largely be due to luck. So, what's the best way to find out how these systems work? Some vehicle handbooks contain schematics of cooling and lubrication flows, but these only aid general understanding. To find out how a flow system works, start at its source – in this case, the water or oil pump. Trace the flow from the inlet to the outlet and note any restrictions, such as a thermostat, a mismatched joint, obstructive

casting flash, or an oil restrictor or one-way valve. A compressed air line, pressurised oil can, and a small diameter rod and flashlight are useful tools to help discovery.

A good example to illustrate coolant and oil flows is the engine from a Nissan 300ZX – a 3-litre V6 with the designation VG30DETT. The Nissan's cooling system is reverse flow – meaning the thermostat is on the pump suction rather than the conventional engine outlet-to-radiator. A belt-driven centrifugal pump mounts on the engine's front. It forces coolant into the water jacket of the dry-liner block, the two water-cooled turbos, and the heads. Before reaching operating temperature, coolant circulates in a closed loop within the entire jacket. This means that with a closed thermostat, coolant is not taken from, or circulated to the radiator. When the thermostat begins to open it is in response to increased coolant temperature: hotter coolant flows

through the pump and impinges on the thermostat. The pump and crankshaft pulley diameters are 118.00mm and 154.00mm respectively.

The engine's oil system is wet sump (oil is kept in a reservoir in the oil pan) from where it passes through a coarse strainer to a crankshaft-speed crescent pump that incorporates an integral pressure relief valve. This pumps oil through a 13.00mm diameter outlet pipe to the filter, and thereafter to the crankcase galleries that supply the crankshaft, the turbos, six squirt jets, and the cylinder heads. The squirt jets are pressure-operated nozzles that spray oil on the underside of the piston crowns: each jet nozzle is 1.30mm diameter. Each cylinder head has two separate supplies: a 2.20mm diameter check valve which supplies the hydraulic buckets and cam bearings, and a 1.30mm restrictor that feeds the hydraulically-operated variable valve timing via the hollow intake camshafts. These details will be referred to later.

COOLANT TEMPERATURE AND ENERGY LOSS

Referring to Chapter 1, part of the principal theory that makes power increases possible is 'to convert as much of the heat released by combustion into energy.' Combustion heat carried away by coolant is waste energy, and overcooling only worsens this condition. A coolant temperature around 82-83 degrees C will prevent proper fuel vaporisation, which may lead to fuel leaking past pistons and oil dilution – this will result in a loss of power and reliability. On the other hand, excessive temperature reduces the weight of an incoming charge, which decreases volumetric efficiency. Heat removal need only be sufficient to prevent overheating and distortion. In general terms, seek an outlet coolant temperature of 94 degrees C to 99 degrees C. There is little leeway to alter the cooling on non-fan cooled, air-cooled engines. Increasing the cylinder head oil supply in an effort to dissipate heat is risky as it raises concerns about oil leaking into cylinders or starved bottom ends. Sand blasting leaves a dull finish, which, like matt black, is better at dissipating heat. Changing from mineral to synthetic oil may also help. Due to improved lubrication, engine oil temperature is always reduced when using synthetic.

SYSTEM PRESSURE AND THERMOSTATS

A production engine uses a thermostat to regulate its coolant temperature, but a race motor relies on adjustments to radiator airflow: by eliminating a thermostat, there is one less part that may fail. A vehicle intended for road use must have a thermostat, otherwise premature bore wear, oil sludging, and, in some cases, overheating, will result. A road engine, however highly tuned, has

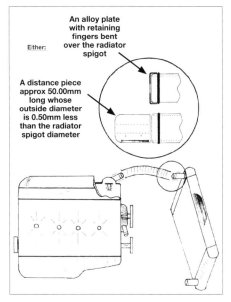

Fig 7-1: A restricted coolant system. A restrictor in the coolant outflow raises the block pressure. A pressure of 35psi to 40psi helps cooling by reducing the formation of steam pockets. This increases horsepower.

a wide speed range, and produces a similarly wide range of waste heat. Such an engine, if not fitted with a thermostat, would produce insufficient waste heat at low-speed to maintain the best coolant temperature. When seeking maximum power, broadly speaking, make the coolant temperature as high as possible, without causing overheating.

Additionally, fit a restrictor so that the block is pressurised between 30psi to 40psi – measured at maximum rpm. Mismatched coolant passages, casting flash, surface roughness and the remnants of casting sand impede coolant flow. This interferes with the transfer of heat from castings to the coolant, which can aggravate localised heating, and is one reason why a block must be pressurised.

A restrictor can take several forms, but in essence it is no more than a sized bung with one centrally-drilled hole. In all types of systems fit the restrictor plate in the engine outflow pipe. A restrictor could be a snug-fitting aluminium distance piece about 30.00mm to 40.00mm long, which is slightly larger than the internal diameter of the radiator spigot. This can be slid inside the top radiator hose. Alternatively, cut the top radiator hose and install a specially-made hose splice that incorporates a restrictor. On the other hand, a 20-gauge aluminium plate, made with four slender fingers, could be slipped over the radiator spigot. The hose holds it in position, which should be double-clamped for safety. On a race motor, an engine converted for racing or a reverse flow system, sandwich a 20-gauge plate between the engine and the rigid outlet pipe. This corresponds to the space occupied by a thermostat in a top-mounted system.

Measure the coolant temperature and system pressure where coolant exits the engine. Non-reverse flow engines have their thermostats installed in the coolant outflow (where flow exits the top of the engine). Take readings immediately before the thermostat (it is a restrictor), as captive block pressure needs to be measured not incoming radiator pressure. To check the pressure, drill-and-tap or weld in position a pressure gauge fitting. A mechanical Bourdon-type pressure gauge is more robust than an electronic unit. For accuracy, the gauge should be scaled zero to 50psi.

If live testing (on the road) rather than on a dynamometer, second or third gear will be sufficient, but allow a long enough pipe for the gauge to reach the dash cap, so that it's visible to a passenger riding in the vehicle. Before testing, ensure the coolant is at operating temperature and that the thermostat is fully open. Concerning the size of the central hole in the restrictor,

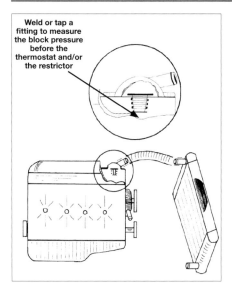

Weld or tap a fitting to measure the block pressure before the thermostat and/or the restrictor

Fig 7-2: Measuring block pressure. Read pressure at maximum engine speed in a low gear.

5.00mm to 7.00mm is often enough for a 4-cylinder engine, and around 17.00mm or less for a V12. To test the pressure, drive in a low gear and bring the engine speed to 1000rpm less than the maximum. Note the pressure, which must be 30 to 35psi. Increase the engine speed to maximum, and the pressure should increase to around 40psi.

To illustrate the value of pressurising a block, in the late 1970s a sacrificial cylinder head from a competition 2-litre Alfa Romeo was drilled in selected places and fitted with temperature probes. At a constant 90 per cent load on the dynamometer the exit coolant temperature on the common rail was 91 degrees C, yet, adjacent to the exhaust valve seat on number 4 cylinder, the temperature was 134 degrees C. Fitting a 5.00mm restrictor in the coolant outflow raised the system pressure to 28psi. When re-tested at the same load the seat temperature was 121 degrees C and the engine provided a 2 horsepower gain.

This modification requires a bit of

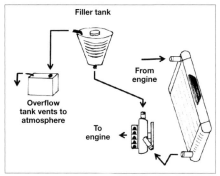

Fig 7-2a: An example of a production vehicle's cooling system.

patience, and one might experience the occasional 'facial' courtesy of hot steaming coolant, but head joint reliability and horsepower will improve. What will be the horsepower increase? This is a question without a definitive answer, as fine tuning largely results from testing and trial. However, increases could range from 1.5 per cent to 4 per cent. This means that if an engine produced 250 horsepower before modification and 258 horsepower after fitting a restrictor, the increase would be 3.2 per cent.

Finally, and of great importance, modifications to system pressure and redirecting coolant flow should be done together as they complement each other and hold out the prospect of even greater power gains (see this chapter 'Directing coolant flow').

RADIATOR CAP AND OVERFLOW

A pressure radiator cap prevents a hot cooling system overflowing at slow engine speed – it has nothing to do with the, previously discussed, system pressure. There is little to be done to improve cap integrity but modifying the overflow is worthwhile. In most modern production vehicles, when an engine overheats pressure overcomes the cap, and steam and aerated coolant escape

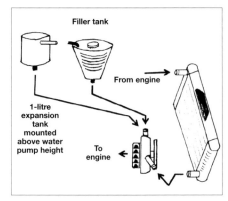

Fig 7-3: A recharge cooling system. If an engine suffers temporary overheating, aerated coolant vents to the expansion tank where it condenses. It then recharges back into the system.

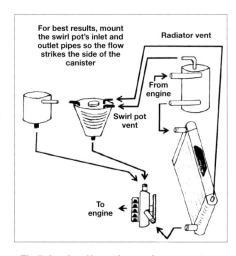

Fig 7-3a: A self-venting recharge system. The swirl pot attempts to vent aerated coolant. The flow strikes the pot's side allowing air to vent to the header tank. In addition, air bleeds form the top radiator vent.

to an overflow tank. If the engine were switched off, coolant would continue to expel until the radiator pressure had subsided. As the system cools to ambient temperature it would contract and draw the expelled coolant back into the radiator via the cap's vacuum valve. On the other hand, if the overheating engine were kept under load (it was still driven) more and more coolant would be expelled until the engine would catastrophically overheat and stop.

Situations may arise when a race car, for example, is held up by a slower vehicle or circulating under a caution flag or a road car is in traffic. In such a situation there is less airflow through the radiator and the engine may begin to run hot. A modification is possible to return expelled coolant to the system without stopping the engine. Instead of routing the overflow pipe to a remote tank mounted below the height of the radiator, fit a 1-litre capacity tank above the height of the water pump. Feed the overflow pipe into the top of the tank and plumb a separate pipe into the tank's base whose other end connects to the suction side of the water pump.

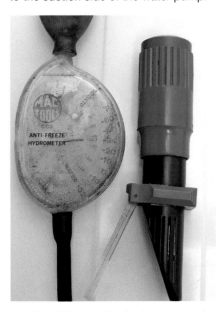

Plate 7-1: A coolant hydrometer and refractometer.
Ethylene glycol concentrations greater than 70 per cent will not remove heat so efficiently. A 70 per cent mix raises the coolant's boiling point 6 degrees C higher than a 50-50 concentration. Measure the mix with a hydrometer or refractometer.

Then, when aerated coolant and steam reach the tank, it condenses and falls to the bottom where suction from the water pump returns it to the system. This way, if an engine loses coolant due to overheating, the loss is automatically made-up: this is a recharge system.

Ethylene glycol, (anti-freeze), raises the boiling point of water, and, with additive packages, it also acts as a corrosion inhibitor. Manufacturers' mix-ratios are usually around 50 per cent: equal amounts of anti-freeze and water. A 70 per cent glycol mix will raise a coolant's boiling point 6 degrees C higher than a 50-50 mix. Do not exceed a 70 per cent mix, as higher concentrations will not abstract heat so efficiently. For high performance applications, generally speaking, seek a coolant and water mix around 40-60 to 60-40. Check the concentration with a coolant hydrometer or with a handheld refractometer. The former measures a liquid's specific gravity while the latter measures its refractive index.

DIRECTING COOLANT FLOW

Coolant needs directing to the areas of an engine that produce most heat. An obvious statement but some engines have basic cooling systems that have not been fine tuned for performance: fine tuning raises production costs. By redirecting the flow, horsepower and reliability can be improved. A highly loaded engine can suffer localised overheating, especially to its rear cylinders. Yet these are furthest away from incoming coolant, and in some designs they are also the last to receive pressurised oil: oil also acts as a coolant. On many engines (the 300ZX included) the coolant stream floods in at the front of the block and makes its way up into heads with little direction. Combustion chambers are the hottest

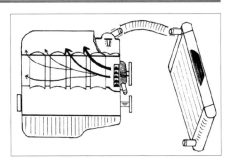

Fig 7-4: Coolant flow on a typical system. Coolant enters the engine's front lower part and makes its way to the head through equal-sized gasket holes. The hotter rear cylinders are cooled less than the cooler front cylinders.

Fig 7-5: Coolant flow on a modified system. Sized holes in the gasket direct more than 50 per cent of the flow to the rear of the head. Additionally, a restrictor in the top radiator spigot ensures positive block pressure, thereby minimising hot spots.

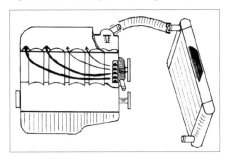

part of an engine, yet on most designs coolant has already absorbed heat from cylinder liners before reaching the chambers. Ideally, coolant should flow to heads first. The concept is not new – such a design was pioneered by the British car maker, Armstrong Siddeley in its 1940s, Star Sapphire engine.

As an example of how altering the flow can improve performance, a situation arose when a V8, 450 Maserati Khamsin engine suffered from overheating. Months before, it had been rebuilt and dynamometer tested. Yet in summer temperatures it sometimes

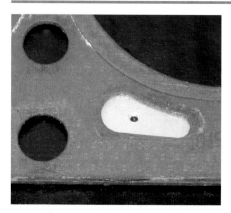

Plate 7-2: Redirecting the coolant flow. The hotter rear of the head needs more coolant than the front. One way to restrict the flow is to epoxy-glue restrictors to the gasket.

overheated when driven hard, but the overheating was inconsistent. The engine was removed and an attempt was made to improve flow to the cylinders furthest from the coolant stream. New gaskets were modified to restrict flow to the front three cylinders on each bank. When dyno-tested a second time the engine provided a 3 per cent increase in horsepower, more than on the previous test. After the engine was refitted in the vehicle it did not overheat. It's clear, then, that not all cylinders have the same cooling demand.

A modification that will help an existing cooling system is to direct coolant to the rear cylinders and the water jacket around the exhaust valves: this is where combustion heat is most intense. Cooling the cylinder liners, especially on their lower section, is not so important. For more on this topic refer to (Chapter 5, 'Block grouting'). Lack of positive flow to the exhaust seats can cause a condition named 'water hammer,' and lead to the formation of steam pockets. This will increase combustion temperature and the risk of detonation, which could

result in piston or head gasket failure. Such uncontrolled combustion limits the conversion of heat into useful energy and, as a consequence, an engine makes less power.

It's common knowledge amongst builders of performance engines that around 60 per cent to 70 per cent of a pump's flow should go to the rear cylinders. Redirecting the flow can be done by fitting a different head gasket that has water holes around 1.50mm to 2.00mm diameter for all the cylinders except the rear, which have 8.00mm. Sometimes 'competition' head gaskets leave something to be desired regarding water flow; some have equal sized holes or even larger holes than a standard gasket! If quality-designed gaskets are unavailable an engine block's water holes can be tapped and fitted with suitably-sized restrictor plugs. Blocks with uneven (non-circular) water holes cannot be tapped. Fill such holes with a two-part metal epoxy, and drill the requisite sized hole. On the other hand, open deck blocks do not have water holes; so there is nothing to plug. The answer is to plug the water holes in the head or modify the gasket. To modify a gasket, fashion a piece of thin aluminium sheet or heat-proof plastic so that it covers the water opening in the gasket. Drill the chosen size of hole in the sheet, and then epoxy-glue it to the gasket's underside. The best size of hole can be surprisingly small. Typical sizes for all but the rear cylinders are in the region of 1.50mm for the intake and 2.00mm for the exhaust with 2.50mm considered as maximum. The openings for the rear cylinder can be between 8.00mm to 10.00mm.

WATER PUMPS AND SPEEDS

Internal combustion engines use centrifugal water pumps to move

**Plate 7-3: Measuring water pump clearance.
When the impeller-to-cheek plate clearance is more than 0.50mm to 0.76mm the pump churns, rather than pumps, coolant. Test the clearance with a feeler gauge or solder wire.**

coolant: in their most common form these are open vane. When primed with liquid, suction develops due to the action of a spinning impeller relative to a precisely mating cheek plate. When the cheek plate clearance is too wide a pump tends to churn rather than pump coolant. Test the cheek plate clearance with a feeler gauge or thin solder wire. To close the clearance, press the impeller along its shaft or machine the pump housing. The normal clearance is 0.50mm/0.020in to 0.76mm/0.030in: the difference is due to axial bearing play. Quality impellers are cast in bronze or cast iron. Avoid after-market pumps with plastic or sheet steel impellers.

If a pump impeller turns too fast coolant may be circulated too rapidly for heat to transfer from hot castings to the coolant. This will raise engine temperature but not coolant temperature and result in a loss of power. A high-speed impeller can also be subject to 'cavitation,' a condition whereby the pump tries to circulate more fluid than is possible. When this happens, a low-

Plate 7-4: Types of water pump impellers. Use bronze or cast iron impellers. Open vane is normal (top), but some older vehicles used closed vane (bottom).

pressure vortex develops in front of the impeller, which then leads to a pressure drop and aerated coolant. Bubbles of boiling coolant can then form, which, when they burst, release pressures of 60,000psi as they pass through waterways. This erodes water jacket surfaces as pieces of metal chip off due to the collapsing bubbles. Owing to the reduced delivery of coolant, overheating or head gasket failure will probably take place. What's more, an over speeding pump robs engine power as it churns a high volume of coolant; although with ineffective results. Power produced by combustion heat drives a water pump, and this is wasted power: a parasitic loss whose energy is better transmitted to the driving wheels. Engineers estimate the parasitic loss of a water pump to be around 7 to 28 horsepower

– the difference depends on speed and design.

Most water pumps rotate at grossly high speeds, and are recognisable by having the same size, or even a smaller sized pulley compared to that of the crankshaft. Due to the cavitation problems inherent with the design of high-speed centrifugal pumps, industrial pumps rarely have speeds above 3000rpm. In a cap-pressurised closed system of an automotive engine it is wise to aim for a pump speed of 3500rpm to 4500rpm. When investigating pump speeds it's useful to make comparisons with ratios. For example, seek a ratio of 0.55:1 (pump speed divided by crank speed). Although, depending on volume and system pressure, this may need to be adjusted up or down. To use the Nissan engine as an example, its pulley diameters were: crankshaft 154.00mm and water pump 118.00mm. The engine redlines at 7000rpm. To find the water pump speed at 7000rpm, multiply the driving pulley diameter (crankshaft) by its rpm, and divide by driven pulley diameter (water pump):

$$\frac{(154 \times 7000)}{118} = 9135rpm$$

Thus, when the Nissan is pulling 7000rpm the pump is revolving at 9135rpm – or a ratio of 1.3:1. To gear down the pump, fit a larger pulley. To work out the pulley diameter for a specific rpm, for example 3850rpm, multiply the driving pulley diameter by its rpm and divide the product by the specific rpm, 3850:

$$\frac{(154 \times 7000)}{3850} = 280mm$$

Consequently, fit a 280.00mm pulley to drive the pump at 3850rpm – this is a ratio of 0.55:1.

Another way to lessen pump speed

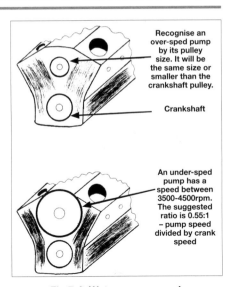

Fig 7-6: Water pump speed.
Most water pumps turn too fast, which has three main disadvantages:
1) Coolant circulates too quickly to transfer heat from the castings to the coolant. This raises engine temperature but not coolant temperature.
2) The pump may cavitate, leading to a pressure drop and aerated coolant.
3) Churning coolant wastes power.

is to fit a smaller crank pulley. This is only an option for engines without a vibration damper (harmonic balancer) incorporated in a pulley and few driven ancillaries. Pulley size influences the belt's efficiency to transmit load – lack of belt wrap around a small pulley will limit its power transmission ability. Given the option, it's best to increase rather than decrease pulley size. Nevertheless, solely as an example rather than a suggestion, to achieve a 0.55:1 ratio by changing the crankshaft pulley while keeping the same size pump pulley: multiply the diameter of the driven pulley (water pump) by its rpm and divide by the rpm of the driving pulley. In that case, the Nissan's water pump pulley was 118.00mm and it needs to turn 3850rpm at a crank speed of 7000rpm, therefore:

$$\frac{(118 \times 3850)}{7000} = 64.9mm$$

Consequently, the crank pulley needs to be 64.90mm diameter: clearly, this is an unworkable option!

DRIVE BELTS

According to engineers, the efficiency of toothed belts (synchronous belts) is 98 per cent. They are excellent for ancillary drives, such as a vacuum or an oil pump. To prevent debris entering between a belt and pulley, shield low-mounted drives with tight-fitting guards, as a single small stone caught between the teeth of a pulley can cut a belt. Although synchronous belts appear a good choice for the drives mentioned, unexplained tooth breakages have been observed, especially when dyno-testing. This might be due to the sudden shifts in engine speed that are possible on a dyno, and the resulting clash between torque and inertia in driven components.

V-belt efficiency is around 93 per cent, but this can increase to 98 per cent when a drive is at a steady speed. Although dependable in most automotive applications they can be unreliable in high-speed on-and-off the throttle situations, as V-belts can spin off pulleys unless deeply-grooved. The groove on some pulleys can be deepened on a lathe, or a new steel pulley can be turned from solid. Aluminium V-belt pulleys are not too durable, especially in off-road applications, and they wear quite rapidly, which can result in a belt twisting 180 degrees and running on its back. In the interests of safety, it's a good idea to duplicate belts.

A V-ribbed belt, also known as poly-V or serpentine (a single belt driving all accessories) is the belt of choice for most drives due to its compactness and strength. However,

do not use a serpentine-type design for competition or modified engines. These tend to have long unsupported runs, and the large torque variation of driven components places severe demands on any belt. Instead, rig-up individual drives for the oil and water pumps, and the generator. Buy custom belts and pulleys from industrial suppliers or power transmission specialists. After fitting different pulleys the old drive belt may be the wrong length. To work out the correct length, measure the circumference of each pulley (π x diameter) add them together then divide the total by two. On a two-pulley drive, measure the shaft centre distance, multiply by two and add this to the pulley dimension. Where there are more than two pulleys, add but do not multiply the shaft centre distances.

LUBRICATION SYSTEM: PUMPS AND SPEEDS

In the first decade of the 20th century the motor manufacturer, Lanchester, introduced an engine that had a gear oil pump feeding oil to the crankshaft bearings via oil galleries. The crankshaft bearings of other period engines were splash or hand fed. Gear lubrication enabled narrow width big ends and a shorter crankshaft. Although all engines now have pressurised lubrication there are some design variations, most notably 'dry' and 'wet' sump systems. So much has been written about the design of these two systems that a great deal of the information could be termed 'common knowledge,' and to go over such old ground in detail is unnecessary.

Feed pumps are driven off the crankshaft by gears, chain, or a toothed belt. Pumps rotate at less than crankshaft speed, but a few particular engines use engine-speed pumps: pumps driven at crankshaft speed. For their given size, crankshaft-speed

pumps transfer large volumes due to their high-speed. But to stop over oiling at high-speed, in some designs, low-speed delivery may be compromised. Pumps only work due to the closeness of their components; for this reason, inspect parts for scoring or abrasive wear. As feed pumps draw directly from a sump or an oil tank, the oil they draw has only passed through a coarse strainer: the oil is screened but unfiltered. This worsens pump wear due to the presence of solid particles suspended in the oil. Pumping systems are more dependable when they are pumping, rather than drawing, oil through a filter; oil passes through an element from the outside and exits the centre. On a dry sump engine, a good addition is to fit a second filter in the scavenge line that returns oil to the tank, as this reduces feed pump wear.

All engine lubrication systems incorporate a pressure relief valve, without which managed pressure (oil pressure) would not exist. Imagine a system where a pump sucks up oil and pumps it to lubricate components. If such a system had measurable pressure it would be dictated by oil thickness, the fit of the bearings, and the size of the oil galleries. This is the design of gearbox oil pumps. Yet, if a spring-loaded valve were installed in the pump supply line the pump would pressurise all the galleries until it overcame the spring tension of the relief valve. Then the excess oil would return to the oil reservoir. Hence, it is the spring tension of the relief valve that sets oil pressure rather than the oil pump. A relief valve can be located in the oil pump or the filter housing, or in a crankcase oil gallery. Examine the piston, bore and spring of a relief valve for scoring, notching or weakness. In certain positions, pistons can jam in their bores or become stiff. This is more common on engines that have been used without air filters, due to abrasive action. On non-adjustable valves, fit a stronger spring or add a distance piece to raise the oil pressure.

RESTRICTING FLOW

On some engines major reliability improvements can be had by redirecting the oil flow. Referring to the Nissan, it had a 13.00mm oil outlet feeding all the engine components. Theoretically, if the pump were pumping to the capacity of the outlet, 13.00mm could be considered as 100 per cent delivery. From this point, subtract all the other measurable engine bleeds. For example:

13.00 Oil outlet
07.80 - 6 / 1.30 Squirt jets
02.60 - 2 / 1.30 Valve timing restrictor
<u>04.40</u> - 2 / 2.20 Hydraulic bucket
   restrictor
01.80 Negative

If this were converted to a percentage, 1.80mm is 14 per cent negative flow (13.00 x 14 per cent = 1.82). In other words, if the outlet were flowing 100 per cent the engine's demand would be greater than the delivery. It should be noted that the crankshaft and turbo demands were not included in the calculation – they should be considered part of 14 per cent negative. Arguably, the engine oil demand at high-speed is suspect.

This theory is supported by evidence. Experience shows that when these engines have high-speed big end failures, invariably they are either on cylinder number 5 or 6, or both cylinders 5 and 6 together. Big ends 5 and 6 are farthest away from the oil supply. It is a similar story with the straight-6 Nissan Skyline engine, as big end failures usually occur on cylinders 1 and 6. This is not remarkable when one realises that

Plate 7-5: Restricting the oil supply can improve reliability.
A stock restrictor (left), and modified (right). Decreasing the oil flow to the head increases it to the highly stressed crankshaft.

the crankshaft oil supply feeds from the middle of the block, so bearings 1 and 6 are the last supplied. To lessen the problem, restrict the cylinder head oil supply. In the case of the V6, replace the 1.30mm restrictor in each head that supplies the variable valve timing with a 0.50mm restrictor. Such a modification increases the oil flow by 12.5 per cent. The description is engine specific solely to illustrate a key point: decreasing the head oil supply, increases delivery to the crankshaft.

Decreasing the head oil supply might sound alarming but lubrication to any surface is finite before the excess is wasteful. Technically, cam lobes, chains, and ball and roller journal bearings are lubricated elastohydrodynamically (EHD). This is a state where sufficient oil film thickness exists to support efficient operation. Compare this to hydrodynamic lubrication, where plain bearing rotation draws in oil between bearing surfaces and forms an oil wedge. EHD lubricated components need an adequate supply to maintain film thickness and anything more is excess.

Engineers claim that oil viscosity at working temperature is important to EHD lubricated components as low viscosity promotes separation,

which leads to rapid wear. As a result, use thick oil wherever possible to promote film strength. However, in hydrodynamic lubrication, high viscosity is not so important. Additionally, from a performance point of view there is the power sapping effect of thick oil – it's a frictional loss. Consequently, plain bearings need a steady pressurised supply of oil, whereas cam lobes rely on mist or immersion.

Others claim that restricting the oil supply on pushrod engines may lead to the loss of temper in the lower coils of high poundage valve springs. Their reasoning is that the loss of oil cooling overheats the springs and causes them to become brittle and break. It is a valid concern but does it stand investigation? During manufacture quality springs are generally tempered twice: before and after coiling. Final tempering takes place around 380 degrees C to 470 degrees C, and so cylinder head surfaces would need to reach similar temperatures to draw a spring's temper. The lower valve spring seat is separated from the combustion chamber by the water jacket and with race engine coolant temperatures around 100 degrees C it seems unlikely that 380 degrees C can be reached at the coils.

The idea of restricting oil flow is not new. Racing engines from the 1950s commonly had a 50-50 split: half of the total pump delivery to the heads, and half to the crankshaft. Yet by the 1970s and 1980s, in many competition engines, the cylinder head oil supply had been reduced to around 18 per cent to 24 per cent. Redirect the oil supply so that 20 per cent of the total oil delivery goes to the heads. This is adequate for most engines. To work out what is 20 per cent of an engine's total delivery, measure the feed pump outlet. Sometimes the feed gallery is slightly smaller to allow for misalignment between the pump and the gallery. In such cases, whatever a pump's capacity, its volume is limited by gallery size; so use the gallery diameter as datum. If an engine had two cylinder heads and the pump outlet size was 15.00mm:

15.00 x 20 per cent = 3.0 ÷ 2 = 1.50mm

Each head needs a 1.50mm restrictor fitted to limit the theoretical oil supply to 20 per cent. If the engine were fitted with hydraulic tappets it may require a slightly larger percentage, perhaps 24 per cent or 25 per cent delivery. This modification is especially important on pressure-charged engines where the bottom end is under severe loading.

Plate 7-6: Measuring the oil pump outlet. When the diameter of the other oil feeds are subtracted from the pump outlet size, the oil demand of different areas of the engine can be measured.

OIL PRESSURE AND TEMPERATURE

Oil pressure need not be greater than engine demand, as too much pressure disturbs the EHD balance. Excess pressure can also raise the oil temperature when oil is trapped in galleries, and is forced to escape between close-fitting rotating components. The oil pump is also under great load as it attempts to push oil into

an over-pressurised system. The result is an increase in oil temperature. Excessive oil pressure has other drawbacks:

1) Loss of power – because the oil pump is under heavy load it consumes more power
2) High pressure, especially when the oil is cold, can rupture the crimped seam on a spin-on oil filter
3) Oil leaks, blown seals, premature bearing wear, and leaking oil gallery caps can also be linked to over-pressurisation

It could be suggested that it's of little consequence to pistons, gears, chains or cam lobes if the oil pressure is 20psi or 60psi, so long as the oil supply is adequate. For plain bearings a working oil pressure between 60psi to 80psi is typical. Others recommend 10psi per every 1000 crankshaft revolutions. Engines with roller big ends are different, as they can operate with pressures as low as 10psi to 15psi.

For maximum power the oil temperature of mineral oil needs to be around 115 degrees C to 120 degrees C, and synthetic oil about 150 degrees C to 160 degrees C, or hotter. Mobil Oil states that 180 degrees C is the maximum continuous operating temperature of Mobil-1. Overcooling lubricating oil is just like running a cooling system too cold, it wastes the heat generated by combustion.

Test oil thermostats to make sure they open at 120 degrees C; if not, they need modification. In a non-racing vehicle it may be difficult to maintain enough load to keep the oil at such a temperature. In such a situation a person might question the usefulness of oil coolers on road-going vehicles.

OIL RECOMMENDATIONS

Oil does not wear out, as such, but

rather it degrades with use as it becomes contaminated with combustion by-products. Synthetic oil is less volatile and has a slower rate of degradation than mineral oil, so oil change intervals can be extended. Use commercially available synthetic oil in 4-stroke engines as it offers better protection due to its wide temperature range and high film strength. The latter refers to an oil's ability to resist the pressure of two adjacent surfaces. Switching from mineral to synthetic oil translates to a drop in oil temperature around 15 degrees C to 20 degrees C: this is due to reduced friction. Arguably, any power increases may also be due in part to superior piston ring sealing and reduced combustion chamber deposits, which result in less demand being placed on the fuel octane. The general consensus is to break-in a new or rebuilt engine on mineral oil as the lubricity of synthetic oil prevents the rubbing action necessary for bedding-in piston rings (see Chapter 10 'Breaking-in and testing'). The minimum running time on a dyno before changing to synthetic would be around thirty minutes; this is roughly equivalent to fifty road miles.

SUMP MODIFICATIONS AND BREATHERS

A spinning crankshaft throws off oil yet a residue remains clinging to the shaft, this upsets the balance and slows rotation. Thrown oil also clogs cylinder walls increasing blowby and crankcase pressure. This condition is known as windage. When driven hard, the pressure inside some wet sump engines (measured at the dipstick tube) can be surprising: 2psi to 5psi is not uncommon. To lessen windage, remove clinging oil from a crankshaft and reduce crankcase pressure. Fit a contoured baffle in the sump, made of 18 or 22-gauge steel plate (aluminium

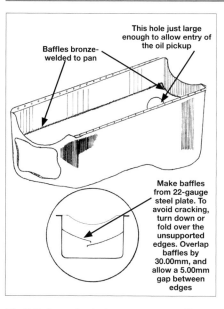

Fig 7-7: An anti-windage wet sump oil pan. Full-length baffles separate the oil reservoir from the crankshaft. Oil thrown off the crankshaft strikes the baffles and drains to the reservoir.

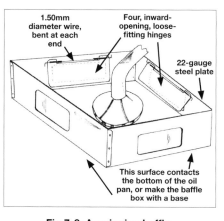

Fig 7-8: A swinging baffle. A baffle box helps to prevent oil starvation on wet sump engines by maintaining a pool of oil around the pickup.

plate tends to crack) that separates the oil reservoir from the crankshaft. Bronze or MIG weld it in position, or secure it with bolts if the sump is aluminium. A practical design could have a single drain slot, and a snug-fitting recess

for the oil pump pick-up. Brace or strengthen baffles with swages, if necessary, and radius or turn down their edges to hinder the formation of cracks. In a competition, or on a performance engine used during a track day, a non-baffled sump can cause air pockets around the pick-up screen. A swinging baffle can help to retain oil in the area of the pick-up.

Some people advocate fitting a scraper. This is a steel plate shaped to contour the outline of the crankshaft so that it avoids the counterweight throws by approximately 0.50mm. A scraper's purpose, plain enough, is to help remove clinging oil. The benefit of a scraper is debatable. It's time-consuming to construct and one wonders if it's worth the effort. This appears to be a view shared by some racing concerns because the writer has never seen one in a 'works' sump. In addition, the un-swaged edges of a scraper are subject to stress, and so liable to crack.

To help relieve wet sump pressure on a street vehicle, rig-up an evacuator breather. The effect of the exhaust can be harnessed to create a depression that lessens crankcase pressure. To make an evacuator breather, drill a hole in one of the exhaust manifold runners approximately 100mm from the head. Take a length of steel pipe (12.00mm/0.50in is a good size), cut one end to a 45-degree angle and thread the other. Insert the 45-degree end into the manifold, in line with the gas flow, and weld it in position. Thread a heat-proof one-way valve, fitted with a short length of pipe, on the other end. A smog-pump valve is good; although the spring for the check valve may need to be trimmed to reduce tension. Keep the existing breather and connect a hose from the pipe to a new baffled port. Some vehicles may need a box-and-baffle system to prevent oil mist

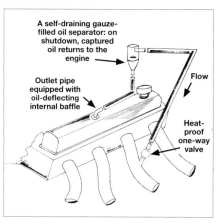

Fig 7-9: An evacuator breather. Exiting exhaust gases help to reduce engine breathing.

entering the exhaust. While baffled tanks can be made, the cyclone valve or oil separator that is sometimes fitted to some production vehicles can often be adapted to fit in line between the rocker cover and the one-way valve.

An engine with dry sump lubrication uses two oil pumps, one to feed oil to the engine and another to return (scavenge) it to a remote tank. Some motorcycle engines are the exception as they use a single pump and an integral crankcase tank. So, once oil has been pumped to the engine it drains by gravity to the crankcase tank. Windage is easier to manage on a dry sump system, as the scavenge pump reduces crankcase pressure. Some race motors use two or three scavenge pumps (two- or three-stage scavenging) each with their own sump pick-up. Windage is lessened as little oil exists in the sump, and the scavenge action can draw a vacuum in the crankcase.

Any wet sump engine can be converted to dry sump. Kits are marketed for popular engines but when a kit is unavailable to convert an engine, these are the parts required:
1) A different or modified sump pan
2) A feed and a scavenge pump

3) An oil tank
4) Braided hose and fittings
5) A remote oil filter (optional)

The feed circuit sequence is: tank, pump, filter, engine/relief valve. The scavenge circuit is engine, tank; although, if needed, an oil cooler and an additional filter can be fitted in the return line. Gear pumps are not self-priming, as dry gears do not generate suction. To overcome this problem, mount oil tanks to ensure gravity supply to feed pumps, and site scavenge pumps low in the sump or at a similar level if they are externally mounted. For custom, one-off conversions, the easiest method is to buy an externally-mounted combination feed and scavenge pump that is driven via a toothed belt. The feed pump on a combination pump has an integral pressure relief valve. When using a combination pump, discard the old wet sump pump, and make up a flange and plumb in a hose that goes from the feed gallery on the block to the new external feed pump. Alternatively, blank off the old pump mounting and fit an aluminium oil cooler adapter (widely available from accessory suppliers) to the oil filter housing. Plumb a line from the adapter to the feed pump. This way, oil feeds from the pump to the filter, via the adapter, and from the filter to the engine. Another option is to keep the existing wet sump pump, and substitute an adapter and hose for its pick-up. Fit the other end of the hose to the oil tank feed.

When doing a conversion, a remote oil filter can be a practical option especially when using a generic pump. A remote filter has a flanged aluminium housing that can be bolted in a suitable location and plumed in with hose. Some housings incorporate an adjustable pressure relief valve. The capacity of each scavenge pump must

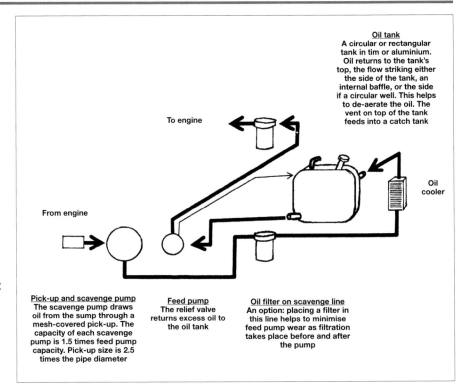

Fig 7-10: A dry sump oiling system.
There can be up to three scavenge pumps. Increasing the scavenge capacity equals more oil aeration but less pumping losses as a vacuum may exist in the crankcase. The pressure relief valve is usually sited in the feed pump or engine oil gallery.

be 1½ times the feed pump capacity, otherwise over-oiling results. The larger the scavenge capacity the greater the vacuum that may exist in the crankcase. The disadvantage to large scavenge capacity is aerated oil, but this can be overcome by good tank design. Arrange the scavenge pick-up screens so they sit from 3.00mm to 5.00mm off the sump floor. Their shape is immaterial, but to prevent clogging their size must equate to 2½ times the pipe diameter.

Concerning the oil tank, an aluminium tank will be expensive, but a black-painted tin tank does the same job. To help de-aeration vent the tank and arrange the return line so oil strikes a baffle or the tank's side. Use Aeroquip hose for the supply and return lines as this has an external braid, so there

is less chance of chafing. Eight- and twelve-cylinder engines need -16 size hoses, and four-cylinder -12. The size of Aeroquip hose is measured in imperial units using a dash (-) system, and each (-) corresponds to 1/16in. Consequently, a -16 hose is 16 x 1/16: in other words 1.00in inside diameter. Although it should be noted that the inside diameter of fittings is less. In the case of a -16 fitting, its inside diameter is a little less than 7/8in.

SEAL RETENTION
For performance applications, single-edged lip seals are adequate. Rubber-like Nitrile is a common seal material, and can withstand temperatures of 150 degrees C. Seals and O-rings made of fluoropolymer, known under the

trade name Viton, can withstand more intense heat; 200 degrees C. As a result, replacing Nitrile seals for Viton is a sensible upgrade. Bonded seals (rubber covered) are best to prevent leaks between a housing and a seal's outside diameter. They are also more tolerant to misalignment, which is an important consideration when a seal does not abut a housing register. On a performance engine, always Loctite or stake seals in position. Stake seals with a small custom-made retaining plate or the head of a screw, or peen the casting with a chisel. This is just a safeguard to ensure that seals remain in position even when they are subject to internal pressure or high temperature.

On rally engines, or high service motors the lip of the seal can wear a groove in a shaft. A reclamation sleeve is a thin metal liner pressed over a worn journal that restores diameter – but not all sized are available. Aside from lapping a damaged journal with crocus paper, fitting a positive-action seal can help, as its helical ridges offer greater latitude to a slightly out-of-round shaft. Another option – a performance modification even – is to replace a single seal with two thin seals side-by-side. For example, replacing a 6.00mm wide seal with two 3.00mm seals; this is a type of labyrinth. But narrow seals are more prone to misalignment so it is important to stake them in place. This is also a good modification for wet sump and pressure-charged engines as they are more likely to operate with some crankcase pressure, and as a result, leak oil.

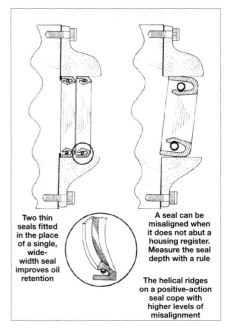

Two thin seals fitted in the place of a single, wide-width seal improves oil retention

A seal can be misaligned when it does not abut a housing register. Measure the seal depth with a rule

The helical ridges on a positive-action seal cope with higher levels of misalignment

**Fig 7-11: Lip seals.
To stop seals blowing out or losing their fit, Loctite or stake them in position.**

Chapter 8
Ignition & management systems

IGNITION OVERVIEW

An intense spark of long-duration helps combustion. This is a simple notion to keep in mind when dealing with technical jargon like multiple spark, wasted spark, double wasted spark, and so forth. Such systems have their merits; but ultimately combustion needs a big, long-lasting spark delivered at the right time. The component manufacturer Mallory claims that sparks from certain of its coils last for 500 microseconds, and have 55,000 volts. This is about five-times longer and twice the voltage of a spark delivered by a production vehicle's coil. The amperage on all systems, for reasons of safety, does not exceed 10 amps. Yet high voltage without sufficient amperage is like shallow breathing when running – eventually one is oxygen-starved – in essence, the spark is weak. When a high voltage low amperage spark has insufficient pressure to jump the contacts of an over-wide sparkplug gap, it leads to a weak spark. For this reason, it's

important to match the ignition or coil to the type of engine, the number of cylinders, and the crankshaft speed.

To measure amperage, disconnect a high tension wire (HT), connect an amp meter in line and run the engine. **Caution!** Do not attempt to raise the amperage of any HT circuit as electrocution may result. Instead, fit uprated components. The HT voltage of production vehicles is around 13,000 to 20,000 volts. A higher voltage sports coil that delivers more than 20,000 volts leads to a stronger spark, better combustion and more horsepower. Companies like MSD, Delco-Remy, Mallory, Autocar Electrical, Pectel, DTA Competition or Aldon, to name only a few, supply diverse ignition and management components. Their contact details are listed in Useful Addresses.

DETONATION AND PRE-IGNITION

Detonation takes place when multiple flame fronts collide in the combustion chamber. This raises cylinder pressure and temperature. The collisions set off shock waves that sound like bolts jingling in a tin can, the so-called 'pinging.' Severe detonation raises the cylinder temperature enough to break sparkplug insulators or piston lands. NGK Spark Plugs suggests that severe detonation may raise plug temperatures to 3000 degrees F. Less severe, yet long-lasting detonation erodes piston crowns, which leads to weakness and interferes with the spread of the flame. The most common causes of detonation are:

1) Low octane fuel
2) A lean fuel mixture
3) Over-advanced ignition
4) Too high compression
5) Too high boost pressure
6) An incorrect sparkplug

Reduce the chance of detonation

by matching the best possible air-to-fuel ratio with the compression, the quench, and the ignition advance. Practically, there is a limit to the modifications that can be done to a design, but on performance engines a common cause of detonation is compression that is too high for the capabilities of the chamber.

The purpose of a device called a 'knock sensor' that is fitted to many cars is to guard against detonation. Whenever the sensor detects a vibration that is in the sensor's range of frequency, it retards the ignition. Sensor frequency is generally 3 to 15 kilohertz. Retarded ignition is noticeable on turbo vehicles by falling boost pressure or failure to get full boost. On non-turbo vehicles, the only sign of retarded timing is loss of performance. On some engines this may elicit feedback so subtle that a loss of power may not be noticed. This could bring about a situation where the power delivery is less than the best, but the engine might be considered to be without fault. For this reason, on modified or standard sports engines, where maximum power is the object, disconnect the knock sensor. This may seem risky, as a monitoring device has been removed, but for an attentive driver, a knock sensor is largely unnecessary. The sound of detonation is hard to miss – even in an open-cockpit car. Detonation, when it takes place, is loudest in third or fourth gear, around three-quarters maximum engine speed, and especially when accelerating up hill.

When dynamometer testing an engine in an acoustic cell, pinging is harder to hear. A crude but effective device to detect pinging, although its construction might alarm the orthodox, is a reel of ⅜in copper pipe and a large disused food can. Flatten and drill one end of the pipe, and bolt it to the rear of the engine – to an intake or exhaust

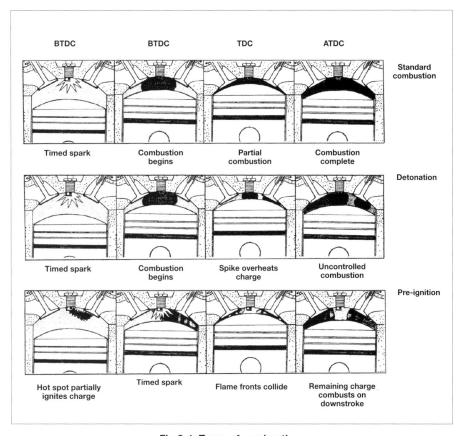

Fig 8-1: Types of combustion.

manifold stud or some other convenient place close to the combustion chamber. Unwind the reel so the other end is adjacent to the dyno operator's panel. Make a hole in the can's closed end and insert the pipe. Bend over the end and solder the pipe to the can. The noise of detonation travels down the pipe and is amplified by the can. Alternatively, use an electronic detector, like MSD's excellent, Engine Knock Alert 8964.

Pre-ignition, as the word suggests, is the ignition of a charge before the point of timed ignition: a cylinder fires by itself rather than due to an electrode spark. In such a case, because the ignition is early, the explosion tries to force the piston back down its cylinder. The piston however, is still moving upwards by mechanical action. The

un-timed explosion and the mechanical action are opposing forces that act on the piston and move it rapidly from side-to-side. Severe pre-ignition usually leads to a melted piston crown.

Common causes of pre-ignition are:

1) An incorrect sparkplug
2) A lean mixture
3) Glowing carbon deposits on an exhaust valve
4) An overheated edge on a valve margin or a piston crown
5) An overheated engine

To reduce the chance of pre-ignition, radius any sharp edges in the combustion chamber, such as on valve reliefs or the exhaust valve margin. Sparkplug heat range is another concern as fitting a low heat plug to a well running engine can cause pre-ignition. For more on sparkplugs (see Chapter 10 'Reading plugs').

POINTS IGNITION

Although these days manufacturers have replaced contact breaker points with more reliable solid state electronics, doing so on a classic or custom machine could compromise provenance. For performance applications, though, a distributor or magneto points system has some inherent reliability problems. Shaft movement, for example, affects the breaker point gap, and worn bearings negatively affect the precision of a timed spark, making the timing irregular. Points are high maintenance; they wear out and require regular replacement to keep working. At high engine speed, the fibre heel of the moving point may have difficulty following the cam profile; instead, it may bounce back-and-forth, which can lead to misfire. To overcome this problem some manufacturers, Ferrari, for example, fitted V12 engines with two distributors and two ignition coils – since one 12-lobe distributor triggering one coil would have been unworkable. Ferrari went a stage further, however, as each distributor had three instead of six lobes, but two sets of points. Therefore, each set of points fired three cylinders.

A quality single-point distributor on a 4-cylinder engine will work up to 7500rpm (crankshaft), and, on some performance engines this might be enough. Converting from a well-maintained points system to electronic does not necessarily carry with it an increase in performance: spark length and pressure are just as important as the triggering method.

Some distributor shafts run in bushes rather than ball journal bearings. Most distributor bushes from about

1960 onward were made of sintered bronze, which has self-lubricating properties. Sintered bronze bushes can be turned on a lathe from bar stock, but they cannot be honed or reamed as this closes the material's pores, resulting in rapid wear during service. Phosphor bronze is an alternative material to make custom bushes. New bushes in phosphor bronze needs to be honed to final size rather than reamed. As the shaft-to-bush running clearance is in the order of 0.008mm/0.0003in to 0.013mm/0.0005in getting the right gap can be tricky. Rather than replacing bushes, in some cases it may be possible to affect a cure by removing the old bushes and lightly tinning their outer surface with an even layer of solder. Once reinstalled, the increased compressive force of the tinned bushes' outer diameter will decrease their inner diameter, and thereby reduce the running clearance.

The easiest way to adjust and test a distributor is on a distributor test machine, such as those made by Marquette, Sun or Sincrotest. These rotate the shaft of the distributor under test at specific speeds, which enables readings to be taken. Such machines do appear for sale on internet auction sites. When a distributor machine is unavailable, you can test the accuracy of the unit on a running engine. Connect a dwell meter to the system: this measures the average points gap, whether it has four, six or eight lobes. Set the dwell at idle speed and take a reading. Slowly increase the engine speed to about 4500rpm and take a second reading. Ideally this will not have altered but, in reality, a small variation is not uncommon. A large difference is usually due to worn bearings and/or a worn shaft. Alternatively, without a dwell meter, use a feeler gauge to average the gap between all the lobes. Fit the unit, set the base timing and

start the engine. Shine a timing light on the timing reference mark, which must appear stationary at steady speed (1000rpm). Increase the engine speed in stages, for example 2000rpm, 4000rpm and 5000rpm. If the reference mark fluctuates when the engine is held at a steady speed, then the distributor needs attention.

A distributor cap vent is a useful modification as it provides an escape path for ionized air and moisture. Ionized air comes about when an atom or molecule either loses or gains an electron or electrons: this makes them either negatively or positively charged. Electrically charged air, captive in a distributor, can lead to electrical interference and misfire. To fit a vent, find a suitable section of hard plastic tube around 20.00mm long that has an inside diameter of 3.00mm to 4.00mm. The best solution is to make a pipe on a lathe so that it has a flanged spigot. Make it from a piece of synthetic stock like Tufnol or Urtilite (the latter is readily available in various diameters and is

Plate 8-1: A vented distributor cap. A distributor vent allows ionized air and moisture to escape. Ionized air, captive in a distributor, can lead to electrical interference and misfire.

excellent for making custom bushes). To complete the job, drill the requisite sized hole in the cap and epoxy glue the spigot in position. If needs demand, fit the vent with a length of rubber hose.

ADVANCE CURVE AND TIMING

To produce useful power an engine needs more ignition advance as its speed increases – 10 degrees BTDC at 1000rpm (referred to as static), for example, increasing to 40 degrees BTDC at 4000rpm (full advance). This type of progression is called the advance curve. A centrifugal advance in a distributor consists of two spring-loaded bob weights that begin to open at some point above idle speed. At idle speed, the springs stop the weights from opening. As engine speed increases they open in a synchronous movement that is linked to the rotational speed of the distributor, until reaching their fully open position. This position is early in the engine's torque period. Depending on the type of engine this could be anywhere between 2800rpm to 6000rpm. The act of opening rotates the distributor cam, which advances the ignition.

Modified engines need a different advance curve to exploit their freer revving potential: usually more advance at lower speed. The distributors on many production engines are equipped with a vacuum advance unit. The purpose of this device is to advance the ignition at low engine speed, when the throttle is partially open – but it has more to do with emissions and economy than making power. The advance curve of a competition distributor is the result of back-to-back dynamometer tests, which is when the setting of a single component is altered and an identical test is performed to check the result. It's possible for the amateur to experiment;

to do some on-the-road testing and come up with good results, but it's time consuming. A better solution, in general, is to buy tried-and-tested parts rather than to attempt a conversion.

On a very old or unique engine nothing can be done other than to experiment – so proceed as follows. Check the advance with a timing light and note at what rpm full advance takes place. This should be around the beginning of the torque period, but if an engine has non-stock cams then this period will be located differently. In such a case, find the new torque period by on-the-road testing or consulting with the cam supplier. On-the-road testing consists of setting the timing to the manufacturer's full advance figure. This means that if full advance takes place at 4000rpm, hold the engine speed to 4000rpm, and check the timing with a timing light. If possible, use an adjustable non-digital timing light as they are unaffected by electrical interference. An adjustable timing light enables all measurements to be taken from the TDC mark on a flywheel or a front pulley, thereby increasing accuracy. Wear safety glasses and ear protection as flecks of grit can fly off, and proceedings are inclined to get noisy. Then drive the vehicle in second gear at a steady 1800rpm. Open the throttle sharply and note the speed of acceleration. A point will be reached in the speed range when the vehicle begins to accelerate quicker. This can be very sudden and distinct. The start of this sudden increase is the beginning of the torque period.

Following on, then find the best ignition at idle. Start by setting the ignition to the manufacturer's base timing, for instance 10 degrees BTDC. Set the idle to around 1000rpm and then make 2-degree changes to the ignition noting the increase or decrease

in engine speed. Re-adjust the idle as necessary to stop the bob weights from opening. If this were to take place it would alter the timing in an unstructured manner. When the engine speed no longer increases, retard the timing to the highest speed setting. If the engine were found to run best at a figure like 14 degrees BTDC, the distributor would need to be modified. Failure to modify the distributor could lead to engine damage as the maximum advance has also been changed during the adjusting process. To explain:

Stock timing
10 degrees static
40 degrees full advance

Reset timing
14 degrees static
44 degrees full advance

Forty-four degrees advance may lead to detonation at high engine load. The answer is to modify the low-speed centrifugal stop. Such a modification takes advantage of improved low-speed running while keeping the same degree of full advance. The best advance curve is harder to establish and can only be found during back-to-back testing when experimenting with lighter bob weight springs. The object is to have full advance at or just before the torque period. Each bob weight has its own spring but one will be stronger than the other. The weaker spring controls low-speed advance and the stronger, high-speed. Replace the low-speed spring with a weaker one, but ensure it has enough tension to return the bob weight to the closed position. There must be no slack in the mechanism otherwise centrifugal action at idle will advance the ignition. For more on ignition timing (see Chapter 10, 'Break-in and testing').

After a finished engine has been

broken-in but before final testing, check full advance. If a manufacturer states 40 degrees BTDC at 4000rpm, check the advance with a timing light at 4000rpm.

Plate 8-2: Changing bob weight springs When modifying a stock distributor, find the best advance by back-to-back testing, experimenting with weaker bob weight springs.

Over-advanced timing at high-speed can lead to engine damage. Low-speed timing and the advance curve, although important, are not critical like full advance. When an engine is built some people set the static timing and assume that full advance will follow, as it's internally set. Another way to set the timing when building an engine is to wedge the advance weights fully open, and set the timing to the point of full advance. No matter what method is used, before final testing check full advance at the stated rpm.

The following two accounts are described in an attempt to show why full advance is important. During the early 1980s a certain American V8 engine was developed for oval track racing. Due to its construction and relatively low crankshaft speed, it was found that the engine needed full advance at medium engine speed, around 2000rpm. In addition, dynamometer tests showed that

full advance at speeds above 2000rpm was not consistent: it appeared to alter randomly. Eventually, this was linked to engine flex and mechanical strain due to the engine's state-of-tune. A modified distributor cured the problem. The centrifugal advance was locked to provide full advance at all engine speeds – even at start up. It should be noted that the race car had separate crank and ignition switches to enable the motor to be spun, and then energise the ignition. During racing conditions the distributor modification proved 100 per cent reliable.

Some years later, the distributor from a certain V6 Ferrari Dino engine was examined. The engine had been fitted to a hill climb racer but the motor had blown, and been brought in for repair. The top of one piston had broken off and there was extensive detonation damage to the other pistons and the combustion chambers. The engine needed rebuilding and detailed repair to the heads. On examination it was found that the centrifugal advance of the distributor had been locked to full advance: a modification that was an evident failure. Arguably, locking the advance was unsuccessful due to the broad speed range over which the engine had to operate, and its light crankshaft assembly. The vehicle had to accelerate uphill out of medium speed corners, plus negotiate high-speed runs, all on full advance: clearly too much for the engine. The implication of these two examples is: think of the effect to other systems before making a modification. For example, for each 10 degrees of ignition advance the temperature of a sparkplug increases by approximately 70 to 100 degrees C. This extends the burn time and raises combustion heat, and when combustion becomes uncontrollable, as in the Dino's case, it can lead to destruction.

ELECTRONIC IGNITION

Electronic ignition systems on production vehicles came about due to stricter Environmental Protection Agency standards. Federal regulations in the USA called for vehicles to operate for thousands of miles without recourse to major servicing: a level of reliability unobtainable with points ignition. Most early electronic systems used mechanical advance weights to control spark advance; on later systems an Electronic Control Unit managed advance.

Capacitive discharge systems accumulate voltage before release. This results in a spark with good pressure, which allows the use of a wider plug gap. Solid-state discharge controls are made that are add-ons to existing systems: for example, Enhancing Spark, Programmable Advance and Rev Limit. It's not possible to be specific because deciding on one system over another depends on factors such as: the cost, the engine/vehicle use, the state-of-tune, the type of fuel, and the number of cylinders. As a result, seek advice from a recognised supplier or engine specialist rather than experiment with a generic system. No matter what, a first-rate ignition system must produce a long, high-voltage spark. The companies named in 'Ignition Overview' are just a few who can offer guidance.

PLUG WIRES

High tension (HT) plug wires on older engines were copper multi-strand cored – copper is one of the best known electrical conductors – they work well and last a long time. On the down side, a copper-cored HT wire causes electromagnetic and radio frequency interference. To lessen interference, manufacturers changed to silicon shell, carbon-coated fibreglass-cored wires. The normal outside diameter of quality

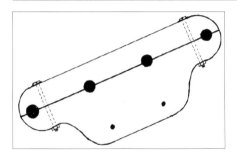

**Fig 8-2: A plug wire separator.
To avoid voltage leaks, make fibre clamps
to separate wires by 7.00mm. A voltage
leak can lead to a misfiring cylinder.**

HT wire of this type is 8.00mm. The carbon core has a controlled resistance, typically around 32,000 ohms-per-metre, that suppresses electrical interference when high voltage passes along the wire. But where there is resistance there is heat, and, as voltage transfer drops in old wires so an engine loses performance. Plug wire life depends on heat – high temperature shortens life. On non-turbo production vehicles, three to four years is an average life before performance begins to suffer.

A superior type of HT wire is spiral core mag wire. This type of wire is made in three different outside diameters: 8.00mm, 8.50mm and 10.00mm. A bigger diameter wire better insulates the core from the destructive effects of heat. Spiral core wire has a ferromagnetic core wrapped with copper/nickel alloy wire. The core has a resistance of around 1600 ohms-per-metre; so it passes more voltage than a carbon-cored wire. Where possible, use this type of HT wire on a performance engine. Although for maximum voltage, copper wire is still the best. This is something to keep in mind – grandfather's plug wire on his 1930s Rudge Ulster had less resistance than modern equivalents!

Whatever the wire some voltage leaks to ground or to other cables: this is termed a 'crossfire leak.' A crossfire leak reduces voltage at a plug and can lead to a misfiring cylinder. To reduce crossfire leaks separate wires from each other and keep them away from metal surfaces. Maintain at least a 7.00mm gap between wires and surfaces by using non-conductive spreaders or custom-made fibre clamps. Cable spreaders can be bought from plug wire manufacturers, but for competition use they often need modifying to cope with vibration and heat.

SPARKPLUGS

Replacing a well functioning sparkplug with a new one of the same type will not raise power. To its credit, NGK in its public literature makes this point clear. Some manufactures claim their innovative designs are superior to a conventional single point plug, but ultimately firing a charge comes down to voltage, and the size and duration of the spark. There is, though, some doubt concerning fine wire plugs like those with platinum or palladium alloy electrodes. These may give a marginal spark advantage as electron passage is less restricted when passing from a sharp-tipped centre electrode. Such a plug may be most helpful on period machinery whose ignition systems generate lower HT voltage.

For maximum power, make plug gaps as wide as possible because a large gap means, potentially, a big spark, and this helps combustion. However, as amperage on the low tension side of ignition circuits is below 10 amps for safety, a large gap can only be bridged by high voltage. Hence, voltage demand is analogous to gap size. Higher voltage is the justification for sports coils or multi-coil ignition. High compression or dense combustion charges, as in turbo engines, can blow out a spark that is attempting to jump

**Plate 8-3: Coil on plug ignition.
Coil on plug ignition reduces connections
and electrical interference. It increases
coil soak, which permits a wider plug gap,
a bigger spark, and better combustion.**

a large gap. On such engines, set plug gaps to around 0.70mm to ensure reliable ignition. For non-pressure-charged engines equipped with a single coil, increase the gap to 1.00mm. These figures are only recommendations, and are suggested as starting points from where testing can begin. Plugs on multi-coil systems should be able to tolerate a wider gap; try increasing the setting from the manufacturers' stated gap.

Resistor plugs are only needed where electrical interference would be a problem. A plug's internal resistor, or 'pill,' hinders voltage flow, and is typically around 10,000 ohms. Like suppressed HT wires, pills deteriorate with use, thereby increasing resistance and reducing voltage. Interestingly, high voltage sports coils hasten pill deterioration.

Modified engines often need plugs

of a different heat range; although fitting a free-flow air filter or a sports exhaust will not usually require a change. Plugs' heat range is 'hot' or 'cold,' also referred to as 'soft' or 'hard': both generic terms that amount to the same. They represent thermal performance – the plug operating temperature or more precisely, a plug's ability to extract combustion heat. For example, cold/hard plugs remove more combustion heat than hot/soft plugs. Race motors use hard plugs and production engines soft plugs. Plug manufacturers use different letter, and number classifications to denote the type of plug and its heat range.

In NGK's classification, a number represents the heat range. Use a soft plug like B5ES on a modest state-of-tune, low compression engine. Raising the state-of-tune (especially the compression) increases the combustion pressure and temperature. Therefore, the same engine but with a higher compression may cause a 'number 5' plug to overheat, this may result in pre-ignition. In such a case, fit a harder plug, like a B8ES – but there is always a trade-off. Harder plugs foul more easily – plugs need an operating temperature of 500 degrees C to 850 degrees C to burn off debris and keep clean (un-fouled). To lessen the risk of fouling, if space allows between the piston crown and the electrode, use a projected tip plug: 'BP' in NGK's classifications. These plugs operate 10 degrees C to 20 degrees C higher than standard plugs.

On production engines it's sensible to follow manufacturers' recommendations. Knowledgeable people may argue that, generally speaking, plugs are too hard, especially on Sports and Super Sports models. This is logical as the speed range of any production engine is too broad to encompass the best combustion temperature within the heat range of

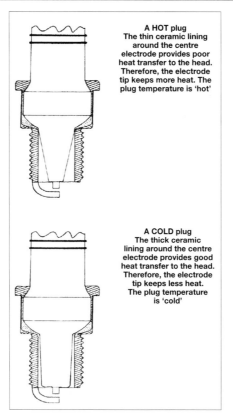

A HOT plug
The thin ceramic lining around the centre electrode provides poor heat transfer to the head. Therefore, the electrode tip keeps more heat. The plug temperature is 'hot'

A COLD plug
The thick ceramic lining around the centre electrode provides good heat transfer to the head. Therefore, the electrode tip keeps less heat. The plug temperature is 'cold'

Fig 8-3: Hot and cold sparkplugs. A plug must run hot enough to burn off deposits at low speed but not too hot to cause pre-ignition at high speed. A plug transfers heat from the centre electrode to the cylinder head.

a single plug. For this reason, some manufacturers used to recommend two types of plug – one for urban driving, and another for the open road. Similarly, when taking part in a track day or speed trial, no damage will be done by fitting harder plugs, in going from, for instance, a '5' to a '6,' but without advice, never go the other way.

When an engine has been modified a manufacturer's recommendation no longer applies as its testing was done on a standard-tune engine. Nevertheless, use its suggested plug as a starting point for slow-speed tests but go to harder grades as the speed

and load increase. Be cautious during maximum power testing when trying to find the best heat range. The safest way is to fit very hard plugs then work back to soft until the best heat range is found. For an explanation on how to examine a plug see Chapter 10, 'Plug reading.' As a final comment, it is not uncommon to find an over tightened sparkplug. This can lead to gas leakage and deterioration of the plug hole threads. For 14.00mm plugs in aluminium, use a midrange torque of 19 to 21ft/lb.

PLUG INDEXING

Combustion benefits if an electrode's open end faces towards the intake valve. To experiment, draw a mark on the insulator with a felt tipped pen in line with the open end of the electrode. Add plug washers so that a torqued plug stops with the open electrode towards the intake valve. Though, as not all engines are the same, finding the best position for a particular motor must be found by back-to-back testing. The benefit to engines with centrally-mounted plugs appears patchy, but on offset plug chambers others claim increases of 0.5 per cent to 1.0 per cent of engine output. Ultimately, any benefit depends on the amount of time and trouble a person is willing to invest.

Plate 8-4: Plug indexing. Combustion can benefit if the electrode's open end faces the intake valve. Draw a mark on the insulator and add washers so a torqued plug stops with the electrode towards the valve.

IGNITION COILS

To make a high pressure spark requires high voltage. Any resistance or escape path in a high voltage circuit, such as cracked plug wires or faulty connections, leads to loss of power or misfire. Fewer connections and decreased electrical interference are two reasons for coil-on-plug ignition: each plug has its own coil. In these systems, high voltage wiring is 'circuit compressed.' In plain language this means that wiring from the coil to the plug is reduced or eliminated; this lessens the possibility of resistance or misfire. Another advantage of coil-on-plug designs is the increased time a coil has to re-energise. Each time the secondary, high tension, circuit delivers a spark the primary circuit must re-energise the coil before another spark can be delivered. For example, a 4-stroke engine needs a spark every second revolution. The spark demand of a 6-cylinder engine at 7000rpm is:

7000 ÷ 2 x 6 = 21,000 sparks per minute, or 350 sparks-per-second

Except for ignition specialists, the figure of 350 sparks-per-second conveys little information other than the number is big. By implication such a big number illustrates a potential weakness in a single coil system: the coil may have insufficient time to re-energise. When this takes place plugs operate on reduced voltage, and at high rpm this may lead to a misfire or loss of power. To help fix this problem fit a higher voltage sports coil. Coil windings, and their ratio to each other in primary and secondary circuits, affect the delivery voltage. Manufacturers of sports coils, like Mallory, usually state primary and secondary voltages and burn time – so make comparisons.

MANAGEMENT SYSTEMS

The companies named in 'Ignition Overview' are just a few suppliers able to provide ignition or combined ignition and fuel management systems. Stock Electronic Control Units have a plug-in or soldered-in management chip, the so-called Erasable Programmable Read Only Memory (EPROM). Specialist suppliers may be able to supply an EPROM that delivers more robust performance than a standard chip. A generic management system can be made engine specific by having its settings adjusted to suit a particular engine in a certain state-of-tune. Generic units offer adaptability as a single type can fit a variety of engines or number of cylinders. In the end, it's all about precision, as even a quality preset unit, it could be argued, may need fine adjustment to achieve the best delivery.

An on-board controller can adjust simple systems, or add-ons, as mentioned in the section, Electronic Ignition. Others need 'mapping' on a dynamometer, or 'live mapping' on a racetrack or runway. Arguably, live mapping is the most precise, as engine conditions, like temperature and airflow, are scalable to real use, such as airflow through radiators, ram air through intake air vents, or oil circulation through coolers. Programming, in its simplest form consists of dividing throttle movement, from fully closed to fully open, into percentages or load sites: 0 per cent equals fully closed, and 100 per cent fully open. Each load site represents 10 per cent; so throttle movement consists of ten positions. Engine speed is brought to each position, maximum load applied consistent to maintain speed, and a reading taken via a laptop. A graphic fuel map then exists – or fuel and ignition if both are programmable. The map is then adjusted via the laptop to lean or enrich the fuel and advance or retard the ignition: this is fine tuning. In reality, to aid fine tuning, a mapped engine would have more than ten load sites. Mapping needs specialist equipment, but, barring problems, reprogramming takes between four to six hours.

Chapter 9
Exhaust & carburetion

EXHAUST SYSTEMS

Don't look at an exhaust in isolation, but rather think of it as part of an engine. The exhaust's effectiveness is linked to the intake system, chamber design, cam profile, and piston speed. Exhaust shape results from dynamometer and track testing, and is tailored to impart certain characteristics, e.g. altering the point of maximum torque. Specific recommendations on what to bolt on are not possible as this depends on engine type, state-of-tune, and intended use – seek the advice of a specialist.

Making an exhaust to save money or to test a theory might appear tempting, but the skill and investment in time and equipment to form pipe sections soon mounts up – this tests the patience of all but the most committed. In addition, even after making a custom system the power-producing results will probably not be greater than that of quality over-the-counter parts. This is especially

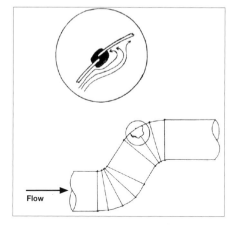

Fig 9-1: Welded sections on an exhaust pipe.
Curves made by welded sections leave internal roughness. This disturbs gas pulses.

true with turbo vehicles, which often suffer clearance difficulties due to their large diameter exhaust tubing. Other concerns about homemade systems are kinks or ripples on the inside of bends, or rough curves made by sectional cuts.

Such internal roughness dampens gas pulses, which affects gas frequency, and, therefore, the exhaust's usefulness. According to exhaust specialists, and from observation, elements of dynamic exhaust tuning are un-calculable – it is a matter of cut-and-try. As a result, by the time a workable self-fabricated exhaust has been perfected, a ready-made system might as well have been bought.

EXTRACT AND RAM

A brief overview of some important points to consider when choosing exhaust components might be useful at this stage. Laurence Pomeroy, the designer of the 1910 Prince Henry Vauxhall, which, in larger form became the 100mph 30/98, said: "Getting gas out of the cylinder is a simple pumping action, but it is getting it in that makes the engine either a pig or a horse." Engineers have moved on from this singular notion of pumping out exhaust gases.

Assuming an engine were to fire just once, the exhaust pressure would exit the exhaust valve into the atmospheric pressure of the pipe. The gas slug would then pressurise the pipe, and travel along its length to the tailpipe where the gas would disperse. Atmospheric pressure would then re-enter the pipe. If the engine continued to fire, its opening and closing valves would regulate expanding and compressing gasses as pressure waves, bounced to-and-fro from the intake air trumpet to the exhaust tailpipe. Tuned exhausts harness the pressure-wave inertia of a high velocity pulse as it passes down a pipe, losing speed and pressure, before it returns as a low pressure wave, only to be met by another high velocity pulse. The pressure waves' cyclical action creates an area of low pressure (less than atmospheric) in the exhaust port just prior to the exhaust valve opening. This 'extractor' or 'scavenging' effect helps to remove gasses when the exhaust valve starts to open. Scavenging continues towards the end of the exhaust stroke when exhaust gas, under its own inertia, continues to travel.

A tailpipe ending in a cone shape alters the speed of a gas pulse. A megaphone allows the gas pulse to expand gradually rather than abruptly exiting at the tip of a parallel pipe. This affects the strength of the returning pressure wave, in other words the speed of the gas as it bounces to-and-fro, and this influences the engine's power characteristics. A megaphone is a type of expansion chamber. A long megaphone with a slow taper gives an engine a broad range of power, and, conversely, a short, steep-angled megaphone narrows the range towards maximum power. A variation is the two-angle, reverse cone megaphone, which attempts to adjust the pressure

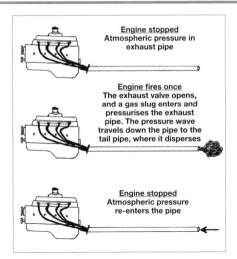

Engine stopped
Atmospheric pressure in exhaust pipe

Engine fires once
The exhaust valve opens, and a gas slug enters and pressurises the exhaust pipe. The pressure wave travels down the pipe to the tail pipe, where it disperses

Engine stopped
Atmospheric pressure re-enters the pipe

Fig 9-2: Gas movement when an engine fires once.
The exhaust pipe design is unimportant.

Fig 9-2a: The pressure waves on a running engine.
Opening and closing valves regulate pressure waves as they bounce to-and-fro from the intake air trumpet to the exhaust tailpipe. A tuned exhaust uses the wave action to remove gasses when exhaust valves begin to open, and to help draw in an incoming charge when the intake and exhaust valves are open during overlap. Therefore, the exhaust pipe design is important.

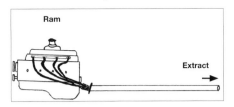

Ram

Extract

wave by a small amount. A reverse cone welded to a megaphone tip speeds up the exiting gas, which can fine tune midrange performance.

Interconnected with exhaust gas scavenging is intake 'ram.' The idea of ram is to maximise cylinder filling by using exhaust gas inertia. Not only does exhaust inertia help to extract leftover combustion chamber gas, but it can

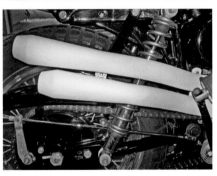

Plate 9-1: Types of megaphone.
1) To broaden the power band, fit a long, slow-tapered megaphone (top).
2) To narrow the power band towards maximum power, fit a short, steep-tapered megaphone (middle).
3) To fine-tune the mid-range power, fit a reverse cone megaphone (bottom).

also help to draw in an incoming gas charge when both valves are open during overlap. This is most helpful at higher engine speeds, when the depression created by exiting gas helps to start the movement of a new charge. Telescopic inlet pipes that change length with engine speed, the rotary manifold, and the Helmhiltz Resonator, are all inventions aimed to maximise induction frequency.

On the other hand, a large overlap at low engine speed develops positive pressure in an exhaust that worsens the idle and fuel consumption. Variable valve timing can help to improve such a condition by providing short overlap at modest rpm but longer overlap and higher rpm. However, the extractor and ram effect that exists in a tuned system only takes place over a narrow engine speed. As engine speed increases, so does exhaust gas speed. At 8000rpm, for example, an exhaust wave travels faster than at 4000rpm. Hence, a single system cannot be tuned for all speed ranges, and a choice must be made between an exhaust that provides better midrange or better top end performance. As a result, choose pipes with care. Do not put a roadrace pipe on a vehicle used for urban driving. Use a smaller pipe for torque, or a larger pipe for high-speed power.

PUMPING LOSSES

Restrictive exhaust tubing may lead to a pumping loss. This is where the tubing bore is too small to pass exiting gas; so it is forced out by the piston. A condition may then arise, at the end of the exhaust cycle, where cylinder pressure is above atmospheric – this is a pumping loss. Cylinder pressure obstructs the intake charge and reversion takes place. This blows some of the charge out of the intake stacks. When reversion takes place it can sometimes be seen on a running engine as a thin mist hovering about a hand's width above the intake stacks. This reduces cylinder filling, and, as a consequence, there is a loss of power.

Pumping loss takes place in any engine, to a greater or lesser extent, and this also influences volumetric efficiency. For instance, a single-cylinder engine with a bore and stroke of 87.00mm x 75.70mm has a 450cc swept volume. If the cylinder's clearance volume were

55.50cc, its total volume would amount to 505.50cc. Therefore, the cylinder, even at a theoretical 100 per cent volumetric efficiency would still only contain 89.02 per cent fresh charge at atmospheric pressure (505.50 x 89.02 per cent = 450.00cc). Spent gas makes up the remainder. As a result, one of the functions of a tuned exhaust is to help evacuate the remaining 10.98 per cent of spent gas, which allows greater room for a fresh charge. This is the so-called, gas pulse tuning.

HEADER AND EXHAUST PIPE SIZE

The tube diameter of extractor headers (a tubular exhaust manifold) affects gas speed. A small diameter pipe increases gas velocity, and this lowers the rpm point where maximum torque takes place. Therefore, the midrange torque of an engine could be improved without adversely decreasing maximum horsepower by fitting small-pipe headers. Conversely, an engine tuned for high speed would have large bore headers and long duration, long overlap timing because, with cams of this type,

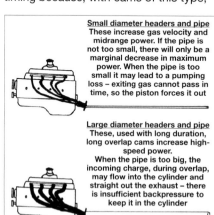

Fig 9-3: Restrictive and un-restrictive exhausts.
Fit a small pipe for midrange or a large pipe for high-speed power.

gas pulse harmonisation happens at high engine speed. In contrast, an unrestricted exhaust allows an incoming charge, during overlap, to flow into the cylinder and straight out of the exhaust – there is insufficient back-pressure to keep the charge in the cylinder.

Tubular headers are paradoxical. They are freer-flowing than cast iron manifolds, yet their tight bends impede flow. A header for a 4-cylinder engine has four equal length primary pipes that come together in a collector box. A single pipe exits the collector to the exhaust pipe: this is a 4-into-1 system. A variation is a 4-into-2-into-1 system, which decreases high-speed power but improves the midrange. It is not uncommon to find this last mentioned system fitted to rally engines. A 4-into-1 system is probably best for most uses. Four points to check when buying or making such a header are:

1) Look for large rather than small radius bends, especially coming off the exhaust manifold joint

2) Examine the bends for kinked, rippled or deformed tubing

3) Shine a light down the pipes and look for welding splatter and unmatched joints

4) Make sure the primaries are the same length: such as 36 inches

Although the four points are different, they tackle the same concern: to ensure equal primary flow from each pipe. This is the reason each primary is the same length. The problem, though, is the distance from the manifold flange to the collector: the distance from number 4 cylinder is less than from numbers 1, 2 and 3. The answer to this problem is to bend the pipes as

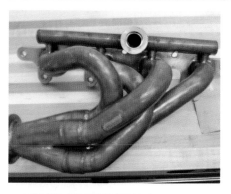

Plate 9-2: Different sized exhaust manifolds.

The pipe diameter and primary length of the header at the top maximises gas harmony for a given engine speed. The turbo engine at the bottom discharges more gas, so it needs bigger piping.

necessary. But a pipe that has more bends than another is more restrictive, so the flow is less. So, even though the four primary pipes are the same length, they flow different amounts. An equal flow header could be made whose pipe distances, including bends, were found by flow testing – but this is an unworkable solution except for the determined. The answer is to compromise, and buy a quality header, paying attention to the four above mentioned points.

Regarding the exhaust pipe, fit an expansion chamber on the single pipe from the collector. A chamber lets the exhaust gas expand and cool, and helps silencing. Ideally, its size would be equal to the swept volume: e.g. a 2-litre engine = a 2-litre chamber. Finding space for such a sized chamber on the underside of a vehicle can be a problem. Good designs are pan-shaped or oval, whose smooth internal surfaces flow to graduated inlet and exit points. Such an expansion chamber could be empty, but some engines need silencing; therefore layer the sides with fibreglass sheet, held in place by a spider-frame. Use dense fibreglass sheet to pack the silencer, not attic insulation or shredded particles – the former is an ineffective insulator, and the latter will be blown out of the exhaust. With the exception of track vehicles, a pipe for a 4- or 6-cylinder engine needs 2 to 3 silencers, and that for an 8- or 12-cylinder engine 3 to 4 silencers. Choose pipes and silencers to help the flow by going from smaller to larger-sized tubing. Where a bend is unavoidable, choose pipes with the largest radius, and select silencers with smooth internal curves.

EXHAUST MODIFICATIONS

Modifications to existing systems are limited to smoothing the gas flow by removing obstructions, such as casting flash, and accurately matching turbo-to-manifold and head-to-manifold joints, including repositioning or opening up gaskets. If possible, position the head-to-manifold joint to have a 2.00mm to 3.00mm reversion step on the lower edge – such a step benefits performance.

On a naturally-aspirated engine, check the exhaust's free-flowing ability with a combination vacuum/pressure gauge or a low pressure gauge graduated from zero to 25psi. This test is particularly important on engines with

Plate 9-2a: Exhaust thermal wrap. Hot gas moves faster than cooler gas. Wrapping piping reduces heat loss and preserves gas velocity that may help scavenging.

raised power output where existing systems are thought to be restrictive. Some stock manifolds are already fitted with threaded connections adjacent to the manifold flange for the AIR (smog pump) lines. Ideally, plumb in a gauge to the AIR line, as this links all manifold runners. On an engine fitted with tubular headers or a cast iron manifold without a take-off point, tap or weld a fitting in position 30.00mm to 40.00mm from the manifold-to-head joint. A reading from one runner gives an idea, but a fitting from each runner leading to a common take-off enables an average measurement. Do not read from the oxygen sensor fitting due to the exhaust's possible venturi effect. Take pressure readings at full load with the throttle wide open. A free-flowing system, generally speaking, should not register a pressure higher than 1.80psi. On the other hand, grossly enlarging the size of piping can cause another, previously mentioned problem: the charge pressure may be higher than exhaust back-pressure, and pass straight through the cylinder into the exhaust.

Some people like to wrap the tubes of a header in thermal tape, arguing that heat improves gas velocity. Hot gas moves faster than cooler gas, and wrapping may help scavenging. Wrapping provides a shield that reduces heat loss and preserves gas velocity. On certain vehicles it may also help to reduce the temperature inside an engine compartment, which improves the air density and performance. Thermal wrap usually comes in a bandage-type reel rather than a tube. To wrap a header, soak the reel in a pail of water for 30 minutes before binding it around the tubes. Wrap goes on tighter when wet, and, consequently, when it dries out it is likely to stay in place. Secure the ends of the tape with stainless steel lockwire.

CARBURETION

Vacuum created by a piston descending on the intake stroke draws air through a carburettor venturi. A venturi is a restriction in an otherwise parallel bore, which increases the air speed. The increased air speed, in the case of a carburettor, pulls fuel through metering jets and helps to atomize fuel – but vacuum stops when the intake valve closes. The intake valve of a single-cylinder engine turning 6000rpm closes 3000 times-per-minute. Therefore, the vacuum on a single-cylinder engine is not smooth, yet it steadies on a multi-cylinder engine that is fed by a single carburettor due to the greater number of open intake valves. When the vacuum is steadier it raises the airflow through the carburettor. But on such an arrangement problems arise equalising the fuel flow to each cylinder via the common intake manifold: some cylinders will be richer, and others leaner. One remedy to this problem is to fit carburettors having one-venturi-per-cylinder.

Given a choice, fit one-venturi-per-cylinder carburettors, which, in effect, means each cylinder has its own carburettor. Except where regulations disallow such carburettors, one-venturi-per-cylinder units are the

Plate 9-3: One-venturi-per-cylinder carburettors.
The four Dell'Orto units (top), and two the Weber carburettors (bottom), each feed a 4-cylinder engine.

carburettor of choice on most racing cars and motorcycles. Although, for the swept volume of a cylinder, the venturi size needs to be large to meet the air demand because the vacuum is not smooth. One-venturi-per-cylinder enables more accurate fuel regulation than with a single carburettor, or multiple carburettors, feeding through a multi-branch manifold. Fuel economy and drivability increase due to harmonised inlet piping, which, as a consequence, broadens the power band.

WEBER AND DELL'ORTO CARBURETTORS

The manufacturers Weber and Dell'Orto make one-venturi-per-cylinder downdraft and sidedraft carburettors that have removable venturis. There is some variation between the two makers in venturi size and graduation, for example they may be available in 1.00mm or 2.00mm increments.

The ability to fit different venturis, to increase or decrease airflow, allows fine tuning to suit particular conditions or demand. Downdraft carburettors have the designation DRLA (Weber) and IDF (Dell'Orto). Sidedraft carburettors have the designation DCOE (Weber) and DHLA (Dell'Orto). These carburettors are made in three sizes. The size indicates the inside diameter of the throttle body, and, allowing for variation, venturis are available in a range of sizes for any particular carburettor size:

Downdraft IDF and DRLA

Venturi	range
36/40	26-36
45	32-39
48	38-42

Sidedraft DCOE and DHLA

Venturi	range
40	24-36
45	26-40
48	41-46

Although one particular type or design of carburettor can make more power than another, performance differences between Weber and Dell'Orto carburettors are negligible. The carburettors are so similar, in terms of design and quality, that preference, rather than superiority, determines choice.

A carburettor is basically a metering unit that, in its simplest form, needs only a main jet and a means of regulating the airflow. Weber and Dell'Orto designers have increased the number of jets and sophistication of fuel delivery, and it is the design and range of adjustment from idle to wide-open throttle that makes these carburettors superior. Jets regulate fuel, but in these units air is introduced, aerating the fuel flow via idle air bleeds and main jet emulsion tubes. The idle jet supplies aerated fuel at idle speed via the idle mixture screw.

On opening the throttle, the butterfly exposes small progression holes drilled into the lower carburettor body, subjecting them to vacuum. Fuel flows from the idle jet enriching the mixture via the progression holes. This continues until the throttle position is wide enough for aerated fuel to flow from the main jet. At the same time, the accelerator jet assists enrichment by injecting fuel via its jet. Jet size provides coarse flow control, whilst the discharge valve hole provides fine regulation.

At high engine speed, in the last 500rpm to 700rpm before maximum rpm, the air corrector jet fine-tunes airflow and, consequently, mixture. Auxiliary venturis assist airflow through the main venturi, and aid the smooth transition from inlet stack to intake port. There is, of course, more to the functioning of these carburettors, but the main point regarding their use is adaptability – both types provide a basic carburettor body, whose internal components allow broad alteration to suit demand.

CARBURETTOR SIZE

Selecting a one-venturi-per-cylinder carburettor for a particular engine depends, amongst other issues, on the number of valves, the cam profile, the stroke, and the piston speed. In the absence of professional advice select a carburettor by using the cylinder swept volume, measured in cubic centimetres, correlated to venturi size. For any given cylinder volume, a large venturi will result in slower airspeed, less atomization, and more wet flow (see Chapter 4, 'Porting'). A large venturi will flow a large quantity of air, and, with the right jetting, may make more power, but the advantage will only be in the upper 12 to 15 per cent of an engine's speed range. In addition, at lower rpm – from idle to around 50 per

Plate 9-4: The four parts of a Weber main jet assembly.
From the top: the emulsion tube holder; the air corrector jet; the emulsion tube; and the main jet.

cent maximum engine speed – drivability will be less than ideal. A roadrace machine competing on a fast circuit with sweeping bends and long straights benefits from a large venturi, as the engine speed is always high. The engine of a rally car or slow-circuit machine needs a broader spread of power, and so a smaller venturi. So, resist the seemingly natural tendency to fit big carburettors with big venturis.

Plate 9-5: An auxiliary venturi.
The auxiliary venturi smoothes the airflow from the inlet stack to the main venturi. The number 30, is the diameter of the main venturi in millimetres.

The following suggestions are starting points for modified engines; these will give moderate top end and good midrange performance. Choosing a smaller venturi moves the point of maximum torque lower down the speed range, and conversely, it is raised by fitting a larger size. For an unlisted cylinder size, for example 275cc, go to the closest smaller size, in this case 250cc and a 28mm venturi.

Cylinder size	Venturi size
200cc	28mm
250cc	28mm
300cc	30mm
350cc	32mm
400cc	34mm
450cc	36mm
500cc	37mm
550cc	38mm
600cc	39mm
650cc	40mm
700cc	41mm

750cc	42mm
800cc	42mm
850cc	43mm
900cc	43mm
950cc	44mm
1000cc	45mm

Compare the suggested venturi size with the range available for a chosen style of carburettor. There is a grey area concerning carburettor size where the venturi dimension is close to maximum. For instance, a 38mm venturi on a downdraft unit fits a 45 or 48 carburettor. A small carburettor ensures good midrange, but top end performance may suffer. In general, if the suggested venturi dimension is within two sizes of maximum, move up to a larger carburettor but verify the available dimension with the manufacturer. A starting point for a main jet, in millimetres, that is broadly compatible with a venturi size is to multiply the venturi size by 3.9 and divide by 100.

OVERHAULING CARBURETTORS

Webers and Dell'Ortos often appear on internet auction sites and at auto jumbles, and buying used units is cost effective. Do not buy imitation Weber or Dell'Orto carburettors, though, as quality can be suspect, and, compared to authentic units, they may make less power. Each authentic carburettor has a serial number stamped on the top cover. If possible, buy carburettors with consecutive serial numbers, as fitting two or more units with sequential numbers ensures uniformity of the body drillings. This is especially important when it comes to progression holes. Consecutive serial numbers or not, faulty carburettors of the same type are uncommon, though buying carburettors without consecutive serial numbers might represent a small

Plate 9-6: A Weber serial number. Each authentic Weber or Dell'Orto carburettor has a serial number stamped in the top cover. Imitation carburettors may make less power.

risk. Nevertheless, no matter what the condition of a used carburettor, strip and overhaul it to verify its internal workings. Modestly priced overhaul kits, in the main, contain all the parts necessary to restore full function.

Examine carburettor bodies for stripped threads, cracks around the screw holes, and warped flanges. Helicoil damaged threads and skim warped flanges on a milling machine. Screws fitted without washers damage aluminium bodies and form burrs around screw holes. This makes screws hard to remove. Get rid of sharp edges with a small countersink rose or the tip of a diamond-point scraper. Strip the bodies of all jets, screws and major components. Clean them with paint thinner, scrubbing the exterior with a very fine brass-bristle brush, or ultrasonically (see Chapter 2, 'Cleaning'). Venturis usually come out of bodies easily, as they are only a slip-fit. However, when tight, use ratchet circlip pliers to grip a venturi's inside diameter then rock it from side-to-side to remove. Blow through every hole with compressed air (90psi plus) to clear debris.

Only a couple of parts are subject to wear, and they are the throttle shaft bearings and the accelerator pump pistons (Weber). Shaft bearings do not wear in the conventional sense

but they become loaded with grit and road detritus. After cleaning, check for smooth operation and replace any that show signs of roughness. Although grooving can occur on Weber accelerator pump pistons and bores, it does not appear to affect operation adversely. Fit new pistons if in doubt. Along with gaskets, seals, and the needle valve, it's prudent to replace the throttle return spring. Reassembly is a reversal of disassembly – make sure to fit aluminium washers under jet heads. The titles of two tuning guides are listed in Appendix 1.

INLET STACKS

Inlet stacks, also known as bell mouths, trumpets or air bells, harness gas

Plate 9-7: An intake stack. A stack exploits gas waves, encouraging pressure behind the inlet valve just before it closes: this helps cylinder filling (top). Replacing a stack with a filter, improves engine life, but lessens performance (bottom).

waves of compression and expansion as they pass through the intake, the opening and closing valves and the exhaust. Valve timing and tuned-length manifolds, optimise bouncing gas waves by causing a high intake pressure behind inlet valves just before they close, thereby maximising cylinder filling. Short stacks, generally speaking, improve high-speed power and long stacks improve flexibility and midrange. In reality, air filter design often dictates stack length – long stacks cannot fit into close-fitting air boxes. Where space allows, most engines respond well to stacks around 80.00mm to 100.00mm in length – measured from the carburettor body to the stack tip.

AIR BOXES AND FILTERS

Engines make more power when breathing cool dense air. Production engines often have water or exhaust-heated intake manifolds to warm the intake air, but these reduce the air density and lead to impaired performance. Arrange air box intakes to catch the outside air stream. Some air boxes, downstream of the filter, have internal baffles or bracing. To smooth the airflow, remove baffles but be careful this does not weaken the air box. Some small diameter intakes restrict flow – drill a hole in the top of the air box, and add another intake. To duct ram air from a fairing to an air box, use single ply neoprene hose reinforced with galvanised or stainless steel spring: this is very flexible and withstands temperatures of 150 degrees C.

Always fit air filters, the exception being when it comes to the provenance of classic machines. To maintain performance, road-going vehicles without filters need attention to piston rings or valve guides after approximately 10,000 miles. Crankshaft bearings

also wear prematurely due to the abrasiveness of grit, so fitting effective filtration makes sense. Cotton-and-gauze filters are robust semi-rigid filters that can be stub-mounted, therefore eliminating an air box. To be effective, cotton-and-gauze filters (as well as foam filters) need oiling, as oil is an external particle barrier. To clean them, brush with a cleaning solution then with warm soapy water, and air dry – do not use compressed air as this may rupture the filter membrane. When dry, re-oil with a light mineral oil. The fit of some foam filters is not ideal. Air leaks can develop in the air box where the foam and/or the internal support meet. Leaks can sometimes be sealed with grease or adhesive-backed weather-stripping. As foam is pliable, a rigid internal support prevents the element collapsing due to engine vacuum. Make sure that any support is accurately fitted.

THROTTLE LINKAGES

Cable or rod linkages are both practical options. On an engine with multiple carburettors, a rod or cable connects the throttle to a quadrant. This transfers throttle movement to other carburettors via a linkage. To guard against breakage, duplicate the cable from the throttle to the quadrant. Use throttles with an adjustable stop: cable nipples will be torn off and linkage rods may bend if the position of a wide-open throttle is unregulated. On linkages, do not use plastic joints or stiff PTFE-lined rod ends (rose joints) as the former are liable to crack and the latter will cause a throttle to stick. Instead, use rod ends that have bronze inserts with free-moving carbon steel balls. Use ball joints (spherical bearings) retained by R-clips or spit pins rather than spring clips. To balance a set of carburettors use a vacuum balance gauge to synchronise each carburettor so it passes the same quantity of air, then tighten the linkage.

Plate 9-8: Wide-open throttle stops. When a throttle has no stop, its cable or linkage limits the wide-open movement. This can break a cable or bend a linkage.

Stop the engine and have an assistant open the twist grip or press on the gas pedal to maximum. Check the slide or butterfly position: this must be wide-open. Then adjust the linkage, as a unit, or the throttle stop screw as necessary. Ultimately, with the throttle held fully open against its adjustable stop, the butterfly or slide must also be at maximum. At the same time, cables must have a small amount of slack, and linkage rods must display no tendency to bend or flex under throttle pressure.

FUEL PUMPS, FUEL PRESSURE AND FILTERS

Electric fuel pumps are either constant speed (continuously pumping) or pressure sensitive (they pump subject to demand). On modified machines use constant speed pumps as they meet the broader demands of supply and pressure. The manufacturers, Facet and Mallory make two types of electric pumps ideally suited for modified engines. Facet's cylindrical pump, sometimes called 'Interrupter,' is self-priming; so installing it above the fuel level presents no problem. Its quality stainless steel and brass internals means it has no rubber diaphragm – so eliminating a wearing part. On large displacement engines, or to guard against failure, mount two pumps side-by-side and have them each draw fuel, and either discharge into a common or a separate delivery pipe. Listed are the two most relevant pumps. The suggested engine size is an approximation as distinctions do not apply. The flow rates are in Imperial Gallons:

Mallory's 'A Series' pumps are high volume gerotor pumps – the pump unit resembles the gear and rotor of an oil pump. This means they are not self-priming and fail or burn up if run dry. Unlike a diaphragm pump, a gerotor pump does not easily handle solids – it can be damaged by grit. Mallory suggests fitting a filter in the pump suction line. This goes against usual hydraulic practice, which is to push rather than pull fluid though a filter. When fitting such a filter, seek advice from the manufacturer. To avoid running dry, mount a gerotor pump below the lowest fuel tank level. Mallory pump specifications are as follows. The flow rates are in Imperial Gallons:

The working pressure of Weber and Dell'Orto carburettors is 1.75psi to 2.5psi, in other words, sufficient for demand without flooding. In reality, if a regulator were adjusted to 2.5psi at idle speed this may equate to 0.5psi at high engine speed – this is insufficient. Low pressure leads to a low float bowl level, which can cause a weak misfire as there's not enough fuel to combust. But when the pressure is too high, fuel can overcome

Facet, fuel-pump-to-engine-size			
Facet pumps	**psi**	**flow rate**	**engine size**
Silver Top	5psi to 6psi	27gal/hr	2.5 litre
Red Top	6psi to 7.25psi	35gal/hr	3.5 litre

Mallory, fuel-pump-flow-to-engine-size:			
Mallory pumps	**psi**	**flow rate**	**engine size**
Series 70	6psi	58gal/hr	4 to 4.5 litre
Series 110	7psi	91gal/hr	4.5 to 5.7 litre
Series 140	12psi	116gal/hr	over 5.7 litre

the float valve and cause flooding. Then there is the risk of fire and a rich mixture.

The size of fuel lines also influences fuel delivery. At high engine load, for example, a seemingly well-performing pump may be delivering an insufficient quantity of fuel, and the problem might be due to restrictive fuel lines. On engines of 2000cc or less, use a fuel line that has a ⁵⁄₁₆in/8.00mm inside bore and on larger engines, ½in/12.70mm.

Regulate fuel pressure rather than relying on the pump and lines to restrict the flow. Fit a regulator between the fuel pumps and the carburettors. Measure the fuel pressure after the carburettor furthest from the fuel pump: a dashboard-mounted fuel pressure gauge is the most practical. To adjust the pressure begin by setting the idle pressure (engine running) to 2.75psi to 3.0psi, then check it at high load. A rolling road dynamometer is best, but failing that full throttle in a high gear going up a long hill gives a good indication. Firewall-mounted regulators are best as they're able to pass high volumes and are less susceptible to vibration than small inline regulators. The units made by Filter King and Fispa are almost identical; some of the models include a pressure gauge. Firewall-mounted regulators have large diameter diaphragms that enable very fine pressure regulation. They also maintain the set pressure without alteration – an important consideration when a machine is subject to rough treatment.

A problem can arise on engines of 2500cc or larger during hard acceleration, where pressure fluctuations can take place quicker than regulator response time. This causes a drop in fuel pressure. Such a modified machine can sometimes benefit from a two-pipe system. This entails fitting a fuel tank return line from the rail. On a two-pipe system, install a filter before the carburettors and a regulator after. The regulator, being after the carburettors is less susceptible to sudden pressure changes. The effectiveness, or not, of a two-pipe system is due to its fuel pumps. However, fitting an accumulator between the pumps and carburettors may be necessary to dampen small changes in pressure.

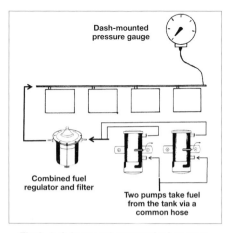

Fig 9-4: A four-carburettor fuel system. Use -10 Aeroquip for the common hose, and -8 for all others.

Chapter 10
Assembly & testing

MOCK-UP: ENGINE ASSEMBLY

A mock-up is essential unless an engine was stripped solely for inspection or the most mundane repair. It is an initial build, a coming together of new (and or dissimilar) components and making them into a working engine. An engine may have been converted from wet- to dry-sump, for example, or have different rods or pistons, or a different type of head gasket. The fit of such parts and of items like hoses, pipes and brackets must be checked. Then there are clearances like those of the main and big end bearings or the quench and valve drop. On some engines, a seemingly insignificant thing like fitting hardened washers under the heads of big end bolts may cause the bolt heads to come into contact with the oil pan – find such problems during mock-up.

Building a racing or modified engine so it delivers reliable power has many snags. Clearances are close, components are clamped tightly together, and custom made parts are untested. When an engine is in service, fluid and combustion temperatures will be high, and the engine highly stressed. The chances are that any irregularities or shortcomings in the build are sure to surface. Resist the temptation to pass over items; such as whether an O-ring is seated in its recess or a circlip located in its groove: double-check these and other parts. Failure to verify such items may cause anguish later; though there is a profound intellectual distinction between checking the same item twice, or even three times, and false confidence: doing the job, and then worrying. Confidence that has the ring of authenticity accumulates little-by-little. Nonetheless, the experienced are as fallible as the inexperienced; and, to reduce mistakes, it's good to split jobs into smaller operations. For example:

Task one: fit all pistons to rods

Task two: fit all circlips
Task three: double-check all circlips
Task four double-check piston and rod orientation

This way the mind focuses on one operation at a time rather than four. This reduces error as, only on completion of one task does the assembler move on to the next. Throughout the whole assembly, adopt the habit of carrying out one whole task at a time. Do not trust to memory, but record data, as this simplifies verification. Use the various build sheets at the rear of this book.

Cover the engine when suddenly called away or when finished work for the day as this prevents the ingress of dust or debris. Certain jobs should be done before a mock-up, and listed below is a typical example of the compulsory and optional checks-and-operations. This is a general list whose spirit is meant to cover air-, and water-cooled engines. So, for some types of engine it is natural there will be omissions and then for others, additions. Each list is in order, which means do the first job listed, first, and so on. As a general rule, leave cylinder head assembly until after mock-up to allow for the necessary checks to the valve position.

Engine block: compulsory

• Remove gallery and core plugs, clean and rod-through oilways.
• Check for cracks between liners (when cylinders are set close together) and main bearing saddles.
• Check the condition of mating surfaces, including the deck, the block, and any head stud corrosion.
• Measure the bore for ovality, taper and liner protrusion (if applicable).
• Check the deck for straightness and signs of head gasket leakage.
• Check the main bearing saddles for straightness, and the saddles and caps for signs of fretting.
• Check the condition of bushes, e.g. cam or idler shaft, timing gear, and chain sprocket.
• Measure the stud-lengths, then remove all fasteners and dowels and check the thread condition.
• Check for fasteners breaking into the water jacket, e.g. head studs.
• Check the liner seals and abutments (open deck blocks with slip-fit liners).
• Carry out any machining.
• De-burr surfaces, remove flash and chase threads.
• Chamfer the top of cylinder liners.
• Check for residual magnetism.
• Clean and paint parts.
• Clean the cylinder bores with paper towels or a chamois leather soaked in brake cleaner. Repeat until no graphite trace remains.

Engine block: optional

• Check the bearing crush.

• Crack test; including cylinder liners.
• Pressure check.
• Measure the cylinder wall thickness.
• Check the alignment axis of: the deck, the bores, the main bearing bore.
• Treat cryogenically.

Crankshaft: compulsory

• Crack test.
• Measure the journals.
• Check for straightness.
• Check the front pulley, the flywheel, the alternator rotor (motorcycle) for signs of fretting.
• Check fasteners, key ways, and pilot bearing, if fitted.
• Check any counterweights for signs of movement.
• Lap journals.
• Check for residual magnetism.
• Remove cross-drilling plugs, clean and rod through drillings.
• On a new crankshaft: check its relevant dimensions, the flywheel bolt pattern, the pilot bearing recess, check for straightness and residual magnetism, and crack test.

Crankshaft: optional

• Lighten and polish.
• Balance.
• Heat-treat and (or) treat cryogenically.

Con rods: compulsory

• Remove fasteners and crack test (including bolts if re-using).
• Check big end eyes for fretting.
• Check each wrist pin bush for tightness in its rod, oil hole alignment, and the pin running clearance.
• Check bolt threads for elongation and signs of over tightening.
• Check the condition of the big end cap dowels.
• De-burr mating surfaces.
• Check each rod's total weight and equalise the engine set.

• Check for residual magnetism.

Con rods: optional

• De-burr flanks.
• Balance end-to-end.
• Shot blast.
• Use upgraded fasteners.
• Treat cryogenically.

Pistons: compulsory

• Crack test: if using old components.
• Check the wrist pin fit.
• Check the piston ring fit and depth in the grooves.
• Check the skirt clearance of all pistons, and selectively assemble to the respective bore.
• Measure each piston's total weight (piston and pin) and equalise an engine set.

Pistons: optional

• Lighten.
• Waist the ends of wrist pin bores.
• Apply a ceramic coating.
• Treat cryogenically.

Camshaft: compulsory

• Inspect all lobes for wear.
• If hollow, de-plug and scrub bores with a gallery brush.
• Measure and record the lobe lift.

Camshaft: optional

• Graph lobes.
• Check lobe indexing.

FASTENERS AND DOWELS

Do not use air tools during mock-up or final assembly, as they remove any sense of feel. The power of an air tool can improperly tighten a fastening or cause damage when fitting a component. Major studs and bolts that are screwed into aluminium, like main bearing or cylinder head fasteners, need special care to prevent the softer

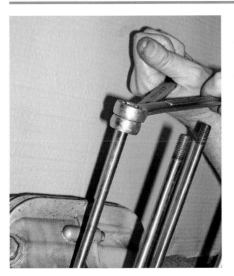

Plate 10-1: Fitting an interference stud. The threads on some studs are interference: they cannot be hand tightened. Fit two nuts against each other and use them to tighten the stud.

material tearing away. The intentional thread interference on some studs (see Chapter 1, 'Bolts, screws and studs') can be a problem that increases the chance of damage to the softer material.

To avoid breakage, never use Loctite when screwing in an interference-thread stud. Instead, thinly coat the threads with an anti-seize compound, either full strength or diluted with thin oil, and use the 'double-nut' method or a suitable thread lock tool to screw the stud in position. Do not be overly generous with the compound either, as any excess trapped in the bottom of a blind hole may act hydraulically and split the casting. Tighten 10.00mm to 12.00mm studs to around 20ft/lb torque, and measure their lengths to ensure uniformity. Be careful when tightening lubricated fasteners. If a fastening needs to be tensioned to 20ft/lb, lubricant may lower the friction between the two threads so the real tension can be higher.

When assembling studs or bolts,

lay them in line on a workbench to check their lengths as some engines have odd length main bearing, cylinder head or front cover fasteners. Always match fastener length to hole depth. Fit dowels to castings and check that their lengths are not greater than the combined depth of both holes, plus the gasket thickness. Lap tapers with fine compound, 500-grit or finer, diluted with oil. No matter whether a taper is keyed or otherwise, it is sensible to check the fit. In addition, avoid greasing tapers before assembly: it could be argued that this lessens fit as air spaces may be formed within the grease.

SEALERS AND GASKETS

The following is a good range:

- General purpose gaskets: RTV Silicone (clear).
- Joints subject to movement: Hylomar.
- Face-to-face joints: Loctite 504 Flange Sealer.
- Exhaust flange joints: Loctite 510 Flange Sealer.
- Head gaskets: K & W Coppercoat.
- Manifold and carburettor gaskets: Wellseal.
- O-rings: Silicone grease.
- Gallery and core plugs: Loctite 504 Flange Sealer.
- Lubricate fasteners with molybdenum disulfide grease, moly grease (as used to lubricate CV joints).

For older or unusual engines, gaskets may not exist and will need to be made. Quality gasket paper like Fibreflex or Oakenstrong is soft, available in various thicknesses, and easily conforms to surface irregularities. To make a gasket for a component, lay it sealing surface down on the paper and mark the screw holes with a fine pen or pencil. Use a hollow punch to make the

Plate 10-2: Making gaskets. Make paper gaskets out of Fibreflex or Oakenstrong. Use hollow punches to cut accurate holes.

holes with the paper resting on the end-grain of a piece of hard wood. Transfer the paper to the component and insert screws to check the fit. With the screws in place, rub along the inner sealing surface with a thumb or screwdriver handle to get an impression. Draw the outer surface line. Cut to the lines with a pair of scissors. When the component is finally fitted, trim any overhanging paper with a razorblade knife.

Another option is to do away with gaskets and have face-to-face joints sealed with a thin bead of flange sealer. Greater rigidity exists between two metallic components when not separated by a paper gasket. This is a good modification for components like motorcycle crankcases and cylinder barrels, or hard-to-seal parts like tin sumps and valve covers. For more on sealing see (Chapter 7, 'Seal retention').

MOCK-UP: THE CRANKSHAFT

Check all main bearing running clearances (it's risky to measure one journal and assume the others will be the same – bearings can be miscoded). Measure the bearing clearances with Plastigauge. Some prefer to assemble each bearing and measure its inside diameter, and then subtract the journal

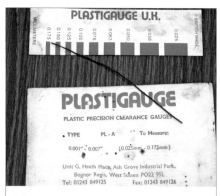

Plate 10-4: Bearing shell alignment.
Check that the bearing shell oil hole aligns with the block oil hole.

Plate 10-5: Measure the crankshaft end float.
Rotate the crankshaft one revolution, measuring the end float every 90 degrees. To get an average, add the four readings and divide by 4.

Plate 10-3: Plastigauge.
Measure bearing clearances with Plastigauge. This is a crushable material of precise diameter whose width, after crush, can be measured on a scale (bottom).

diameter from the measurement: the result being the running clearance. This method may be marginally more accurate but it takes specialist measuring equipment; so it is only mentioned in passing. Plastigauge is a pliable plastic-like material of precise diameter, whose width after compression corresponds to a specific dimension. It works on a similar principal to lead wire but instead of measuring the diameter of the crushed wire with a micrometer, with Plastigauge, measure the width of the crush.

To measure the running clearance fit all the upper main shells in their saddles but apply no oil. Check that the block oil delivery hole aligns with the hole in the bearing insert. Grooved shells usually fit in the saddles; although there are exceptions. All the main bearing caps must be accessible without turning the crankshaft. To aid this, on a workbench, align the shaft to the best position then insert it in the block. Centralise the crankshaft visibly or by fitting one or both thrust washers, but do not rotate. Attach a piece of Plastigauge to each un-lubricated main journal, aligned along the crankshaft axis. Fit the caps and their bearings, lubricate the threads and heads of the fasteners with moly grease, and tighten to 20ft/lb less than the recommended torque. Check the numbers on the caps and saddle, and the cap alignment in the register. Then tighten each fastener to full torque by maintaining a constant pull on the wrench when approaching the torque break-point. Loosen and re-torque each fastener four-times as the act of tightening-and-loosening reduces friction. On an engine with cross-bolts,

tighten them after torquing the main fasteners, then unscrew the fastenings and remove the caps. Measure the crushed Plastigauge using the chart supplied with every packet. Typical main bearing clearance is 0.0008in per 1.00in of diameter. Consequently, the clearance on a 2.00in diameter journal would be 0.0016in.

Remove the crankshaft; clean off the Plastigauge residue and coat the upper and lower bearings with oil applied using a soft-bristle brush. Re-fit the shaft and lubricate the journals, but fit the thrust washers dry. Fully torque the fasteners and check that the crankshaft is free to rotate. To check the end float, fit a DTI so its stylus rests on one end of the crankshaft, then gently lever against a crank web. Measure the end float at 90 degrees throughout one revolution. Investigate any discrepancy (if there are small discrepancies, add the four measurements together and divide by four to get an average). Typical end float clearance is around 0.003in/ 0.076mm to 0.006in/0.15mm but some air-cooled engines may be as high as 0.50mm/0.0196in. Oil the assembled thrust washers before continuing.

BIG END CLEARANCE

Check the big end running clearance by fitting each piston and rod assembly to the engine. Without a piston, rod movement cannot be prevented, and this would destroy any Plastigauge reading. There's no need to fit the piston rings or wrist pin circlips. Assemble each piston to its assigned rod, and, with a felt-tipped pen, number it on the forward-facing piston boss (towards the front pulley). This is because some rods have an offset – they can only be fitted one way – or the big end numbers should face either the port or starboard side of the engine. The pistons may also have different-sized valve reliefs to match the inlet and exhaust valve heads. Once a piston is correctly fitted to its rod, numbering it on its forward-facing boss is a safeguard against incorrect assembly – when looking at a built engine from underneath, all the piston numbers face forward. The cautious may benefit by using rod bolt protectors – plastic sleeves that slip over the big end bolts to guard against nicking journals.

Start at number 1 cylinder. Rotate the crankshaft to BDC, slip in the upper bearing shell, and orientate and fit the assembly. Usually two piston-and-rod assemblies can be fitted with the crankshaft in one position. Use a similar procedure to that followed when checking the main bearings. Torque each moly greased fastener four times, or use a stretch gauge (see Chapter 6, 'Big end bolts'). Plastigauge each bearing and record the measurement then clean off the residue, lubricate the bearings and fully tighten the fasteners. Rotate the crankshaft at least one full turn to check for tightness before moving on to the next two assemblies. Typical big end clearance is 0.0008in per 1.00in of diameter.

Plate 10-6: Check piston and rod position. With a felt pen, number each piston on its forward-facing boss (top). Check for con rod offset, and the big end eye numbers (bottom). Then assemble the rod to the piston.

When all the big ends have been measured and the piston-and-rod assemblies checked for tightness, turn the engine upside down and give the crank four or five turns. On each cylinder, look at the wrist pin eye position at TDC and BDC relative to the piston bosses. The eye must be centralised with no tendency to rub against a boss. Check the numbers that were written with a felt pen: they must be visible on the forward-facing boss of every piston. When two con rods share a common crankpin, check

Plate 10-7: Rod bolt protectors. To protect journals, put plastic sleeves over the big end bolts.

Plate 10-8: Check for con rod centralisation. Look at the wrist pin eye position at TDC and BDC, relative to the piston bosses. It must be centralised, and not touch either boss.

the big end eye side play with a feeler gauge. Typical clearance for steel rods is 0.30mm/0.012in to 0.45mm/0.018in but for aluminium rods, figures of 0.89mm/0.035in to 1.00mm/0.040in are the order. Ostensibly, a clearance bigger than that recommended is not harmful, but it adds to engine clatter.

SETTING THE QUENCH

The way to find the quench clearance is described in Chapter 6, 'Quench'. Use a lathe to machine material from a quench land. Bolt a plate that is at least 5.00mm thick to a lathe faceplate. Bore a recess in the plate 2.00mm deep, and open the diameter to equal the size of the piston skirt. The skirt must be a snug fit in the recess as it acts as a register to locate the piston. Make up a suitable drawbar to hold the piston in place. This consists of an imitation wrist pin, drilled and tapped to accept the threaded end of the draw bar, which passes through the headstock and is secured on the other end with a nut and washer.

Alternatively, where the difference in clearance between the cylinders is small, swap the pistons from rod-to-rod in an effort to seek a better fit. In reality, the result will probably be a compromise compared to machining. On engines which have the same rod design for all the cylinders, more luck might be had by swapping the rods from cylinder-to-cylinder. Concerning the quench tolerance (the difference between quench heights), strive for zero variation, but 0.05mm/0.002in is acceptable.

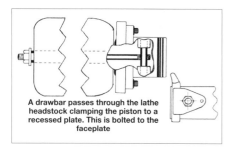

A drawbar passes through the lathe headstock clamping the piston to a recessed plate. This is bolted to the faceplate

Fig 10-1: Machining a quench land on a lathe.

COMPRESSION RATIO

Check the clearance volume by fitting one piston minus its rings. To prevent leakage, coat the lower bore with a smear of grease. Refer to Chapter 6, 'Compression ratio' for a full explanation.

PISTON CROWN CLEARANCES

Apart from quench, measure three other piston crown clearances:

- Valve drop: piston-to-valve clearance
- Circumferential clearance: valve head clearance in the relief
- Crown height: crown-to-chamber roof (domed pistons only)

To measure these clearances, first set the valve timing.

CYLINDER HEAD AND VALVE TIMING

On a single camshaft pushrod engine, set the timing on number 1 cylinder with a DTI's stylus resting on the cam follower. Setting the timing on an overhead cam engine is more complex. On a straight 4- or 6-cylinder engine, set the timing on number 1 cylinder. On a V-banked or horizontally-opposed engine, set the timing on number 1 cylinder and the next cylinder in the firing order. This will be on the opposite bank to number 1.

Check the head gasket fit before proceeding (see Chapter 4, 'The head gasket joint'). Check the block-to-head dowel lengths. Heads and decks that have been skimmed reduce dowel insertion; as a result they may bottom in their holes. When this takes place the dowels prevent full clamping pressure in the block-to-gasket-to-head sandwich. Screw in the head studs and check their lengths: stud thread must protrude above the head clamping register by the requisite amount. Excess thread can cause a nut to bottom on the stud shank or, when using domed nuts, to contact the dome. Both problems will prevent the gasket from being properly compressed.

Find true TDC (see Chapter 3,

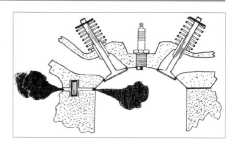

Fig 10-2: Check the block-to-head dowel length.

Skimmed heads and decks reduce dowel insertion. A dowel can bottom in its hole, preventing full clamping pressure in the block-to-gasket-to-head sandwich. This leads to a head gasket leak.

'Top dead centre') once this is found use the lobe centre method to set the timing (see Chapter 3, 'Lobe centre angle'). This technique, as previously mentioned, is simple and accurate and yields precise results no matter whether an engine has incorrect valve clearance, no valve clearance, or is measured on a cam follower.

Concerning the valves, the premise is that only a 45 degree face cut was made to minimum depth after the seats were replaced. Moreover, the valves were not lapped. This course of action makes sense; no one would consider it worthwhile to spend time blending seats, only to discover they need recessing to increase the valve-to-piston clearance. Lapping a valve increases valve drop by approximately 0.10mm/0.004in: so take account of the increase in any calculation. Only assemble valves to the cylinder or cylinders that are to be checked. In that case, a straight-block engine will have the valves assembled to one cylinder and an engine with more than one bank, two cylinders. This way, even on the most complex engine there are only two cylinders to watch. Fit temporary springs or just the inner spring of a duplex set. Do not fit the camshafts to the head at this stage.

Instead, fit the head using a disused gasket – the same thickness as the replacement, where this is not the case make allowances in the calculations.

Arrange the pistons midway down their bores (none at TDC), and fit the head. Torque the head fasteners to 10ft/lb or 15ft/lb less than the maximum torque. Rotate the crankshaft two revolutions to verify there is no piston-to-head contact then, if there is more than one, fit the other head. Set the pistons midway down their bores and install the camshafts. Pay close attention to valves contacting pistons – valves bend easily but with care, this can be avoided. When checking the timing on some engines it may be possible to loosen cam bearing caps to reduce valve opening or when setting the timing on one bank, to freewheel the cam drive on the other. To move camshafts, tap the lobes with a hard-faced plastic hammer or when fitted with vernier holes, use a suitable turning tool. Such a tool is shown in Plate 1-10.

VALVE DROP

Once the engine is timed, measure the valve drop by either:

• Pressing down on the valves while measuring the movement with a DTI – strong springs require a depression tool
• Use Play-Doh shaped into small balls and placed strategically in the piston relief. As Play-Doh is not easy to measure accurately, allow a tolerance of 0.10mm/0.004in

Increase the valve drop clearance by recessing the valve seats or fly cutting the piston reliefs – this has to be done equally to all the seats or to all the reliefs. A rotary burr, guided by careful hands, can also be used to remove material from reliefs when the

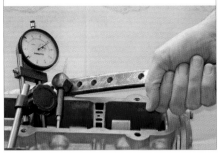

Plate 10-9: Two ways to check the piston-to-valve clearance.
1) Place balls of Play-Doh on the piston, then rotate the crankshaft (top).
2) Press down on the valves, and measure the movement with a DTI (bottom).

amount is small. Polish out marks and equalise the volumes. Variations in piston height and valve depth should be slight, in the order of 0.10mm/0.004in at the most. As a result, the valve drop on number 1 cylinder should be the same for all the other cylinders; within the tolerance mentioned. Where the valve drop is liberal the temptation is not to bother to remove and re-fit the head (or heads), install all the valves and check every valve drop clearance. This incurs risk, as anything unmeasured that can be measured is an unknown, and potentially, a problem. Ultimately, it comes down to personal choice ...

CIRCUMFERENTIAL CLEARANCE

Not only must a valve have clearance between its underside and the relief,

Plate 10-10: Circumferential clearance. Use a pair of spring bow dividers to measure the clearance between the valve head and the relief.

a gap has to exist circumferentially between the valve head and the edge of the relief. Commonly, only one piston is checked per bank, even though an argument could be made that every piston should be measured. To perform the check, fashion an accurate point on an old valve stem or a sized piece of silver steel. Rotate the crankshaft to 5 degrees BTDC, insert the tool through the exhaust valve guide and gently centre punch the piston crown. Rotate the crankshaft to 5 degrees ATDC and perform the same task through the intake guide. Engineers' Blue, lightly coated on the tool's tip helps to locate the indentation. Remove the head and set a pair of spring bow dividers to half the valve head diameter, and scribe an arc. An overhead camshaft engine needs a minimum circumferential clearance of 0.64mm/0.025in, and a pushrod engine 1.00mm/0.040in. Enlarge reliefs by milling with a fly cutter or, for the cash-strapped, it is not such a crime to remove small amounts with a flat scraper and then polish out any marks.

CROWN HEIGHT

Place a ball of Play-Doh about 10.00mm in diameter on the piston crown. Fit the gasket and head, and fully tighten

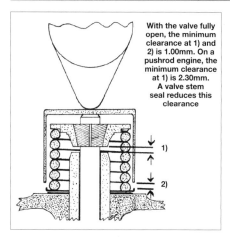

With the valve fully open, the minimum clearance at 1) and 2) is 1.00mm. On a pushrod engine, the minimum clearance at 1) is 2.30mm. A valve stem seal reduces this clearance

Fig 10-3: Valve cap and bucket clearances on an assembled engine. Set the valve clearance before checking for room at places 1) and 2).

the fasteners. Rotate the crankshaft over TDC, remove and measure the compressed Play-Doh – figures of 4.50mm to 8.50mm are typical. Close clearances may call for skimming the crown or machining a fire groove (see Chapter 6, 'Modifications and what to buy').

OTHER VALVE INSPECTION

There are two other inspections that can cause embarrassment if overlooked:

• Check for spring-cap-to-guide clearance between the top of the guide and the bottom of the spring cap at full valve opening. It's worth noting that a valve stem oil seal reduces this clearance
• Check for clearance between the bottom edge of the valve bucket and the lower spring seat. Fitting high lift cams reduces this clearance and the two parts can make contact, especially if the spring seat has a raised lip

At both places, on overhead camshaft engines, seek a minimum

clearance of 1.00mm/0.040in. The minimum spring-cap-to-guide clearance on a pushrod engine is 2.30mm/0.090in. To increase this clearance, spot face the top of the guide. In the case of the bucket and spring seat, remove material from the bottom of the bucket by turning or grinding.

MANIFOLDS AND MISCELLANEOUS

If the decks or heads on a V-banked or horizontally-opposed engine have been skimmed, the intake manifold (or manifolds) may be too wide to fit into the space made by the heads' included angle. The answer is to machine the manifold flanges. Make sure the head gaskets fitted for the mock-up are the same thickness as those for the final assembly.

Match the manifold runners to the intake ports, otherwise there may be a step that interrupts the airflow. For one-venturi-per-cylinder carburettors this presents little problem as a light can be shone down the manifold to see the join. One-piece manifolds like those routinely fitted to American V8s cannot be visibly matched without a borescope. Where a borescope is not available, match the runners on a one piece manifold with Engineers' Blue. There are two ways to do this:

Method 1: Match the manifold ports to the head ports by using the gasket as a template

The standard port openings on many gaskets are slightly larger than the port size in the head. If this style of gasket were coated with blue and matched to the manifold the manifold ports would be larger than the ports in the head. Such a step would disrupt the airflow. Another concern is the gasket material. Intake manifold gaskets are often one-

piece, and made of tin incorporating a deformed swage. This conforms to surface irregularities when compressed, and seals the join. Such a gasket can only be used once. Therefore, the gasket used for port matching must be the same thickness as that for the final assembly.

Method 2: Use a sacrificial gasket to match the head ports to the gasket then match the gasket to the manifold ports

Get a piece of tin or aluminium sheet that is the same thickness as the final assembly gasket. Locate the gasket by dowels to the head face. Blue the head face, fit the gasket and then the manifold. Torque the manifold fastenings. Remove the manifold and cut openings in the gasket that conform to the blued impressions made by the head. Refit the gasket to the head. Blue the gasket on its manifold-facing side, and then fit the manifold. Match the manifold openings to the blued impressions. This method takes longer but it is precise.

On engines that have been dry-sumped, all the pump bracketry and pipework needs going through; the same goes for the front pulley and flywheel – if they or the crankshaft have been replaced. With the checks completed, mark the timing gear with an electric pencil or a dot of paint to ease the final assembly, and then disassemble the engine.

FIT PISTON RINGS

Before the final cleaning and painting, check the piston ring gaps. Cylinder bore diameters and the end gaps of pre-gapped rings may differ fractionally. To take advantage of any differences,

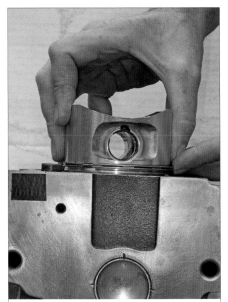

Plate 10-11: Measuring piston ring end gaps.
Use a stepped distance piece or a piston to square a ring in its bore (top). Measure the end gap with a feeler gauge (bottom).

selectively assemble the rings to the bores. Lay out all the rings on a workbench – top ring; second ring; oil expander and the expander rails. Start with the top rings, using number 1 cylinder. Squarely insert one ring approximately 25.00mm to 30.00mm down the bore by using an old piston, a sized distance piece or a custom made tool – one of these is essential. Measure every top ring gap in number 1 cylinder. Repeat this for the second ring and the oil expander; although the

expander has no measurable gap so is more a question of feel. The gaps of expander rails are not measured in the conventional sense, but verify they have not been miscoded and that they do fit the bore.

After measuring all the rings in number 1 cylinder it will be found that some gaps are bigger or smaller than others. From this point, choose a single top ring. This ring, for the sake of example, when fitted to number 1 cylinder had an end gap of 0.38mm/0.015in. Fit this ring to each cylinder, in turn, and note the variation. Some cylinders may be fractionally bigger or smaller than others. Once these cylinders are known, match rings with big gaps to small cylinders, and rings with small gaps to big cylinders.

When ring gaps need to be filed only touch one end as the other acts as a guide. To remove small amounts, use a hand-held diamond lap or a carborundum stone. A six-inch or eight-inch first-cut smooth file is good for larger cuts or use a purpose-made ring file. After filing, de-burr the ring end each time before rechecking the gap. Concerning the clearances, follow the engine or the ring manufacturer's advice. Alternatively, general clearances are listed in Chapter 6 'Piston rings'. Common advice recommends setting a gap to the lowest figure of a specification. This means that if a top ring specification were 0.32mm/0.013in to 0.46mm/0.018in, set the gap to 0.32mm. A problem arises, though, in setting every ring to 0.32mm as there is no longer a tolerance but a single dimension and nothing else. To ease assembly, aim for a measurement 0.254mm/0.001in smaller than the lowest figure of a specification. After eight to ten hours' running on a dyno, which is between 700 to 900 miles, ring gaps increase by 0.001in. Assembly in this way ensures maximum gas seal due to

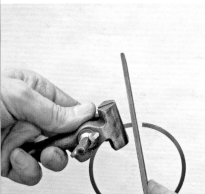

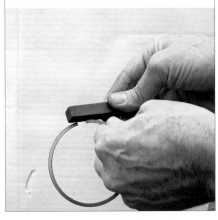

Plate 10-12: To file a piston ring.
The flat base of a ring file makes it easy to keep the end square (top). A hand vice and a single cut file can also be used, centre. Remove burrs with a carborundum stone (bottom).

the closest running clearance within any given range.

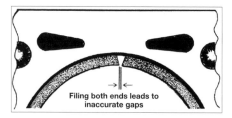

Fig 10-4: Piston ring end gaps.
File only one end of the ring. Then use the
untouched end to help alignment.

Plate 10-13: Piston ring pliers.
To avoid breakage or marking the piston,
fit rings with ring pliers.

Following the above, permanently number each piston's boss with a stamp or an electric pencil. Check the circlips are in place and then fit the rings to the pistons. Double-check the rings are installed the right way up – with a 'dot mark' or the word 'top', uppermost.

CYLINDER HEAD: FINAL ASSEMBLY

If only a 45-degree face cut was made before measuring the upper engine clearances, now is the time to blend the seats (see Chapter 4 'Valve seats'). Always build-up heads on stands to avoid damaging valves and surfaces. Number valves before lapping to avoid confusion. Fit un-lapped valves to the head, and begin numbering at number 1 cylinder, inlet valve. To clarify, a 4-valves-per-cylinder 4-cylinder engine has a total of sixteen valves. The eight intake valves would be numbered from 1 to 8 and the exhaust likewise. So, if

an intake valve were picked up that was marked with the number 4, it would be the second valve in number 2 cylinder. Underline the numbers 6 and 9 (e.g. 6 9) to avoid them being mixed up. Use an electric pencil or number stamps.

Lapping valves presents little problem. Three small dabs of fine grinding paste (350-grit) followed by a few light passes should do the trick, after which thoroughly clean the valve and seat with solvent and thinly blue the valve face. Blueing is essential, as the matt contact ring left on a valve seat after lapping is no indication of a good seal.

The various operations described in (Chapter 4, 'Checking springs' and 'installed height') concern spring pressure and bind: go through the operations. Before assembly, count out all the lower spring seats, the spring caps and the locks: this avoids errors. Assemble valves after thinly coating their stems with assembly grease, graphite

Plate 10-14: Fitting valve stem oil seals.
To avoid damage, use a seal protector and
custom punch to fit valve stem oil seals.

grease or engine oil. Install all the lower spring seats and packing shims, if fitted, followed by the valve stem oil seals, suitably shielded by a seal protector. Good practice when installing valve locks is to make sure their ends do not touch, it makes no difference in reality, but adds a professional touch. Do not coat locks with silicone. Check the seal of the assembled valves on a vacuum tester or fill the chambers with kerosene, and look for leaks.

ENGINE: FINAL ASSEMBLY

Give the various components a final clean. It's important to have a can of spray lubricant to hand to coat the cylinder bores if they are splashed with water. As before, clean cylinder bores with paper towels or a chamois leather soaked in brake cleaner then oil them using a soft bristle brush. Paint cast iron engines any colour that appeals or that maintains provenance; though tin sumps are mostly black (see Chapter 2, 'Painting'). Aluminium engines are either painted silver or remain un-painted. Paint miscellaneous parts and fit the core and gallery plugs, lock wiring or staking them in position. In a similar way, stake or Loctite seals and bearings. Core plugs have a plated finish, and ought to remain un-painted. To improve aesthetics, paint un-plated fasteners and plugs black.

Assembly follows almost identical lines to the mock-up: lubricate fasteners before tightening and Loctite or lockwire all internal non-stretch fasteners. During assembly, some fasteners may need removing and replacing several times before being finally tightened. Name these fasteners on a check list or leave them severely backed off as a visible sign of their looseness – this reduces errors. Fit the crankshaft and all the pistons. Pay particular attention

Plate 10-15: Fasten components. Fasten seals or bearings with Loctite (top), screws, or staking.

to the different coloured ends of the oil ring expander – both colours must be visible. It is easy for the expander ends to overlap, and then in essence the ring is out of operation. Once the pistons are installed, go systematically from the back to the front of the engine checking the main bearing then the big end fasteners. Recheck the big end side play (two rods on a common crankpin), the permanent numbers on the pistons

Plate 10-16: Paint flywheel marks. Painting the timing marks on a flywheel or pulley makes them easier to see on a running engine.

(all must face front and be numbered consecutively) and the wrist pin eye centralisation.

Fit any oil restrictors and install the heads, tightening the fasteners in three stages until the final torque. If the engine has domed head nuts, pay attention that stud thread does not bottom in the nuts and prevent full clamping. If this occurs, the remedy is to add a washer; although stud length should have been checked. Before fitting the sump and valve gear, it's prudent to fill and pressurise the water jacket to check for leaks (see Chapter 4, 'Crack testing and repair'). Gaskets and seals may appear to fit, but their bond can only be verified by pressure checking.

Valve clearance can only be set accurately when a head is fully tightened. At this point in the build it may be easier on an overhead camshaft engine to set the pistons midway down their bores, and rotate the camshafts by hand when setting the valve clearances rather than assembling the timing drive, and then adjusting. Assembling the valve gear is a repeat of the mock-up, though check the timing with a DTI, as inscribed lines or paint marks are only accurate to 3 or 4 degrees, and chain tension also alters the timing. Set the

static ignition timing with an ohm meter. Stipple the flywheel or front pulley timing marks with paint, and then immediately wipe over with a cloth to highlight only the incised marks – this ensures accuracy. Fit the ancillaries and seal off any openings, such as air intake and oil lines. Finally, turn the crankshaft to TDC firing stroke on number 1 cylinder to align the timing marks. This is a vital reference point when the engine is to be dynamometer tested.

BREAK-IN AND TESTING

Engine tests need to be circumspect and severe enough to stress the engine to prove it delivers the necessary levels of performance. However, as with any custom engine, keep in mind the scope and complexity of any modifications and the engine's intended use. A broad list of items to check during testing could include:

- Adjust oil pressure
- Check for oil and coolant leaks
- Regulate water flow and pressure
- Verify static ignition timing and fuel settings
- Set timing chain tension
- Re-torque fasteners
- Recheck valve adjustment
- Test and find the best ignition advance
- Set the fuel mixture (maximum rpm)
- Set the fuel mixture (idle, midrange and progression to maximum rpm)
- Adjust the boost pressure and airflow through coolers
- Read sparkplugs

Before starting a freshly-built engine make sure there is oil delivery by rotating the pump drive or by cranking the engine with the sparkplugs removed. Also, check that there is sufficient voltage to the fuel pumps and the ignition system. Set the base fuel pump pressure, mixture and ignition. Breaking in is a process that removes micro high-spots left from the machining processes, and establishes a burnished work-hardened skin on cylinder walls. Some people consider thirty minutes running on a dyno sufficient to break in the engine: a debatable point that may have validity in certain types of build. Perhaps the factor that mostly dictates run-time is cylinder bore finish. Three to five hours running is common, the latter figure roughly equalling 450 road miles. Whatever the time, it's important to load the engine progressively to get gas pressure behind piston rings. This is comparable to driving in a high gear up a long hill at around half to two-thirds throttle.

Breaking in will take longer when driving a vehicle on the road as the engine cannot be constantly loaded: for most engines, 750 miles would be enough. Another point about road testing is a vehicle's gear ratio. For high-speed performance, the best top gear ratio is that which allows maximum revs in top. In other words, if a machine were travelling on an endless straight, in its highest gear, with the throttle wide open, the engine would be turning at its maximum permissible revs (red line). This is referred to as a 1.0:1 ratio. Modern non-racing machinery is often over-geared, as this reduces revs in top gear, thereby improving gas mileage. Such a ratio is less than 1.0:1. A situation arises on such an over-geared machine where it is slower in miles-per-hour in top than in the next lower gear. Consequently, the engine is not fully loaded in top, and it may be difficult to set the best ignition and fuel mixtures. For maximum power seek a gear ratio closest to 1.0:1. Manufacturers' literature often states vehicles' gear ratios. On the other hand, the gearing on a racing machine is dictated by a racing circuit. Generally speaking, the highest gear ratio will equate to the engine turning at maximum

revs at the end of the longest straight or downhill run. Reaching maximum revs half way down a straight means the driver has to throttle back to avoid the engine over-speeding.

Towards the end of the necessary hours or miles of running, test the engine for high-speed performance. This entails adjusting the ignition advance, maximum power fuel mixture, and the cooling system pressure. But neither the ignition nor the fuel mixture can be set for maximum power independently of each other (for mapping the engine see Chapter 7, 'Management systems'). Ideally, carry out all high-speed testing with the oil and coolant outlet temperatures at:

Mineral oil	115 to 120 degrees C
Synthetic oil	150 to 160 degrees C
Coolant	94 to 99 degrees C

Adjust the ignition advance first by making all adjustments at the point of maximum advance. Set the timing to specifications and make an 80 per cent

Plate 10-17: Adjustable timing light. An adjustable timing light enables all measurements to be taken from the TDC mark, thereby increasing accuracy.

power run, either on a dyno or a similar speed test in top gear, and note the engine power.

When an initial advance has been set that delivers reasonable power at 80 per cent load adjust the fuel mixture. Engines develop most horsepower at or near their maximum

rpm. This is the point where the fuel mixture is most critical. An engine's fuel demand depends on its temperature and load. Excess fuel (rich mixture) cools combustion and reduces power. Minimal fuel (lean mixture) heats combustion and raises power. But an engine with a minimal fuel ratio is closer to detonation than one with a richer mixture. So, for maximum performance, run leaner rather than richer mixtures.

The air-to-fuel mixture (ratio) is most easily measured electronically. A Lambda sensor relays a signal to an LCD display on a mixture indicator or a more sophisticated instrument like those produced by Horiba or NGK's AFX. These convert a Lambda signal into Lambda values or as an air-to-fuel ratio. A wide band sensor, like a UEGO or the more affordable Bosch, delivers signals over a broad range. When an exhaust has no fitting for a sensor, weld a threaded boss in the pipe. The thread size of a Lambda sensor is 18x1.5mm. Site the boss no closer than 1 metre from the exhaust manifold joint but before the catalytic converter. Eliminate all air leaks that may exist in between as these will give a lean reading. On turbo engines, fix the sensor after the turbo, as high pressure in the primaries can cause inaccuracy.

For gasoline, the theoretical air-to-fuel ratio for complete combustion is approximately 14.7 parts of air to one of fuel (14.7:1). This is named 'stoichiometric,' meaning the ratio expected from an ideal formula. Stoichiometric in the Lambda Scale is 1.00 Lambda. For maximum power, use a mixture around 0.95 to 0.80 Lambda. On a turbo engine that will be driven hard use a richer mixture for safety, around 0.75 Lambda. Air-cooled engines often run best on a seemingly rich mixture, around 0.70 Lambda. Be cautious at higher readings on naturally-aspirated engines, around 0.90 to 0.95 Lambda.

Such readings, at wide open throttle, may lead to sudden damage.

Comparison of Lambda values and air-to-fuel ratio (gasoline)

Lambda	Air-to-fuel	
0.70	10.3	Rich
0.75	11.0	
0.80	11.8	
0.85	12.5	
0.90	13.2	
0.95	14.0	
1.00	14.7	Stoichiometric
1.10	16.2	
1.20	17.6	
1.30	19.1	
1.40	20.6	
1.50	22.1	Lean

Make a 90 per cent power run and adjust the mixture as necessary. Try fitting different sized venturis if experimenting with the maximum power delivery or to move the engine's torque point. When satisfied with the mixture, make a 100 per cent power run – at this time the mixture can be left a little rich, around 0.75 to 0.80-Lambda.

Before going further with ignition and mixture testing, fine-tune the cooling system (Chapter 7, 'System pressure and thermostats'). Check the pressure at maximum engine speed, as this is where the water pump turns fastest. Make this test with a light load on a dyno, or in second gear if road testing, as it's pointless to stress the engine unnecessarily.

Return to the ignition circuit and set about tuning the advance. The objective is to set the minimum advance conducive to maximum power – anything else adds unnecessary heat. The favoured procedure is to advance the timing in 2-degree increments from the point of initial advance. After each change make a 100 per cent power run while looking at the power delivery and the fuel mixture,

as indicated by the mixture indicator. Enrich the mixture if it becomes lean, and keep advancing the timing in 2-degree increments until maximum power begins to fall: then retard the timing to the maximum power point. For example:

• 297hp @ 36 degrees advance
• 300hp @ 38 degrees advance
• 296hp @ 40 degrees advance

Therefore, set the timing to 38 degrees.

Once the advance, maximum power fuelling, and the cooling system pressure have been set, adjust the idle, accelerator jet, the needle position or other settings pertinent to the progression circuit. When these are satisfactorily corrected, on a non-racing engine, the settings can be left where they are but for authentic maximum power, fine-tune the mixture and the timing using the sparkplugs as a guide.

READING PLUGS

A 'plug cut' is a way of adjusting the timing and mixture by using the sparkplugs as a combustion guide. Setting the timing by using the indicated horsepower on a dyno and the fuel mixture with an analyser, however accurate, is still relatively coarse. Reading a plug after a plug cut uses the human eye to interpret the colour of burnt hydrocarbons and thermal telltales that remain on a plug. When these are 'read,' small changes can be made to the ignition timing, the plug heat range, and the fuel mixture that affect high-speed maximum power running. Plug reading is particularly important on a multi-cylinder engine where one or two carburettors feed the cylinders through a multi-branch plenum – some cylinders may be rich or others lean.

Plug reading is subjective, of course, as the viewer interprets colour

and other subtle indicators, and draws on his experience to form an opinion – inevitably, opinions vary. Trackside sparkplug representatives are usually willing to share their information and offer opinions when problems arise – that is their job. Nonetheless, subjectivity is present on finer points even if a consensus reigns about the basics. Generally speaking, read plugs for maximum power to indicate combustion conditions within the last 700rpm before, and at red line. Maximum heat is generated in this zone, and it is also where the division between reliability and performance is most distinct. A separate plug cut can also be made at midrange throttle but, in such a case, only the part throttle fuel mixture can be read. These are the soot deposits on the nose of the ceramic.

Never use old or sandblasted plugs, as these do not give clear readings. Sandblasting, moreover, dulls the plugs' ceramic surface, and may leave traces of grit. To save costs, on a well-running, multi-cylinder engine, cut only one or two plugs, while the others remain untouched. Plug reading checks:

• Ignition advance
• The fuel mixture
• A plug's heat range

To read a plug, first make a plug cut. The recognised way is to bring the engine to full operating temperature, and replace all or selected plugs with new ones. Start the engine but do not let it idle. Instead, blast the machine down the track at high revs in a high gear: ideally maximum revs in top (1.0:1 ratio). Hold maximum speed for 30 seconds or more and then snap the throttle shut, disengage the clutch and kill the ignition. Restarting the engine confuses a maximum power reading as lower speed deposits will be present. That is the recognised way but in reality, except for a vehicle that has a small displacement engine, it is difficult to find a long enough straight where a machine can be held wide-open top gear for 30 seconds. A compromise is to do two or three 15-second maximum power runs on the same plug. Do not idle or allow the engine to run on part throttle.

It's also possible to read a plug taken from the engine of a vehicle that has been driven hard. Such as, if a new plug were fitted and the vehicle completed a couple of laps on a fast circuit. The plug will exhibit deposits indicative of the various engine speeds used on the track rather than a deposit solely for maximum power. Nonetheless, it should give a good reading. Conversely, perform a plug cut on a dynamometer, bearing in mind at what altitude the machine will be used.

READING IGNITION

After a plug cut, look for ignition advance first, as ignition is largely responsible for sparkplug heat. According to NGK, the normal operating range of plugs is 800 to 1000 degrees F. Use an illuminated magnifying lens with 10 x magnification to observe the plug nose, the centre wire electrode, and the flat ground electrode. A magnifier whose light shines through the lens is easy to use as its image is clear. A cheaper but harder to use alternative, is to buy an illuminated magnifier as used by stamp collectors. A plug with over-advanced ignition will have no carbon deposit on the centre wire electrode, or just a wisp of a deposit that ends a millimetre or two from the tip. A clear tip extending for 360 degrees around the electrode will be visible. Retard or advance the timing until the electrode is covered by a carbon wisp right up to the tip.

On the flat ground electrode, look for a dark-grey colour. With the best timing and heat, a faint blue heat line

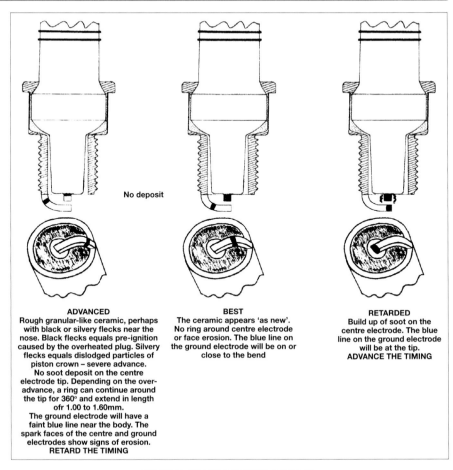

No deposit

ADVANCED
Rough granular-like ceramic, perhaps with black or silvery flecks near the nose. Black flecks equals pre-ignition caused by the overheated plug. Silvery flecks equals dislodged particles of piston crown – severe advance. No soot deposit on the centre electrode tip. Depending on the over-advance, a ring can continue around the tip for 360° and extend in length ofr 1.00 to 1.60mm. The ground electrode will have a faint blue line near the body. The spark faces of the centre and ground electrodes show signs of erosion.
RETARD THE TIMING

BEST
The ceramic appears 'as new'. No ring around centre electrode or face erosion. The blue line on the ground electrode will be on or close to the bend

RETARDED
Build up of soot on the centre electrode. The blue line on the ground electrode will be at the tip.
ADVANCE THE TIMING

Fig 10-5: Reading ignition advance.
Fuel octane affects the ignition: low octane leads to less advance. Ignition readings are unaffected by plug heat range.

will be visible on or about the bend, just before the electrode contacts the plug's body. An un-coloured electrode denotes insufficient advance, or, with approved advance, a plug that is too cold. On the other hand, a deep blue colour indicates excessive advance or too hot a plug. Once found, the faint blue heat line moves towards the tip of the electrode with retarded timing, or disappears into the thread of the plug's base as the timing is advanced.

READING HEAT CHANGE

Before checking the mixture select the best heat range of plug because a plug

that is not hot enough will not exhibit reliable mixture readings. To find the best heat range, look at the ceramic nose and the ground electrode. On a plug of the correct heat range the ceramic nose will be clean. More concisely, the ceramic will sheen due to heat melting its bonding medium. Concerning the ground electrode, this should have the faintest blue wisp of colour. Conversely, an overheated plug, one that is too soft, is likely to have a blue-coloured ground electrode. The depth of colour depends on the amount of overheating and may range from a deep, to a pale blue. For more on sparkplugs see Chapter 8.

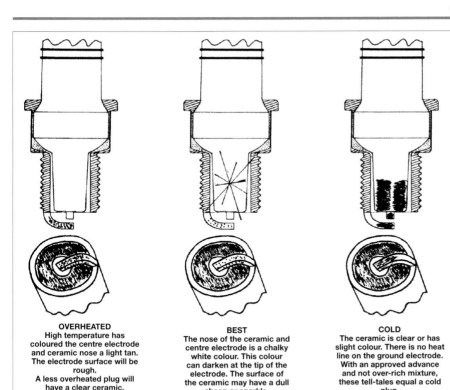

OVERHEATED
High temperature has coloured the centre electrode and ceramic nose a light tan. The electrode surface will be rough.
A less overheated plug will have a clear ceramic. The ground electrode will be dark tan to brown, with a rough surface
FIT A COLDER PLUG

BEST
The nose of the ceramic and centre electrode is a chalky white colour. This colour can darken at the tip of the electrode. The surface of the ceramic may have a dull sheen or sparkle.
The smooth surface of the ground electrode is light tan to dull chalk

COLD
The ceramic is clear or has slight colour. There is no heat line on the ground electrode. With an approved advance and not over-rich mixture, these tell-tales equal a cold plug.
FIT A HOTTER PLUG

Fig 10-6: Reading plug heat range.
A cold plug can lead to loss of spark energy and shorting.

1.00mm and its colour, a pale straw to light tan. Differences exist concerning the best height of the ring and its depth and colour. For example, richer-fuelled air-cooled engines often deliver reliable power with a light tan-coloured ring rising one, to one-and-a-half millimetres from the abutment. For leaner-burning water-cooled engines, such a condition is not appropriate as they may perform best with a deposit that extends only 190 to 280 degrees around the ceramic and of gossamer colour. This change of colour can be almost imperceptible from the ceramic's patina. As stated before, a richer mixture protects against detonation and a leaner mixture can lead to detonation. Detonation is identifiable by tiny black flecks on the ceramic, which, in severe cases, take on a shimmering appearance as they are minute particles of piston crown aluminium.

READING FUEL MIXTURE

To check the maximum power mixture, look at the carbon deposits on the ceramic insulator deep inside the plug's body: where the ceramic abuts the metal casing. Deposits in this area cannot be seen without an illuminated magnifier as bright sunlight or strong artificial light is insufficient to penetrate the 10.00mm depth of the body.

There's no definitive appearance of the size and colour of the lower deposit applicable for all engines. Nonetheless, any well-jetted engine held at maximum revs for around 30 seconds or more ought to display some form of soot ring at the abutment. This may continue partially around the ceramic or extend for 360 degrees. The ring's height may be unclear or judged to be about

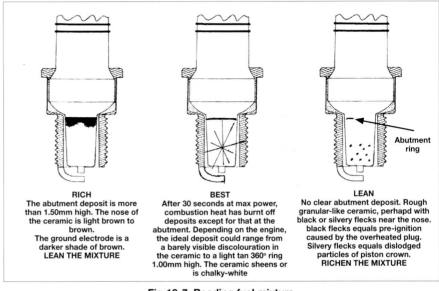

RICH
The abutment deposit is more than 1.50mm high. The nose of the ceramic is light brown to brown.
The ground electrode is a darker shade of brown.
LEAN THE MIXTURE

BEST
After 30 seconds at max power, combustion heat has burnt off deposits except for that at the abutment. Depending on the engine, the ideal deposit could range from a barely visible discolouration in the ceramic to a light tan 360° ring 1.00mm high. The ceramic sheens or is chalky-white

LEAN
No clear abutment deposit. Rough granular-like ceramic, perhapd with black or silvery flecks near the nose. black flecks equals pre-ignition caused by the overheated plug. Silvery flecks equals dislodged particles of piston crown.
RICHEN THE MIXTURE

Abutment ring

Fig 10-7: Reading fuel mixture.
More fuel is a protection against detonation yet it equals less power.

Conclusion

Motorcycles and cars are more than machines made to carry people from one point to another, or solely to race around a track; they also have aesthetic features. To the casual observer, the artistic embellishment on a race car may appear to be little more than the choice of livery. But the creative idea goes further, since, to a greater or lesser extent, each design is just as much an artistic expression crafted by the human hand as is sculpture or literature. Each fulfils a purpose, but, in addition, each has, in varying degrees, the capacity to please – even in an abstract way.

Arguably, concerning a motor vehicle, the sense of taste is the only sense not used in an evaluation. For example, we look at the shape of a vehicle or take pleasure in touching it, but perhaps the senses of smell and hearing are most evocative. The smell given off by a hot engine, or of castor oil, or the sound of exhaust and mechanical noise made by a high-performance vehicle when under load can lead to a lasting memory. For the builder of such an engine, pleasure may be tinged with concern and an added acuteness listening for any unusual sound or change of exhaust note. Even on an engine that is well designed and put together, there is usually a modification or an idea for a possible improvement floating in a team member's head. More can be done, and so, work on the engine has merely been suspended ...

An engine is more likely to fail when under load, as this is when components are most stressed and any weakness in materials or assembly will show. When followed, the techniques and suggestions described in this book will help to reduce the chance of engine failure as stressed components will be working in greater harmony.

However, there is a separate issue: the look and sound of a high-performance vehicle is synonymous with speed, even when posing on the boulevard at 20 miles-per-hour. The street is no place to enjoy the intoxication of speed and sound – it is hazardous and peopled by unpredictable drivers who possess various levels of driving skill. Do not speed on the street. No matter how big an ego or how fast a street driver, there is no comparison with the measured risk, the cold calculation, and the rhythm that exists in the mind of a professional race driver. Driving at a 'track day' is the place to go fast, not the street. A track day is when a race circuit is open to the public. There are usually three levels of driving competence: novice, intermediate and experienced; each of which is allocated different track time. Consequently, a novice and an experienced driver will not be on the track at the same time. That means a person can drive within their limits and without the unwarranted pressure of holding up, or trying to keep up with, faster, more experienced drivers.

Appendix 1
Useful addresses

CERAMIC COATINGS

Kool Coat Ceramic Coating Ltd,
Number 10 - 19695 - 96th Ave,
Langley, BC, V3A 4P3, Canada.
www.koolcoatceramiccoatings.com

Plasma & Thermal Coatings Ltd,
Greenwich Road, Maesglas Industrial
Estate, Newport, NP20 2NN, UK.
www.plasmathermalcoatings.com

CLUTCHES

Alcon Components Limited, Apolo,
Tamworth, Staffordshire, B79 7TN, UK.
www.alcon.co.uk

AP Racing, Wheler Road, Seven Stars
Industrial Estate, Coventry, CV3 4LB,
UK. www.apracing.com

Quarter Master, 510 Telser Rd,
Lake Zurich, IL, 60047, USA.
www.racingclutches.com

Tilton Engineering, 25 Easy Street, P.O.
Box 1787, Buellton, CA, 93427, USA.
www.tiltonracing.com

CONRODS & CRANKSHAFTS

Falicon Crankshaft Components Inc,
1115 Old Coachman Road, Clearwater,
FL, 33765, USA. www.faliconcranks.com

Farndon Engineering, Bayton Road,
Exhall, Coventry, CV7 9EJ, UK.
www.farndon.com

Krem Enterprises, 10204 Perry Highway,
Meadville, PA, 16335, USA.
www.krem-enterprises.com

Pankl Engine Systems GmbH & Co KG,
Kaltschmidstrasse 2-6, A-8600, Bruck
an der Mur, Austria. www.pankl.com

CRACK TESTING SUPPLIES

Ely Chemical Company Ltd, Lisle Lane,
Ely, Cambridgeshire, CB7 4AS, UK, or

Ely Chemical Company Inc, 125 East.
US Highway 12, Michigan City, Indiana,
46360, USA. www.elychemical.com

Burton Power, 617-631 Eastern Avenue,
Ilford, Essex, IG2 6PN, UK.
www.burtonpower.com

Goodson Shop Supplies, P.O. Box 847,
Winona, MN, 55987, USA.
www.goodson.com

CRYOGENIC TREATMENT

Cryogenic Treatment Services Ltd,
The Engine, Sovereign Way, Mansfield,
Nottinghamshire, NG18 4LQ, UK.
www.195below.co.uk

One Cryo, 14514 144th Ave East,
Orting, WA, 98360, USA.
www.onecryo.com

FASTENERS

Allbolts Ltd, Eye Airfields Industrial

Estate, Langton Green, Brome, Suffolk, IP23 7HN, UK. www.allbolts.co.uk

Automotive Racing Products, 531 Spectrum Circle, Oxnard, CA, 93030, USA. www.arp-bolts.com

Coastal Fabrication Inc, 16761 Burke Lane, Huntington Beach, CA, 92647, USA. www.coastfab.com

Light Aero Spares, Exeter Road Industrial Estate, Okehampton, Devon, EX20 1UA, UK. www.lasaero.com

Sps Technologies, 301 Highland Avenue, Jenkintown, PA, PA19046, USA. www.spstechnology.com

Trident Racing Supplies, Unit 31, Silverstone Circuit, Silverstone, Northamptonshire, NN12 8TN, UK. www.tridentracing.co.uk

GASKET PAPER

Fibreflex Packing & Manufacturing Co Inc, PO Box 4646, Philadelphia, PA, 19127, USA.
www.fibreflex.com

Okenstrong Gaskets, Jointine Products (Lincoln) Ltd, Lindum Business Park, Station Road, North Hykeham, Lincoln, LN6 9AU, UK. www.jointineuk.com

GASKETS (PRE-FORMED)

ElringKlinger AG, Max-Eyth-Strasse 2, 72581 Dettingen / Erms, Goetze, Germany.
www.elringklinger.de

IGNITION, FUEL & ENGINE MANAGEMENT

Aldon Automotive Ltd, Breener Industrial Estate, Station Drive, West Midlands, DY5 3JZ, UK. www.aldonauto.co.uk

Autocar Electrical Equipment Co Ltd, 49/51 Tiverton Street, London, SE1 6NZ, UK. www.lumenition.com

Delco-Remy International, 2902 Enterprise Drive, Anderson, IN, 46013, USA. www.delcoremy.com

DTA Competition Engine Management Systems, 10 Boston Court, Kansas Avenue, Salford, M50 2GN, UK. www.dtafast.co.uk

Magnecor Europe Limited, Unit 12, Jubilee Business Park, Snarestone Road, Appleby Magna, Derbyshire, DE12 7AJ, UK. www.magnecor.co.uk

Mallory Technical Service Dept, Mr Gasket Company, 10601 Memphis Ave #12, Cleveland, OH, 44144, USA. www.malloryracing.com

MSD Ignition, Autotronic Controls Corporation, 1350 Pullman Drive, Dock Number14, El Paso, Texas. 79936. USA. www.msdignition.com

Pectel Control Systems, Brookfield Motorsports Centre, Twentypence Road, Cottenham, Cambridge, CB4 8PS, UK. www.pectel.co.uk

Powertrain Electronics, LLC, 6600 Toro Creek Road, Atascadero, CA, 93422, USA.
www.airfuelratio.com

METAL SUPPLIES

MSC Industrial Supply, 75 Maxess Road, Melville, NY, 11747, USA. www1.mscdirect.com

Saxon Steels, Unit 48, Dronfield Industrial Estate, Callywhite Lane, Dronfield, Nr Sheffield, S18 2XR, UK. www.saxonsteels.com

MISCELLANEOUS SUPPLIERS

Burton Power, 617-631 Eastern Avenue, Ilford, Essex, IG2 6PN, UK. www.burtonpower.com

Goodson Shop Supplies, P.O. Box 847, Winona, MN, 55987, USA. www.goodson.com

GPR Motorsport Equipment, Unit 1 Silverstone Technology Park, Silverstone Circuit, Towcester, Northamptonshire, NN12 8TN, UK. www.gprdirect.com

K-Line Industries Inc, 315 Garden Avenue, Holland, MI, 49424, USA. www.klineind.com

PISTON SUPPLIERS

Arias Pistons, Rosier Commercial Centre, Coneyhurst Road, Billingshurst, West Sussex, RH14 9DE, UK.
or
Arias Pistons, 13420 South Normandie Ave, Gardena, CA, 90249, USA. www.ariaspistons.com

PUMPS (WATER & OIL)

Auto Verdi USA, 1260 Logan Ave, Unit A-1, Costa Mesa, CA, 926 26, USA. www.autoverdi.com

Dailey Engineering, 42095 Zevo Drive, Unit 7, Temecula, CA, 92590, USA. www.daileyengineering.com

Davies Craig, 77 Taras Avenue, P O Box 363, Altona North 3025 Victoria, Australia.
www.daviescraig.com.au

Scherzinger Pump Technology Inc, 3-1440 Graham's Lane, Burlington, Ontario,
L7S 1W3, Canada. www.scherzinger.ca

Appendix 2
Inspection & build sheets

Measuring crankshaft and main bearing journals							
Main bearing journals							
A							
A1							

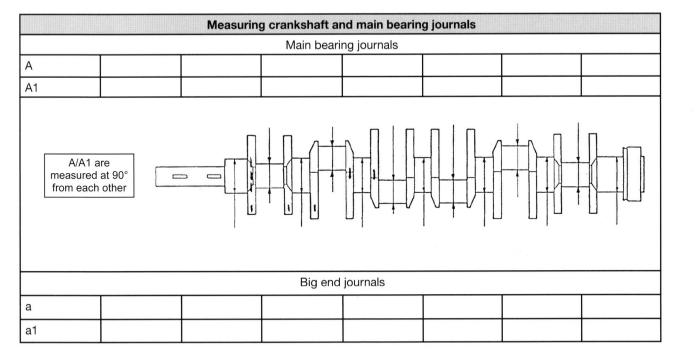

A/A1 are measured at 90° from each other

Big end journals							
a							
a1							

Measuring cylinder bores

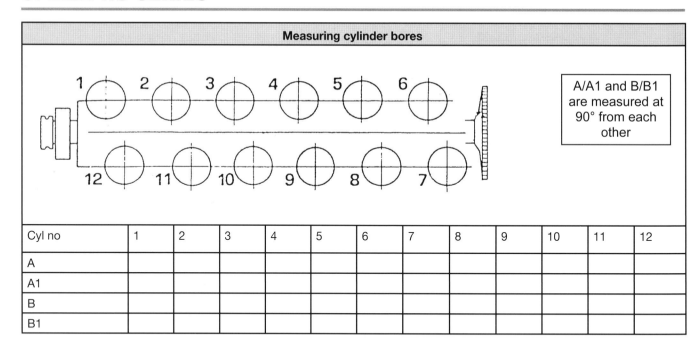

A/A1 and B/B1 are measured at 90° from each other

Cyl no	1	2	3	4	5	6	7	8	9	10	11	12
A												
A1												
B												
B1												

Valve clearance

Bank _____

		Inlet								Exhaust					
		Target clearance _____								Target clearance _____					
Cyl no	Valve no	Valve CL	Shim size	New shim	Valve CL	Shim size	New shim	Cyl no	Valve no	Valve CL	Shim size	New shim	Valve CL	Shim size	New shim
1	1							1	1						
	2								2						
2	3							2	3						
	4								4						
3	5							3	5						
	6								6						
4	7							4	7						
	8								8						
5	9							5	9						
	10								10						
6	11							6	11						
	12								12						

Valve spring install heights

Bank _____

Inlet Target height _____ mm				Exhaust Target height _____ __mm			
Cyl no	Valve no	Spring height	Shim	Cyl no	Valve no	Sprint height	Shm
1	1			1	1		
	2				2		
2	3			2	3		
	4				4		
3	5			3	5		
	6				6		
4	7			4	7		
	8				8		
5	9			5	9		
	10				10		
6	11			6	11		
	12				12		

Piston to valve clearance

Bank _____

Cyl no	Valve no	Clearance	Cyl no	Valve no	Clearance
1	1		1	1	
	2			2	
2	3		2	3	
	4			4	
3	5		3	5	
	6			6	
4	7		4	7	
	8			8	
5	9		5	9	
	10			10	
6	11		6	11	
	12			12	

Conrod weights

Rod number	1	2	3	4	5	6	7	8	9	10	11	12
Little end												
Big end												
Total rod after equalising												

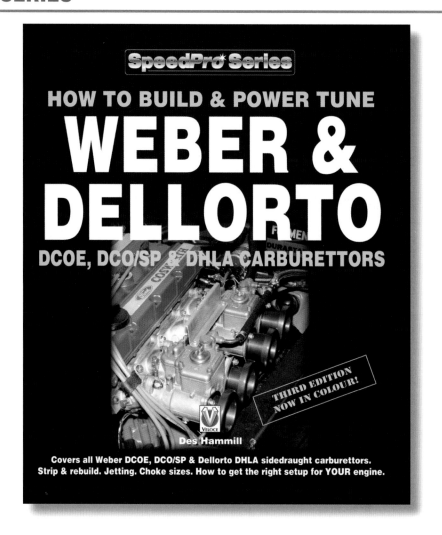

SpeedPro Series

HOW TO BUILD, MODIFY & POWER TUNE

CYLINDER HEADS

UPDATED & REVISED EDITION

Peter Burgess & David Gollan

Expert advice on building and modifying cylinder heads for high performance with reliability • Topics include - horsepower & torque, equipment & tools, airflow, building a flowbench, porting, valves, valve seats & inserts, valve guides, valve springs, unleaded fuel conversion. Includes an overview of camshafts, exhaust system, ignition system and case studies of a selection of popular heads. Covers all types of cylinder heads, except 2-stroke

THE COMPLETE PRACTICAL GUIDE TO MODIFYING CYLINDER HEADS FOR MAXIMUM POWER, ECONOMY AND RELIABILITY. DON'T WASTE MONEY ON MODIFICATIONS THAT DON'T WORK. APPLIES TO ALMOST EVERY CAR/MOTORCYCLE (NOT 2-STROKE ENGINES).

978-1-903706-76-3 • £16.99*

* All prices subject to change, P&P extra. For more information visit www.veloce.co.uk

Index